The Michigan Lake to Lake Bed & Breakfast
Association Proudly Presents:

Michigan
Bed & Breakfast Cookbook

Michigan Bed & Breakfast Cookbook. Copyright © 2013 Trails Books. All rights reserved. Printed in Canada. No part of this book may be used or reproduced in any manner whatsoever without written permission except in the case of brief quotations embodied in critical articles and reviews. Bower House books may be purchased with bulk discounts for educational, business, or sales promotional use. For information, contact Bower House P.O. Box 7459 Denver, CO 80207 or visit BowerHouseBooks.com.

Cover Design: Rebecca Finkel
Text Design: D. Kari Luraas
Editorial Assistant: Loren Szenina
Editor: Mira Perrizo

Front Cover Photos: Breakfast on porch, Hexagon House B&B,
photo by Dan VanDuinen Photographic; Sun-shaped fruit, Adventure Inn B&B,
photo by Sandy White, Innkeeper
Back Cover Photos: Blueberries, iStockphoto; Breakfast in front of fireplace,
Kalamazoo House B&B, photo by Christian Giannelli

The Bed & Breakfast Cookbook Series was originated by Carol Faino and Doreen Hazledine of Peppermint Press in Denver, CO in 1999.

Library of Congress Cataloging-in-Publication Data Available Upon Request

ISBN 978-1-889593-30-2

10 9 8 7 6 5 4 3 2

Homemade meets local flavor
at the corner of fresh and tasty

They say: "Breakfast is the most important meal of the day."

We say: Breakfast can be the **best** meal of the day if you're dining at a bed and breakfast inn.

We promise: Breakfast is even better when it's served at a B&B belonging to the Michigan Lake to Lake Bed and Breakfast Association.

With this cookbook in your hands, what's on our innkeepers' menus can now be on yours. Inside, you'll find recipes as distinctive as these Lake to Lake–member inns themselves. It's not surprising when you consider that Michigan is the second most agriculturally diverse state in the nation, a leader in the production of tart cherries, plums, apples, and a whole lot more really yummy stuff.

Innkeepers draw on a mix of culinary training, traditions passed down by their grandmothers and the cultural ethos unique to their regions. Some may adopt a touch of Provence while others have a flare for the sunnier flavors of Mexico. All reflect the level of quality each must demonstrate to pass regular, professional inspections that Lake to Lake requires.

Michigan Lake to Lake bed and breakfast inns offer more than just breakfast. Did you know B&Bs invented the "endless" cookie jar? It's always full of treats that are both delectable and home-baked. You'll discover the best of them between these pages, from in-season strawberry bread to orchard-fresh fruit tarts and oven-warm scones that burst with Michigan blueberries.

Many innkeepers welcome their guests with an afternoon snack that runs a gamut from seafood dips and zesty salsas to cheese spreads and farm-fresh asparagus wraps. Some B&Bs will pack you a picnic lunch to fuel your day's adventures. Some offer full-course dinners to help you celebrate your special occasions. All their best recipes are here.

Welcome to the wonderful world of bed and breakfast inns, where every recipe is a flavorful find—a treat to treasure, a taste to enjoy.

Contents

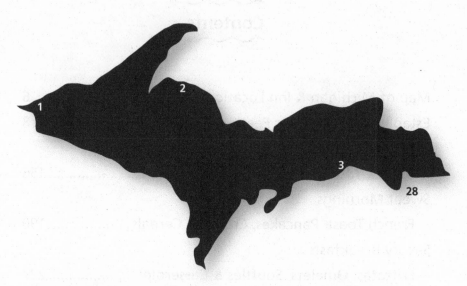

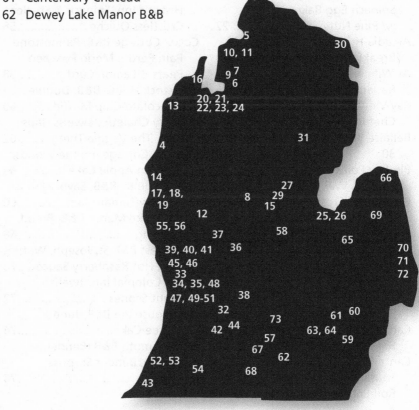

Michigan Bed & Breakfast Establishments and Their Featured Recipes

A Country Place B&B

John & Cindy Malmstrom
79 North Shore Drive N., South Haven, MI 49090
269-637-5523
www.acountryplace.net | acountryplace@cybersol.com
5 Rooms
Wooded setting five minutes from downtown | Walk to beach

This 1860s Greek Revival home has a gracious English country theme throughout the guest rooms and common areas. Touches of lace, accents of floral prints, handsome antique furnishings, and other small collected treasures create a very pleasing ambiance.

The specialty at A Country Place is hospitality, with personal attention given to every guest's needs.

The focal point of the back lawn is a screened gazebo where nature can be appreciated to the fullest. The gazebo is also a perfect place to enjoy a picnic, read a good book, or just relax. It is a perfect setting for those restful and romantic getaways.

A country breakfast featuring home-baked goodies from the kitchen is served at your leisure. Weather permitting, breakfast may be enjoyed on the spacious deck or enclosed summer porch. Spring and fall, breakfast is served in the formal dining area by the fireside. There are complimentary refreshments available throughout the day, with freshly baked goodies for late afternoon and evening snacks.

A Country Place B&B is situated on two acres of woodland with Lake Michigan beach access half-a-block away. Hiking and bicycling may be enjoyed on the thirty-four mile Kal-Haven Trail that links Kalamazoo and South Haven, or guests may appreciate a more leisurely afternoon of shopping, dining, or golfing.

Apple Dapple Cake

Yield: 8–10 servings

"This is our favorite recipe."

Cake

butter, for coating the pan
- 3 cups all-purpose flour
- 1 tsp baking soda
- 1 tsp fine salt
- 1¾ cups granulated sugar
- 1¼ cups canola or vegetable oil
- 3 large eggs, at room temperature
- 2 tsp vanilla extract
- 3 cups Granny Smith apples, peeled, cored, and medium-diced (from about 3 medium apples)
- 2 cups coarsely chopped pecans (about 8 oz.)

Glaze

- ¾ cup packed dark brown sugar
- 4 Tbsp unsalted butter (1/2 stick), cut into large chunks
- ⅓ cup heavy cream

Preheat oven to 325°F and arrange a rack in the middle. Generously coat a 10-inch tube pan with butter (the pan should have a removable bottom), and set aside.

Place the flour, baking soda, and salt in a medium bowl; whisk to combine and aerate; set aside. Place the sugar and oil in a large bowl; whisk to combine. Add the eggs and vanilla to the sugar and oil; whisk until thoroughly combined. Add the flour mixture using a rubber spatula; stir until just evenly incorporated, being careful not to over mix. Stir in the apples and nuts until evenly distributed. Pour the batter into the prepared pan and smooth the top. Bake until the surface of the cake is golden brown and a toothpick or wooden skewer inserted into the center comes out clean, about 60–65 minutes. Place on a rack to slightly cool while you make the glaze.

Place all of the glaze ingredients in a small saucepan over medium heat. Bring to a boil, stirring often until the sugar has completely dissolved. Continue to boil, stirring occasionally, until the mixture has thickened slightly, about 3 minutes more. While the cake is still warm and in the tube pan, pour all of the glaze over it. Let sit until completely cooled, at least 2 hours. To remove the cake from the pan, run a knife between the cake and the perimeter of the pan and the tube. Arrange a sheet of aluminum foil so that it's directly touching the surface of the cake, making a hole in the foil to expose the tube. Flip the pan over and push the removable bottom and cake down onto the foil. Flip the cake and platter over and remove the foil.

A Dove Nest B&B

Bob & Terry Dove
4400 S. Philips Road, Kingston, MI 48741
989-683-8404 | 877-909-3683
www.adovenestbedandbreakfast.com
tdove@adovebedandbreakfast.com
2 Rooms, 1 Suite
112 acres on a lake | 40 minutes to Frankenmuth or Port Sanilac

A Dove Nest is more than a B&B. It is a destination to be treasured. Located in the heart of Michigan's "thumb" area, there are countless opportunities to get out and experience Michigan's natural side. Guests enjoy bird watching and wildlife viewing in the Certified National Wildlife Habitat areas on the B&B grounds. While having breakfast, guests have seen coyotes and herds of deer crossing the frozen lake. Bald eagles often put on a show. For the wildflower lovers, the area is full of common and endangered varieties. Whether walking the trails or riding a bike, hunting and fishing, or stargazing—A Dove Nest B&B will not disappoint.

Breakfast becomes a social gathering served around a 1950s-style table overlooking the lake. The hearty country breakfast includes at least two meat choices, eggs, hash browns, and pancakes or waffles. The innkeepers serve handmade syrups and jellies from wild fruit on the property, as well as jelly made from locally grown blueberries. Pure maple syrup harvested from trees in the area is a wonderful extra, as are the fresh farm eggs from a neighbor. Special dietary needs can be accommodated if the innkeepers know in advance of your stay. Guests write that the breakfasts are phenomenal.

Sausage Quiche

Yield: 6–8 servings

*"I have made this basic recipe with many different variations.
Our guests love this quiche and have asked for the recipe many times."*

1	lb. bulk pork sausage
6	large eggs
2	cups Monterey Jack cheese, shredded
½	cup sharp cheddar cheese, shredded
1	cup ricotta cheese
¼	cup flour
¼	cup butter, melted
½	tsp baking powder
½	tsp coarse ground black pepper
	Parmesan cheese

Preheat oven to 375°F.

Cook sausage until no longer pink; drain. Beat eggs in a large bowl and add cheeses (except for Parmesan), flour, butter, baking powder, pepper, and sausage.

Combine well. Pour into pie plate and sprinkle with Parmesan cheese.

Bake uncovered for 30–35 minutes or until a knife inserted in the center comes out clean.

Tips and variations: You can add 1 cup fresh mushrooms and ½ cup onions if desired. You may also top with some green chilies. Substitute cottage cheese for the ricotta or mozzarella for the sharp cheddar.

A Night to Remember B&B

Dan & Nadine Maliniak
5712 Main Street, Lexington, MI 48450
810-359-7134
www.anighttorememberbandb.com
info@anighttorememberbandb.com
5 Rooms
Ice cream parlor and antique shopping on premises | Harbor town

Whether seeking a peaceful retreat, a romantic getaway, or the experience of country living, guests will find what they are looking for at A Night to Remember B&B. Located near the tranquil shores of Lake Huron, this relaxing B&B is just a short stroll into the quaint resort town of Lexington, where there are charming shops and dining. You might purchase a private cruise on the lake or try out your fishing skills. Come stay here and see why Lexington is considered one of Michigan's best-kept secrets! Leave the stress behind and become immersed in unparalleled relaxation. This historic estate is a soon-to-be favorite for travelers seeking a beautiful, romantic destination.

Wander back to the inn for a visit to "Temptations"—an old-fashioned ice cream parlor featuring Sanders Hot Fudge (a local favorite)! Indulge in a tasty treat while shopping at the fun gift shop and antique barn on the property and relaxing in the majestic gardens.

Enjoy the inn's Breakfast Casserole and an early morning cup of coffee out on the balcony, or join others in the parlor for friendly conversation.

Breakfast Casserole

*"This recipe is one we created for a quick and delicious breakfast.
This casserole can be made in the microwave."*

10	potatoes, Yukon Gold, peeled and diced
	margarine or butter
	salt & pepper, to taste
10	eggs
2	large ham slices, cut and cubed
1–2	cups cheddar cheese, shredded, to taste
2	Tbsp sour cream

Place small potato pieces into a microwave-safe casserole dish. Add
a scoop of margarine or butter; salt and pepper to taste. Cover with
plastic wrap and heat on high for 5 minutes. Remove from microwave;
stir gently. The escaping steam is hot so use caution. Re-cover with
plastic wrap and cook for another 4 minutes or until the potatoes are
tender.

Whisk eggs lightly in a medium bowl. Remove the potatoes from the
microwave and add the eggs and ham pieces along with a handful of
cheese to taste. Mix it all together.

Re-cover and place into microwave for 4–5 minutes. Remove from the
microwave; carefully remove the plastic wrap; stir. The mixture will still
be in a liquid form from the eggs. Cover and place back in the microwave for an additional 3–4 minutes until the eggs are no longer liquid,
but gently set. Remove from the microwave.

Spoon sour cream into mixture and stir gently until it is blended well.
Cover the top completely with the remaining cheese. Re-cover with
plastic wrap and heat another 2–3 minutes until the cheese is melted.

Adrounie House B&B

Don & April Tubbs
126 S. Broadway Street, Hastings, MI 49058
800-927-8505 | 269-945-0678
www.adrounie.com | adtubbs@wowway.biz
6 Rooms
Walk to shops and restaurants | 45 minutes to Grand Rapids

The Adrounie House was built in 1894 as a Queen Anne Victorian with a parlor, a sitting room with a fireplace, and a lovely oak staircase. The staircase has beautifully hand-carved woodwork on the stair paneling and beneath the windows. The front entry and dining room have inlaid floors of oak and birds-eye maple. Four sets of huge pocket doors grace the common areas on the main floor. Numerous antiques and collectibles are found throughout the house.

Guests enjoy "porch sitting" on the comfortable wraparound with early morning coffee or a cup of tea, and a good book in the evening.

The town of Hastings has been listed twice in "100 Best Small Towns in America To Live In." Adrounie House is within walking distance to Hastings' shops, restaurants, and movie theater.

A full breakfast is served, accommodating special dietary needs.

Omelet Sandwich

Yield: 6 servings

*"This favorite recipe is a yummy oven-baked omelet sandwich.
Prepare the night before and stick in the oven in the morning."*

2	cups ham (or chicken, turkey, or tuna), chopped
1	cup celery, chopped
1–2	green onions, chopped (or chives or onion flakes)
1	(4 oz.) can mushrooms, chopped
¾	cup sharp cheddar cheese, grated or shredded
	butter, softened, for buttering bread
12	slices bread with crusts removed
4	eggs
½	cup mayonnaise
½	cup sour cream
2	cups milk
	paprika, to garnish
	basil, fresh or dried, to garnish

Mix first 5 ingredients together in a large bowl. Butter 1 side of the 12 slices of bread.

Place 6 slices of bread, butter side down, in a 9x13-inch casserole dish.

Cover with meat mixture and top with remaining 6 slices of bread, butter side up.

Beat together the eggs, mayo, sour cream, and milk in a bowl. Pour this over the mixture in the casserole dish. Cover with plastic wrap and let stand overnight in the refrigerator.

The next morning, preheat oven to 350°F. Remove plastic wrap and bake 40–45 minutes until puffed and golden. Sprinkle lightly with paprika.

Plate one serving per person and sprinkle with basil, fresh or dried.

Serve while hot.

Tips and variations: If the casserole should appear to be "dry" in the morning, beat together 1 cup of milk and 2 eggs and pour over all before baking.

Adventure Inn B&B

Sandy White & Nicholas DeGrazia
3650 Shorewood Drive, North Lakeport, MI 48059
810-327-6513
www.adventureinnbedandbreakfast.com
stay@adventureinnbedandbreakfast.com
2 Rooms
On Lake Huron | 9 miles to Port Huron or Lexington

Lake Huron is no less blue and no less mesmerizing when the days turn cooler, and then cooler still. After a walk on the beach, perhaps to the wooded trails within Lakeport State Park, return to a crackling fire in the living room's wood-burning fireplace, and get cozy in either of two lake-facing rooms.

When guests make a reservation, they are asked about breakfast preferences, especially dietary restrictions. The innkeepers make every effort to amaze with their choices. Sandy and Nicholas are always adding new recipes using fresh, local fruits and vegetables whenever possible. Breakfast is served either on the sun porch overlooking the landscaped yard and Lake Huron or in the dining room, where the view is similar. On summer days when weather is suitable, the round table on the deck is another popular breakfast spot.

Breakfast features ordinary breakfast tastes served in a way that most people don't take the time to do for themselves at home. It begins with an artful fresh fruit course, usually served with home-made granola. A hot entrée follows. There is a choice of at least four or more juices. Tea and coffee made from freshly ground beans are available for early risers, and it keeps coming so long as there are cups wanting to be filled.

Since there are two guest rooms and consequently up to four guests, it's typical for guests to dine at the same mutually agreed time. Amazing coincidences and great stories are often revealed over a shared breakfast. However, in-room dining is also possible. Accommodations can be made for guests who need to get on the road early.

Orange & Michigan-Cherry Scones

Yield: 12 scones

"Early settlers brought cherries to North America in the 1600s. About 200 years later, cherries became established as a crop in northern Michigan, with the most favorable growing conditions found on the Leelanau Peninsula. No other state produces more tart cherries than Michigan."

2	cups flour
	zest of one orange, finely chopped
7	tsp sugar
2	tsp baking powder
¼	tsp baking soda
½	tsp salt
⅓	cup butter, cold
1	cup Michigan dried cherries
¼	cup orange juice
¼	cup half & half
1	Tbsp milk
1	egg, beaten
	extra flour

Preheat oven to 400°F. Line a baking sheet with parchment paper.

Combine flour, orange zest, sugar, baking powder, baking soda, and salt in a bowl. Using a pastry blender or two table knives held parallel, cut butter into flour mixture until it becomes a coarse crumble. In another bowl, combine cherries, orange juice, half & half, milk, and egg. Add liquid mixture to flour mixture and stir. When a soft, wet dough forms, scrape it onto a floured work surface.

With light hands and fingers, form a ball, then press the ball into a circle. Keeping your fingers floured, fold in the sides of the circle, then top and bottom to form a fat envelope. Press the dough out and repeat the folding and pressing process four or five times. Turn the dough over completely if the bottom is sticking. Add more flour if the whole thing is too sticky to handle. Pat the dough into an oval shape to a depth of about ½-inch. Cut into wedge or trapezoid shapes and place on the baking sheet. Sprinkle scones with sugar.

Bake 12–15 minutes, until a tinge of browning appears. Serve warm.

Tips and variations: Alas, these do not stay moist for very long. The neighbors and guests at our adjacent vacation rental cottage get many of our excess scones.

Albion Heritage B&B

Mary Slater & Richard Lewin
517 E. Michigan Ave., Albion, MI 49224
517-629-3550
www.albionheritage.com | mail@albionheritage.com
3 Rooms, 1 Suite
College town | 20 minutes to Marshall, 30 minutes to Jackson

Albion Heritage B&B is a Georgian Revival home, built in 1912. It has served as a private home since its inception, until the present owners, Richard Lewin and Mary Slater, purchased it with the intent of renovating it to become an elegant home away from home for people visiting the Albion area.

Whether it is for events taking place associated with Albion College, private family affairs, Michigan International Speedway events, touring Michigan's wine country, or just personal time away, Albion Heritage B&B is the place to call home.

With the finest of amenities and gourmet breakfasts, Albion Heritage B&B cannot be beat. Make Albion Heritage B&B a top choice for a place to stay in Albion.

"We spent a delightful weekend at the Albion Heritage Bed and Breakfast. The house was lovely as well as comfortable and welcoming. We really enjoyed the chance to meet and visit with Mary and Dick. Breakfast was really gourmet. Can't wait for the next visit."—Guest

"Hobbit" Eggs with Spinach & Paprika

Yield: 4 servings

         olive oil spray (or butter flavor cooking spray)
1⅓   cup baby spinach leaves, coarsely chopped, divided
   4   extra-large (jumbo) eggs
   2   Tbsp heavy cream, divided
         salt & pepper, to taste
   4   Tbsp shredded cheese (of choice), divided
         roasted paprika, to taste

Preheat oven to 375°F. Generously coat the insides of four (6-oz.) ramekins with olive oil spray.

Put about ⅓ cup spinach in each ramekin and break an egg over the spinach. Drizzle cream over each egg and sprinkle with salt and pepper. Cover each with about 1 tablespoon of shredded cheese.

Sprinkle each with paprika. Bake until the egg whites are firm and the yolks are as runny or firm as desired (10–14 minutes).

Serve immediately with breakfast meat and bread of choice.

Antiquities' Wellington Inn

Barbara & Hank Rishel
230 Wellington Street, Traverse City, MI 49686
231-922-9900 | 877-968-9900
www.wellingtoninn.com | stay@wellingtoninn.com
7 Rooms, 2 Suites, 2 Apartments
Chic, walkable downtown neighborhood

Enter the stately mahogany and leaded glass foyer of Antiquities' Wellington Inn and be transported back in time to an era of quiet and gracious living. A time when life was slower, when families entertained at home, and downtown was a leisurely stroll past elegant neighborhood homes. This 1905 neoclassical mansion was built by one of Traverse City's lumber barons and has been fully restored to its original grandeur featuring period antiques throughout the nine guest rooms, dining room, library, and living room. The inn's unique downtown Traverse City neighborhood location is within a short walk to fine restaurants, shops, recreational trails, and the spectacular beaches of Grand Traverse Bay.

Each morning guests are treated to a sumptuous full breakfast in the turn-of-the-last-century dining room. One can almost hear the sound of fine crystal and great conversation that must have taken place around the massive table that once occupied this room. With its original stained glass windows, ceiling, and wall fixtures, the vintage china and silver used by the innkeepers for breakfasts and private teas seem very appropriate. Refreshments and snacks are always available in the guest kitchen.

Luncheon tea at the Wellington Inn is reminiscent of tearooms that flourished in Britain in the nineteenth century. Guests enjoy an assortment of traditional teas accompanied by beautifully presented split scones with crème frâiche and homemade jams, finger sandwiches, teacakes, tarts and shortbreads.

Spinach Egg Bake with Pine Nuts

Yield: 10 servings

"A favorite with our guests."

- 10 eggs
- ½ cup all-purpose flour
- 1 tsp baking powder
- 1 (10-oz.) pkg. frozen chopped spinach, thawed and well drained
- ¼ cup butter, melted
- 2 (4-oz.) cans green chilies, drained, seeded and chopped
- 2 cups small-curd cottage cheese
- 4 cups Colby/Monterey Jack cheese, shredded
- ¼ cup pine nuts
- 1 red pepper, sliced and sautéed (optional)

Preheat oven to 400°F.

In a large bowl, beat the eggs. Stir in the flour and baking powder. Stir in the spinach, melted butter, green chilies, cottage cheese, and Colby/Monterey Jack cheese.

Pour the mixture into a 13x9-inch glass baking dish. Sprinkle with pine nuts.

Bake for 15 minutes. Reduce the oven temperature to 350°; bake for 25–30 minutes more or until puffed and the center is set. Remove from the oven and let stand for 10 minutes before cutting.

Garnish each serving with a few slivers of sautéed red peppers.

Arcadia House B&B

Greg & Patrice Wisner
17304 Northwood Hwy (Scenic M-22), Arcadia, MI 49613
231-889-4394
www.thearcadiahouse.com | info@thearcadiahouse.com
4 Rooms, Carriage house
Lake Michigan port village along M-22

Arcadia House was constructed in 1910 by the Tondu family, well-known local builders. It was the long-time residence of Charles P. Matteson, who operated the general store next door. Careful restoration has preserved the home's Edwardian elegance and added modern comforts and conveniences.

Antique furniture and accessories throughout the house contribute to the tranquil ambience so valued by the guests. Enjoy cozy fires in the parlor, table games in the sitting room, or relax on the porch with a 1940s novel from the inn's vintage collection.

For further rejuvenation there is an outdoor garden hot tub and on-site massage therapy.

A full service breakfast is served daily at the time of your choosing from 8 a.m.-10 a.m. Breakfast starts with fruit, followed by a main dish and a meat selection. The innkeepers are happy to accommodate special dietary requirements. From soufflés, pancakes, and oatmeal to Virginia ham, potatoes, and scones, the breakfasts at Arcadia House are always a highlight of the day.

Arcadia House is centrally located close to the best that northwestern Michigan has to offer—Sleeping Bear Dunes, Arcadia Dunes Nature Preserve, Arcadia Beach on Lake Michigan, and world-class golf.

Tofu Breakfast Burritos

Yield: 4–6 servings

"Here's a vegetarian dish that all your guests will like."

6   tortillas
4   Tbsp vegetable oil, divided
1   clove garlic, minced
½   onion, finely diced
1   lb. firm tofu, crumbled
1   cup vegetables of your choice (try green onions, tomatoes, mushrooms, and bell peppers), finely chopped
⅛   tsp turmeric
     salt and pepper, to taste
6   oz. faux sausage, crumbled
     Tabasco or other hot sauce, optional

Preheat oven to 200°F. Place tortillas between two wet paper towels, wrap them in foil, and heat them in the oven for 5–10 minutes.

In a large skillet, heat 2 tablespoons of vegetable oil over medium heat. Add garlic and onion and sauté for 2–3 minutes. Add tofu, vegetables, turmeric, salt, and pepper and continue to cook over medium heat for 5–7 minutes.

In another skillet, heat the remaining oil, add the faux sausage, and cook until the "sausage" is browned. Add the "sausage" to the tofu mixture and stir to combine. Scoop the mixture into the tortillas; fold them up; serve immediately with hot sauce.

This recipe has been adapted from www.chooseveg.com.

At Willow Pond B&B

Jerome & Claire Vandenburg
9896 Carlsen Road, Fenwick, MI 48834
989-248-3150
www.atwillowpond.com | innkeeper@atwillowpond.com
2 Rooms, 1 Suite
On 26 acres in an Amish area an hour from Grand Rapids

Guests who stay at At Willow Pond B&B most frequently comment on how peaceful and relaxing they find this country inn to be, situated in "the middle of the mitten."

The B&B's 26 acres nestled in Michigan's heartland is located in a small town Mecca. Nearby orchards and farm stands are just minutes away. Horse-drawn buggies of the nearby Amish and Mennonite communities are frequently seen on the roads and byways. Antique shops and golf courses, lakes and bike trails, cute little stores and old-fashioned movie theaters are all part of the ambiance and landscape.

Claire is the cook at At Willow Pond, and is happy to accommodate special requests or specific diets with advance notice. Her main philosophy is a combination of both healthy and indulgent. The menu starts with the freshest foods possible, such as eggs from the B&B's own chickens; fruit and vegetables grown organically on the property; and as much locally grown food as possible. Claire loves baking her own bread, cookies, muffins, and scones.

Breakfast always starts with a fruit course and includes something sweet, something savory, and of course, juice and coffee, tea or hot chocolate. Breakfast might include sautéed apples, Claire's special recipe for light and fluffy multigrain pancakes, or stuffed French toast and sausage, or maybe a yogurt cream fruit parfait, garden vegetable frittata, bacon, and cranberry scones.

Light Honey-Banana Whole-Wheat Bread

Yield: 2 loaves

"This is a light, just slightly sweet yeast bread (not the more dense, sweet quick bread). It is wonderful toasted with eggs for breakfast, makes a great peanut butter and honey sandwich, and is fantastic as French toast—especially stuffed French toast with Nutella and bananas!"

2½–3	cups bread flour, divided
2	cups whole-wheat flour, divided
2½	tsp active dry yeast
1	cup warm water
2	Tbsp vegetable oil
1	large egg
½	tsp vanilla
¼	cup honey
1	large banana, mashed
1½	tsp salt
2	tsp poppy seeds or flax seeds

Preheat oven to 375°F. Grease a large bowl and two loaf pans.

Stir together ¾ cup bread flour and ½ cup whole-wheat flour with yeast in the bowl of a stand mixer. Mix in water, using dough hook attachment, for 30 seconds, then beat at a higher speed for 3 minutes. Add in oil, egg, vanilla, honey, and banana, mixing at moderate speed until blended. Gradually add salt, poppy seeds, and as much of the remaining flour as needed, until dough begins to come together in a ball, (using both types of flour approximately equally).

Turn out dough on a lightly floured surface and knead 5–7 minutes, adding in any remaining flour until dough is smooth and elastic, and to keep the dough from being too sticky.

Place dough in a lightly greased large bowl and turn over once to coat dough. Let rise until double, about an hour. Punch down dough, divide in half, and allow to rest for 10 minutes. Shape dough into 2 loaves, and let rise in greased loaf pans until doubled again, about 45 minutes.

Bake for 30–35 minutes.

This recipe has been adapted from *Healthy Bread Recipes*, Salton/Maxim Housewares, Inc.

Bay View of Mackinac B&B

Doug & Lydia Yoder
PO Box 448, Mackinac Island, MI 49757
906-847-3295
www.mackinacbayview.com | Bayviewbnb@aol.com
10 Rooms, 3 Suites
Outstanding views | ideal location on iconic island

Come back to yesterday, where grace, charm, and romantic turn-of-the-last-century traditions are complemented by the modern conveniences of today. Just a short ferryboat ride from Mackinaw City or St. Ignace lies Michigan's crown jewel—historic Mackinac Island— and its most romantic and distinctive B&B, Bay View of Mackinac.

Built over a century ago in 1891, Bay View of Mackinac still celebrates her original family heritage in the Grand Victorian style that is truly Mackinac. Beautifully positioned on the bay, Bay View is the only B&B of her type and style resting on the water's edge. Each guest room will embrace guests with its own unique seascape, while the second story sundeck boasts an incredible view of the straits of Mackinac.

At Bay View, guests will enjoy a hot, gourmet, seated breakfast on the veranda; the best homemade cookies served every afternoon; and a generous taste-tempting dessert each evening. And of course, bottomless cups of the famous Bay View Blend Coffee are served.

After many years of requests from their guests, the wonderful recipes from this inn are now available in a lovely book. Guests may purchase a copy of the inn's cookbook, *The Best of Bay View of Mackinac, An Original Mackinac Island Cookbook*, while at the inn or on-line. You will want to add this to your cookbook collection.

Chef Rose's Rolled Omelet

Yield: 6 servings

"A traditional Bay View Bed and Breakfast favorite."

¼ cup each of ham, green and red peppers, and onion
  (other vegetables of your choosing are optional)
6 eggs
¾ cup flour
1½ cups milk
3 Tbsp melted butter
  pinch of salt & pepper
  cheese of your choice, shredded, for garnish
  tomatoes, fresh, diced and seeded, for garnish

Preheat oven to 350°F. Smooth out a large sheet of aluminum foil on a cookie sheet and spray generously with cooking oil.

Dice meat and vegetable assortment and set aside. Place eggs, flour, milk, butter, salt, and pepper in a bowl. Whisk until smooth. Pour batter onto foil and distribute diced vegetables and ham evenly.

Bake 15 minutes.

Remove from oven and sprinkle with shredded cheese and diced fresh tomatoes.

Starting at one end, roll baked mixture away from you. Cut into slices.

Bellaire B&B

David Schultz & Jim Walker
212 Park Street, Bellaire, MI 49615
231-533-6077 | 800-545-0780
www.bellairebandb.com | info@bellairebandb.com
9 Rooms
Village setting in lakes area an hour from Traverse City

Recently voted the 12th Best Overall Bed & Breakfast in North America, Bellaire B&B sits at the top of a hill at the end of a tree-lined drive, located in a tranquil setting with delightful gardens, a hammock, and shuffle-board court.

The goal at Bellaire B&B is to offer a relaxed environment with those warm and caring extras never thought to be found anywhere else but home. The cherry-paneled library is filled with hundreds of books, a blazing fireplace in the winter, and comfortable chairs to relax into, hiding away, dreaming of distant lands and adventure. Discover the sunken garden and enjoy a private sunny afternoon, or gather with other guests on one of the wonderful porches or parlors to share stories over a glass or two of wine.

In the morning, a hearty breakfast is served that features a hot main dish, fresh homemade breads and muffins, fresh fruit, juices, and gourmet coffee, teas, and hot chocolate.

The village is only a short walk away with quaint shops, a movie theater, brewpub, and fine dining. Guests enjoy the convenient location of the inn and are off on adventures that may include golfing, skiing, boating, kayaking, art galleries, antiquing, wine tasting, or hot-air ballooning.

Come and be positively spoiled!

"The room is as welcoming as its host. The rocking chair soothed me as I rocked away the stress and pressure of a busy work week. I wish everyone the same total relaxation I enjoyed in this room and visiting with Jim and Dave and their other guests as we enjoyed the summer breeze on the porch." —Guest

Blueberry Boy Bait

Yield: 8–10 servings

2 cups all-purpose flour
1½ cups sugar
¾ cup shortening (half butter, half margarine)
2 tsp baking powder
2 egg yolks
1 cup milk
1 tsp salt
1 tsp vanilla
2 egg whites
2 cups blueberries (can use fresh or frozen)

Preheat oven to 350°F. Grease and lightly flour a 9x13-inch baking pan.

In a large bowl, blend the flour, sugar, and shortening together with a pastry cutter until it resembles coarse meal. Remove 1 cup of the mixture to use for topping and set aside.

To the mixture remaining in the bowl, add baking powder, egg yolks, milk, salt, and vanilla. Mix until very smooth. In a small bowl, beat the egg whites until stiff. Gently fold the beaten egg whites into the mixture. Pour into the baking pan.

Place fairly dry blueberries evenly on top of the batter. Sprinkle reserved crumb mixture over the fruit.

Bake for about 40 minutes.

Big Bay Point Lighthouse B&B

Jeff & Linda Gamble
3 Lighthouse Road, Big Bay, MI 49808
906-345-9957
www.bigbaylighthouse.com | keepers@bigbaylighthouse.com
7 Rooms
On Lake Superior an hour west of Marquette

Guests at this lovely inn will renew their spirits in unsurpassed beauty as they are treated to a secluded adult retreat from the stress of modern life. Enjoy quiet nights and Northern Lights on Lake Superior shores. Sit before the fire in the living room and recount the number of lighthouses that have been seen. Hike, bike, ski, or snowshoe along the shore or on the many trails in the area. Experience the deep solitude and unspoiled beauty of nature at this lighthouse inn. A good night's sleep is guaranteed, but early risers may be rewarded with close-up views of deer, raccoons, rabbits, foxes, wild turkey, and other assorted wildlife feeding in the meadow at daybreak.

Sitting high atop a cliff jutting into the clear, deep waters of Lake Superior, this unique B&B inn is one of the few surviving resident lighthouses in the country, and is listed on the National Register of Historic Places. For over a century, mariners have relied on Big Bay Point's light to guide them along this remote and rocky stretch of Michigan coastline. Although automated in 1941, the romance and lore of the site are undimmed.

Climb to the lighthouse lantern, 120 feet above the lake surface. From this vantage point, visitors can survey open fields of native grasses and wildflowers, dense hardwood and pine forests, the majestic Huron Mountains looming in the distance and the ever-changing face of Lake Superior. The drama of offshore lightning-bolt dances, ice kaleidoscopes, and dramatic gales, as well as the spectacle of the night sky, and Aurora Borealis are breathtaking.

Chicken Wellington

Yield: 4 servings

"This is my go-to recipe when I want to impress dinner guests. It is a fancy-looking main dish that will impress even the gourmet chefs in your crowd. You can make it ahead of time and be relaxed when your guests arrive. Serve it with an appetizer of baked Brie and crackers, a green salad, buttered asparagus spears, cranberry relish, and your favorite dessert. This menu looks fancy and tastes wonderful. It's easy on you, your time, and your nerves."

½ (10 oz.) pkg. frozen chopped spinach, thawed and well-drained

1 (5.2-oz.) container semi-soft cheese with garlic and herbs

1 frozen puff pastry sheet, thawed

4 boneless skinless chicken breast halves (1¼ lbs)

¼ tsp salt

2 Tbsp fine dry breadcrumbs

.1 egg

1 Tbsp water

Preheat oven to 425°F. Lightly grease a baking sheet and set aside.

In a bowl, stir together drained spinach and cheese. Set aside.

On a lightly floured surface, roll out pastry sheet to a 15x13-inch rectangle. Trim into a 14x12-inch rectangle and reserve trimmings. Cut into four 7x6-inch rectangles.

Spread one-fourth of the spinach mixture over each pastry rectangle, leaving a ¾-inch border around the edge.

Season chicken breast half with salt. Top each pastry rectangle with a chicken breast half, tucking under the thin end to make an even thickness. Sprinkle each breast with ¼ of the breadcrumbs. In a small bowl, beat together egg and water. Brush egg wash onto edges of the rectangles. Gather together the four corners of each pastry at the top of the chicken breast and firmly pinch edges together to form a tight seal. Place packets on prepared baking sheet.

Cut a small decorative shape from the remaining pastry. I use a leaf cookie cutter, but any seasonal shape works. Place on top of pastry packet and brush with additional egg mixture.

Bake packets for 25 minutes or until golden brown. Your meat thermometer should read 160 degrees.

Tips and variations: You can prepare the packets through step 4 up to 24 hours ahead; cover and chill. To serve, bake as directed.

Black River Crossing B&B

Stan & Sue Carr
N11485 Hedberg Road, Bessemer, MI 49911
906-932-2604
www.blackrivercrossing.com | info@blackrivercrossing.com
3 Rooms
Waterfalls, winter sports, and wildlife area near Lake Superior

The Black River Crossing B&B was built in 1997 from white pine logs, and opened as a B&B in January 2002. There are three guest rooms, four fireplaces, and three common areas for relaxation, game playing, and movie watching. Indulge in a full, home-cooked breakfast and at the end of the day enjoy complimentary evening beverages.

The B&B is situated near Ottawa National Forest in the heart of the Lake Superior snow belt. Consequently, it is in a well-known winter sports area with numerous opportunities for downhill, cross-country, and backcountry snowshoe exploration. The annual average snowfall often exceeds 150 inches. The downhill ski areas of Powderhorn, Blackjack, Indianhead, Mount Zion, and White Cap are all within 15 minutes or less of the inn. With 150 waterfalls in the area, there are many to discover while walking the trails. The North Country Trail, spanning several states, passes within several miles of the inn.

The greatest of all the Great Lakes is so big that all the water from Erie, Michigan, Huron, and Ontario together could not fill up Lake Superior. The Porcupine Mountains State Park, Picture Rocks National Lakeshore, and the Apostle Islands are gems of the area. Walk the lakeshores. Pick up rocks and agates at Little Girl's Point. Take a sunset cruise, have a fire at the beach, or go swimming (yes, the water gets warm enough in August).

Cranberry Crumble Dessert

Yield: 5–6 servings

"This is a simple cranberry dessert to serve with ice cream. It is light and delicious. Cranberries are grown locally, so we keep some all year."

Filling
1 cup (or more) frozen or fresh cranberries
⅓ cup sugar
½ cup walnuts, chopped

Batter
1 egg
½ cup sugar
½ cup flour
¼ cup butter (½ stick), melted
cinnamon and cloves for seasoning
cream or maple syrup to thin the batter

Preheat oven to 325°F.

Cover the bottom of a glass pie plate with frozen or fresh cranberries. Sprinkle ⅓ cup sugar and chopped walnuts over the cranberries.

In a mixing bowl, beat egg and sugar. Add flour and melted butter; blend well. Spread over cranberries. Season with cinnamon and cloves. For thinning the batter, add a bit of cream or maple syrup.

Bake until the batter is cooked through, about 45 minutes. Test with a toothpick. Dish will be brown on top.

Serve warm with ice cream.

This recipe has been adapted from a *Taste of Home Magazine* issued a few years ago.

Bridgewalk B&B

Janet & Tom Meteer
2287 S. Main Street, Central Lake, MI 49622
231-544-8122
www.bridgewalkbandb.com | bridgewalkbb@earthlink.net
5 Rooms
Village charm on Intermediate Lake | 30 minutes to Charlevoix

Crossing the footbridge to this charming inn is the first step to a relaxing vacation. Enjoy the spacious grounds, the meandering brook, and the shade of wonderful old maple trees. The porch with its rockers and swing beckon a weary traveler. Casual elegance awaits inside. Built in 1895 by James Cameron, an early settler and lumber baron, the inn reflects the gracious appointments of a more elegant era: large airy windows, pocket doors, high ceilings, and woodwork of birds-eye maple, cherry, and mahogany. The downstairs common area is a place to relax—read in front of the fireplace, play the baby grand piano, or listen to music.

A gourmet breakfast starts a day filled with antiquing, biking, boating, golfing, hiking, shopping, or gourmet dining possibilities. Stroll a short distance to Intermediate Lake, or take a short drive to the shores of beautiful Torch Lake, Lake Michigan, or Lake Bellaire where boating, windsurfing, or kayaking opportunities await. And don't forget the nearby nature preserves: Grass River, Antrim Creek, Seven Bridges, and the Jordan Valley Pathway.

Cream Scones

Yield: 12–15 scones

"Lighter than usual scones and slightly sweeter."

2 cups flour
½ cup sugar
1 Tbsp baking powder
⅛ tsp salt
⅓ cup unsalted butter, cold and sliced into pieces
½ cup heavy cream
1 large egg
½ Tbsp vanilla

Preheat oven to 425°F.

Whisk together in a large bowl the flour, sugar, baking powder, and salt. Cut in butter with 2 knives and a pastry blender (or use food processor) until crumbly. In a separate bowl, beat together cream, egg, and vanilla. Stir into dry mixture until all is incorporated.

Turn out onto a floured pastry cloth, roll out until ¾-inch thick and cut into 2-inch rounds. Place on an ungreased baking sheet. Bake 13 minutes. They should be golden around the edges.

Tips and variations: The dry mixture can be frozen in a Ziploc bag for up to one month. No need to thaw, just add wet ingredients and bake as usual. You can add any nuts, dried fruit, chocolate chips, grated rinds, or flavoring you like.

Butler B&B

Gene & Judy Butler
5774 Main St., Lexington, MI 48450
810-359-5910 | 866-359-5910
www.butlerphotosbb.com | gbutler1235@sbcglobal.net
3 Rooms
Four blocks from Lexington Harbor and village shops

Butler B&B is located along the scenic drive of M-25 in the picturesque harbor-town of Lexington. This historic home was built in 1879 almost entirely out of hemlock, a very straight-grained, strong, weather-resistant wood. The Lexington area was one of the few areas in the state where sufficient hemlock grew to allow almost an entire house to be built of this one type of wood. The house is listed on the Michigan Register of Historic Sites.

The B&B's two acres of beautifully landscaped property provides an ideal setting for outdoor rest and relaxation, and just four blocks away is the scenic limestone harbor providing a beautiful nautical setting for your enjoyment. Shopping downtown or at antique shops in the area is always a draw, as are the free Friday night concerts in the park, or a visit to the Blue Water Winery and Vineyard.

A complimentary full breakfast is served on the weekend with a continental breakfast on weekdays. Breakfast at the Butler B&B is a casual meal among friends. If you were a stranger before, you won't be after—nor will you go away hungry. Coffee, tea, and hot chocolate are available anytime during the day, along with fresh-baked cookies in the evening.

Apple Butter

Yield: 2 pints

3 lbs. apples
1 cup cider or apple juice
3 cups sugar
2 tsp cinnamon
1 tsp nutmeg
½ tsp allspice
½ tsp cloves
dash of salt

Wash, core, and peel apples; cut into eighths.

Divide the apples and the cider or juice into thirds for processing in a blender. Put ⅓ cup cider or juice and 4 or 5 pieces of apple in the blender. Cover and blend for 5 seconds. Add the second third; blend for 5 seconds. Add the final third and blend for an additional 25 seconds. Empty into saucepan.

Add sugar and spices to apple mixture. Cook over low heat about 45 minutes, or until thick; stirring occasionally. Pour immediately into sterilized jars and seal.

Tips and variations: A food processor could also be used.

This recipe has been adapted from a 1968 book that came with the chef's first Waring blender.

Buttonville Inn

Candy & Ron Harsh
3049 W. Saginaw Road, Coleman, MI 48618
989-465-9364
www.buttonvilleinn.com | info@buttonvilleinn.com
3 Rooms, 1 Suite
Rural Amish area setting along Pere Marquette Rail-Trail

Buttonville Inn B&B is a classic, Foursquare, Craftsman-style three-story home. It was built in the 1920s as a country manor roadhouse with French and English country-style furnishings in the common areas.

The charm of this unique B&B surrounds guests with warm, homey hospitality. Wander along the babbling brook, curl up with a good book, or just relax on the covered, wraparound summer porch, screened for convenience. Bask in the elegant yet relaxed and friendly atmosphere, while enjoying the ambiance of gentler times.

Guests are always welcome in the large country kitchen with fireplace, where goodies await the weary traveler. In summer, breakfast may be served on the covered porch so that guests might enjoy all the beauties of nature while savoring their meal.

Adjacent to the inn is an old railroad track that has been converted into a rail trail for biking and hiking. There are 36 miles of paved trail between Midland and Clare. The inn is located in the midst of Amish country, where large spring and fall Amish auctions and flea markets are held. A large casino resort is also only a 20-minute drive from the inn.

Magic Puff Pancakes for Two

Yield: 2 servings

"This is a beautiful presentation when filled with fresh, sliced strawberries and/or blueberries sprinkled with powdered sugar or whipped cream!"

2   Tbsp butter, melted
3   eggs
½   cup milk
½   cup flour
½   tsp salt
¼   tsp vanilla

Preheat oven to 425°F. Spray bottom of Mini Baker (8-inch baking dish or two 5–6-inch ramekins) with cooking spray.

In a large bowl, combine butter, eggs, milk, flour, salt, and vanilla. Whisk until smooth.

Pour egg mixture into baking dish. Bake 25 minutes until it is puffed and golden. Remove from the oven. Slice a thin top layer off of the pancake and set aside. Fill the center of the pancake with sliced fruit such as strawberries, blueberries, or bananas. Replace the top; sprinkle with powdered sugar. You may serve with whipped topping or syrup, if desired.

Tips and variations: Check while baking. You may need to reduce baking time. Kids love these.

This recipe has been adapted from *Let's Eat: A Kids' Cookbook.*

Candlelite Inn B&B

Melanie Barnard
709 East Ludington Ave., Ludington, MI 49431
877-997-0099 | 231-845-8074
www.candleliteinnludington.com
melanie@candleliteinnludington.com
7 Rooms
Walk to historic downtown, sandy beach, pier, and lighthouse

Look no further for a delightfully romantic Michigan B&B with so many special amenities. This warm and inviting B&B is a perfect gathering place whether getting away with a special someone, or reserving some or all of the seven rooms for a larger group of family and friends. The innkeeper continuously strives to add special romantic and pampering touches for her guests. Outdoors, guests can relax on one of two outdoor decks, sink into a settee for two, or spend a few hours in a rocker; laugh at the gray and black squirrels scampering around the backyard, build an evening fire in the outdoor fireplace, or take advantage of the gas grill.

In the morning, wake up to the mouthwatering smells of freshly baked muffins and breads, tantalizing entrées, and cobblers. At Candlelite Inn B&B, guests are never too early or too late for the full, piping hot, delicious breakfast served family style in the lovely sun room overlooking a quiet pond. Melanie prefers to cook with fresh local and organic produce. Her homemade jellies and jams are exceptional and evening desserts of pies or tarts complete the day.

Candlelite Inn is one of the few Michigan B&Bs to be certified by Green Lodging Michigan, and in 2008 was one of the first in northwestern Michigan to become a Green Lodging Partner.

Candlelite Inn is within walking distance to historic downtown Ludington with its one-of-a-kind shops, a huge sandy Lake Michigan beach, pier, marinas, *SS Badger* Ludington, Michigan, car ferry, and North Pierhead Lighthouse.

Upside-Down Blueberry French Toast

Yield: 8–10 servings

"Another great way to use blueberries, especially when they are local and in season."

1	pint blueberries (more if you prefer)
4	eggs
½	cup half & half
1	tsp pure vanilla
8–10	pieces of 1-inch thick favorite French or Italian-style bread
½	cup sugar
2	Tbsp butter
1	tsp cinnamon

Preheat oven to 350°F.

Cover the bottom of a 9x13-inch glass baking dish with blueberries.

Beat eggs, half & half, and vanilla in a large bowl. Add bread slices to egg mixture, turning once to coat each side. Place dipped bread in the baking dish.

In a separate bowl mix sugar, butter, and cinnamon together until crumbly. Sprinkle the sugar mixture on top of soaked bread. Bake uncovered for approximately 30 minutes. Remove when the topping is bubbling nicely.

Tips and variations: This dish can be done the night before. Place dipped bread slices in the baking dish without the blueberries. In the morning, the soaked bread slices have to be removed and replaced once the blueberries have covered the bottom. The sugar mixture for the topping can also be mixed and stored overnight in the refrigerator in a covered dish or a plastic storage bag.

Candlewyck House B&B

John & Mary Jo Neidow
438 East Lowell Street, Pentwater, MI 49449
231-869-5967
www.candlewyckhouse.com
6 Rooms
Lake Michigan resort village | Walk to shops and dining

The Candlewyck House B&B is the perfect place to begin a Lake Michigan or Great Lakes getaway. Built in 1868, Candlewyck House reflects the charm and warmth of Great Lakes lodging from a bygone era, but with all the comforts of the twenty-first century. No one leaves the table hungry at Candlewyck! A delicious 5-course breakfast is made fresh daily. Recipes vary and are never dull, gathered from over 400 cookbooks for new and exciting fare. When guests work up an appetite, there is always a large basket of complimentary snacks on hand and drinks in the refrigerator.

Planning a romantic Michigan getaway, a Lake Michigan beach vacation, or a weekend on hiking or biking trails? How about an art fair, music concert, or a visit to some art galleries?

If so, this Great Lakes B&B is the perfect lodging, and Pentwater is the perfect place. Here, the pace of life slows so that guests may take in the sights, sounds, and smells of a simpler time. With each new day, guests are summoned from a restful slumber by the aroma of a full country breakfast. Relax in the sun on our large brick patio or stroll the plush gardens that surround the entire property. It's a short walk to town where shopping and dining are abundant. Casually stroll the picturesque streets and beaches, or borrow one of the many bicycles available to guests and explore all that the beautiful waterside village has to offer. Candlewyck House provides the most comfortable and convenient accommodations in all of western Michigan.

German Baked Eggs

Yield: 8–10 servings

"This egg recipe is our number one most-requested dish."

12	eggs
½	cup bacon bits
¼	cup flour
1½	tsp baking powder
1	stick butter, melted
¼	cup chives, fresh if possible
½–1	cup milk
6–8	drops hot sauce
2	cups cottage cheese
8	oz. cheddar cheese, grated

Preheat oven to 375°F.

In a large bowl, mix the first eight items thoroughly. Add the two cheeses last.

Pour into a 9x13-inch baking pan and bake 35–40 minutes or until a knife inserted comes out clean.

Let rest 5 minutes and serve.

Tips and variations: Since we often have 12–15 people for breakfast, I stretch this recipe by adding two more eggs and ¼ cup milk for each additional person. I also add a little more of the cheeses and divide into two pans to bake.

Canterbury Chateau

Janet Henry
5050 Kintyre Lane, Brighton, MI 48116
810-516-2120
www.canterburychateau.com | staff@canterburychateau.co
4 Rooms
Far-northwest Detroit suburb studded with parks and lakes

Canterbury Chateau is owned and operated by Janet Henry, who for a time was a Home Economics teacher. This will tell you all you need to know about the accommodations and food at the inn.

Guests and non-guests alike have come to enjoy the 3:00 p.m. check-in time when tea, coffee, and tarts are served—for a nominal charge—by the fireplace in the Hearth Room or on the sun deck, as the weather allows. Sit, laugh, relax, and enjoy the ambience of the Chateau. This is an excellent way to start your stay. Arrangements for the tea/coffee hour are by reservations only.

When guests come down for breakfast at Canterbury Chateau, they often say they were awakened by the pleasant aroma of a hearty breakfast wafting from the kitchen. Coffee is always served for early risers. Coffee is followed by a plated breakfast buffet served on the island in the kitchen and enjoyed either in the sunrise breakfast area or in the dining room. When guests arrive at the inn, they fill out a breakfast request so accommodations can be made for any special diet requests. Breakfast times are flexible to fit guests' travel needs.

After breakfast, plan to visit downtown Brighton. Originally a small settlement near the old plank road that became Grand River Avenue, today Brighton's city center is full of unique, upscale shops, restaurants, and a park to play or stroll in. If there is a golfer in your group, guests at the inn may take advantage of golf privileges at the private Oak Point Golf Course. Prior arrangements are necessary.

Wander back to the inn after dinner in town and enjoy a complimentary dessert saved just for you.

Zesty Hot Sausage, Cheese, & Crescent Roll Egg Dish

Yield: 4 servings

"This savory treat is an all-in-one breakfast dish. Our guests enjoy it so much they want to know how it's made. Now you know, too."

1 large meatball-sized zesty hot sausage

2 small cartons of Southwest Egg Beaters

1–2 cups cheese, shredded, use 3 varieties for the best results (works best with sharp cheddar, mozzarella, Colby Jack)

1 large or small pkg. of crescent rolls depending on number of servings

¼ cup butter, melted and warm (approximate, may use more)

salt and pepper, to taste (optional)

Preheat oven to 350°F. Move the rack to the center and cover the bottom rack with foil to catch any drippings. Select a baking dish sized to accommodate the number you are serving. A 9x9-inch square for 4 servings or a 9x13-inch for 8 servings. Spray bottom and sides with olive oil.

Flatten the sausage and cook on both sides in a large frying pan sprayed with olive oil.

Cut the sausage into small pieces. Add the Egg Beaters to the pan. Scramble the Egg Beaters and sausage together. You may add a little salt and pepper or let your guests season to their own tastes at the table. Go light on pepper because you are using zesty hot sausage. Add shredded cheeses. Blend well.

Place the large ends of the crescent roll triangles around the inside edge of the baking dish and let the pointed ends dangle outside. There should be no crescent roll on the bottom of the baking dish. Pour the scrambled egg mixture into the baking dish.

Make a hole in the center of the mixture with a spoon. Pull the triangle ends that hang over the edge of the baking dish toward that center hole. It is like wrapping the crescent roll over the top of the mixture. Baste the crescent rolls with warm butter.

Bake for 12–15 minutes or until golden brown. Remove from oven and allow it to rest for 5–10 minutes before cutting. Cut in triangles to match your crescent roll design on the top.

Tips and variations: To serve 8, add two additional cartons of Egg Beaters and multiply the other ingredients accordingly.

Castle in the Country B&B Inn

Ruth & Herb Boven
340 M-40 South, Allegan, MI 49010
888-673-8054 | 269-673-8054
www.castleinthecountry.com | info@castleinthecountry.com
2 Rooms, 8 Suites
65 wooded acres with pond | 45 minutes to Saugatuck

Castle in the Country B&B Inn features all the amenities a discriminating guest appreciates. There is an on-site spa for couples' side-by-side massages, reflexology, pedicures, manicures, and facials. The 65-acre secluded wooded estate is the perfect setting for strolls and meanderings. There is complimentary use of kayaks and a paddle boat on the private lake, and a screened gazebo and porch for quiet moments of rest.

At Castle in the Country, breakfast has reached a celebratory status. Served in the dining room overlooking a natural pond, your own table for two will be ready for you. Breakfast offerings are reviewed during check-in when you may select your seating time. Fresh, local ingredients from nearby farms and food purveyors are incorporated into every breakfast, and special dietary needs may be met with advance notice. All breakfasts include a fruit course, baked pastry, and a main entrée. Breakfast meats are always included on the side so that vegetarians can be easily accommodated. For an extra special experience, consider adding an additional value package that includes the upgraded service of breakfast brought to your guest room for one of the mornings of your visit.

There are times when it just isn't worth the drive, the wait, and the expense of going out to a restaurant. Instead, stay in and take advantage of this convenient dinner option. A full dinner for two is prepared with fresh and seasonal ingredients and packed into a picnic basket for you to enjoy in your room, in one of the common dining areas, or in a secluded outdoor picnic spot.

The innkeepers' insider knowledge will ensure that you get the most out of your day trips to nearby towns including Saugatuck, Holland, South Haven, and Kalamazoo. They will pinpoint the best restaurants, wineries, antique shops, and galleries near the inn.

Cherry Chocolate Cream Scones

Yield: 6–8 scones

"While some scone recipes use a combination of milk and cream, we use only heavy cream. The end result is a crispy, more browned crust with a moist interior. Any dried fruit—cherries, apricots, or even raisins—will work, but the vanilla and almond flavors are added because they go so well with cherry and chocolate. The two-step baking procedure is important. The initial high heat yields a higher rise, but if left to bake at that temperature, the bottoms will burn while the interior remains undone."

2	cups all-purpose flour
½	cup brown sugar
½	Tbsp baking powder
½	tsp salt
¼	cup dried cherries, apricots, or raisins and/or chocolate chips, diced into half-inch cubes
½	tsp almond extract
½	tsp vanilla extract
1	cup heavy cream
1	egg, beaten for glaze
	granulated sugar for topping

Preheat oven to 425°F. Line a baking sheet with parchment paper.

In a large bowl, combine flour, brown sugar, baking powder, and salt and mix thoroughly. Add diced fruit and chocolate. In a small bowl, combine almond extract, vanilla and cream; add to flour mixture. Stir with a spatula until large clumps form.

Using squeezing motion with clean hands, press the dough into a ball. Don't over mix.

Place dough onto a large cutting board and press into a disc approximately 1-inch thick and 10 inches in diameter. Cut into 8 wedges and move to the baking sheet. With a pastry brush, coat scones with egg and sprinkle with sugar.

Bake for 10 minutes. Reduce heat to 375 degrees F. Rotate and bake for an additional 10 minutes until golden brown. Allow to cool on a cooling rack for 15 minutes.

Chateau Chantal Winery and B&B

Brian Lillie
15900 Rue de Vin, Traverse City, MI 49686
800-969-4009 | 231-223-4110
www.chateauchantal.com | wine@chateauchantal.com
2 Rooms, 8 Suites, 1 Apartment |
Commanding views of Grand Traverse Bay | vineyards

Chateau Chantal is described as a perfectly charming winery and Old World inn stocked with fine wine and staffed with attentive proprietors whose sole purpose is to provide a space or experience to meet a guest's every need. The inn offers a unique experience in northern hospitality that combines vineyard, winery and B&B lodging. Lunchtime Tapas Tours are held daily mid-June through Labor Day and wine dinners are offered throughout the summer. Cooking classes taught by nationally renown Chef Perry Harmon will help you increase your confidence and creativity in the kitchen and your knowledge of wine pairings.

B&B guests enjoy exceptional amenities, from cozy rooms to spacious suites, views of vineyards and fresh water, terrace or balcony settings, high ceilings, fireplaces, sitting areas, and elegant furnishings. The inn and winery are set in a relaxing rural landscape with trails, quiet country roads, and beaches.

Nearby, in the Grand Traverse region, there are shops, galleries, cultural venues, fine dining, and championship golf. The area offers four robust seasons of activity.

Chocolate Cherry Mocha Muffins

Yield: 2 dozen muffins

"A guest favorite at Chateau Chantal by Chef Sue Greve."

6	eggs
1½	cups oil
2	cups buttermilk
1	cup strong black liquid coffee
2	tsp vanilla extract
⅔	cup cocoa (sifted, then measured)
3	cups white flour
2½	cups whole-wheat flour
2	cups brown sugar
1	tsp baking powder
2	tsp baking soda
2	tsp salt
2	cups chocolate chips
2	cups pitted cherries

Preheat oven to 375°F. Prepare muffin tins with paper liners.

In a large bowl, combine the eggs, oil, buttermilk, coffee, and vanilla; set aside.

Sift cocoa, flours, brown sugar, baking powder, baking soda, and salt into a separate bowl. Add the dry mixture to the wet mixture and combine.

Spoon the batter into muffin cups and bake about 20–25 minutes, or until done. Test with a toothpick inserted into the center of the muffin. When it comes out clean, the muffins are done.

Chelsea House Victorian Inn

Jim & Kim Myles
118 E. Middle Street, Chelsea, MI 48118
877-618-4935
www.chelseahouseinn.com | innkeeper@chelseahouseinn.com
5 Rooms
Walkable small-town setting 25 minutes west of Ann Arbor

Chelsea House Victorian Inn is a restored 1880s Queen Anne Victorian home built with the craftsmanship of a bygone era. The home was originally built for James Gorman, a lawyer and tobacconist who later became a state representative and finally state senator. There was no detail overlooked in the homes of this era. Local lumber experts say that the clear pine used was not unusual for its time. Sugar pine forests were vast in Michigan in the 1800s. Now, however, those forests have long since been depleted.

Located in the vibrant town of Chelsea, there is plenty to keep a visitor busy. You can be active, sedentary, pampered, or entertained all within walking distance of the inn. There are golf courses, parks and lakes, the Chelsea Center for the Arts, and the Jeff Daniel's Purple Rose Theatre. Several vineyards dot the countryside. The University of Michigan's cultural activities are only 15 minutes away. A plethora of restaurants and shops fill the streets of town.

Breakfast at the Chelsea House starts with fruit crêpes followed by a hearty entrée. Dietary restrictions can be accommodated with some advance notice. These innkeepers put the same detail into their meals as they have their rooms and the restoration of their home.

Baked Cinnamon Apple French Toast

Yield: 2 servings

*"If you have leftovers of this dish it is awesome warmed
in the microwave and served as dessert in the evening
with a scoop of vanilla or cinnamon ice cream."*

4 Tbsp cream cheese (regular or light) softened	½ baking apple (Granny Smith) thinly sliced
4–6 thin slices French or Italian bread	3 eggs
3–4 Tbsp light brown sugar cinnamon	⅔ cup milk
	2 Tbsp maple syrup powdered sugar, for garnish

Preheat oven to 350°F. Grease two individual casserole dishes with nonstick cooking oil.

Spread cream cheese on one side of each slice of bread. Layer the bread and cut into 1-inch cubes. In the bottom of each casserole dish, sprinkle a layer of brown sugar and dust with cinnamon. Place a layer of sliced apple over the top. Place in a layer of the cubed bread and again sprinkle brown sugar with a dusting of cinnamon on top. Dice up the remaining apple and sprinkle on top.

In a bowl, mix eggs, milk, and maple syrup and gently pour mixture over bread until well soaked. Mixture should come up half way to the top of the bread when soaked. Cover dishes with aluminum foil and bake for 30 minutes. Uncover and bake for an additional 15–20 minutes until fluffed up and brown on top. Serve with powdered sugar on top. Present with warmed syrup, as an optional topping. You may not want the syrup at all. The finished dish is like a bread pudding.

Tips and variations: The top will be a golden color and puffy like a soufflé when the dish first leaves the oven, but as it cools it will flatten. Don't despair, it is just the nature of the dish. It tastes just as delicious.

This dish offers great diversity and works in all these variations:

- gluten-free bread (we recommend cinnamon raisin gluten-free bread vs. white)
- egg substitute
- almond, soy, and coconut milk have been used instead of cow's milk, and non-dairy guests also get this without cream cheese in the center

Chesny's Keswick Manor

Graham Chesny
1800 Center Avenue, Bay City, MI 48708
989-893-6598
www.keswickmanor.com | innkeeper@keswickmanor.com
4 Suites
On a street of grand old mansions not far from I-75

On June 10, 1895, Fremont B. Chesbrough, noted Bay City lumberman, sold his vacant property to Robert E. Bousfield for $3,600. Bousfield and his brother owned the Bousfield Woodenware Works, the world's largest woodenware factory. They primarily built barrels and kegs. Local legend says that Anna Taylor survived going over Niagara Falls on October 24, 1901, in a Bousfield barrel!

This historic home provides a comfortable surrounding for guests to relax and unwind. Four beautifully appointed suites and welcoming common areas make a stay here truly memorable. Close to many attractions and entertainment opportunities in Bay City and nearby communities, there is much to do while staying at the inn.

An elegant complimentary breakfast for all guests is prepared daily. The Keswick Manor also offers exceptional dining for its overnight guests. Menus and prices can be viewed on-line. The manor is well known for its wonderfully catered parties, weddings, meetings and special events.

Graham's Blueberry Custard French Toast

Yield: 4–6 servings

"This is a creamy, one-dish baked French toast that you prepare the night before and then bake in the morning."

8	slices brioche or French bread, 1-inch thick
1	cup blueberries, rinsed
1	(8-oz.) pkg. cream cheese, cubed
12	large eggs
1	cup milk
1	cup heavy cream
½	tsp salt
¼	cup maple syrup

Arrange bread in a lightly sprayed 9x13-inch baking dish. Sprinkle with blueberries and cream cheese cubes. In a large bowl, whisk together eggs, milk, cream, salt, and syrup. Pour mixture over bread. Cover and refrigerate for several hours or overnight.

Preheat oven to 350°F. Bring the dish to room temperature before baking.

Bake covered for 30 minutes. Remove cover and bake until lightly browned, about 30–35 minutes longer. Serve warm.

Tips and variations: Instead of the milk and heavy cream, you can substitute 2 cups of half & half.

Cobblestone Manor
Luxury Historic Inn

Paul & Heather Crandall
3151 University Drive, Auburn Hills, MI 48326
248-370-8000
www.cobblestonemanor.com | stay@cobblestonemanor.com
8 Rooms, 2 Suites
Intimate retreat in a corporate and education hub

Built in 1840 and recently renovated with all the modern amenities required by professional travelers, Cobblestone Manor offers a pleasing, luxurious, historic atmosphere. The formal living room allows for comfortable relaxation, music enjoyment, or quiet and intimate conversations with friends. Innkeepers Paul and Heather and their Cocker Spaniel, Joe, are committed to providing world-class service at this cozy, historic Victorian-era inn.

Enjoy a wonderful dinner at the award-winning Alfoccino restaurant with a Cobblestone Manor overnight stay. Chef Juno has put together an outstanding menu for this package that includes a bottomless salad and house-made garlic bread, a choice of fifteen delicious entrées to please any palate, and a dessert to share. Entrée selections include a choice of several outstanding pastas, their signature ribs, New York strip steak, perch, shrimp, salmon or whitefish, or a number of their sumptuous Italian specialty dishes. Don't forget to save room for one of Alfoccino's mouthwatering desserts to share with a date!

Spinach & Shallot Crustless Quiche

Yield: 8–10 servings

"At Cobblestone Manor, we serve this fluffy, rich, delicious entrée with mini-muffins (often cranberry orange muffins) and a breakfast meat such as bacon or sausage links, and an assortment of lovely fresh fruits cut up on the side of the plate. The recipe is requested very regularly and we rarely have leftovers on the plates."

1	large (or 2 small) shallots, finely diced
	butter, to sauté the shallots
1	(10-oz.) pkg. frozen chopped spinach
2	cups grated Swiss cheese (packed)
16	eggs
3	cups heavy cream
2	tsp salt
¼	tsp cayenne pepper
2	tsp sugar
1	Tbsp Frank's Hot Sauce

Preheat oven to 375°F. Grease a 9x13-inch baking dish.

Sauté shallots in a small amount of butter until translucent. Scatter evenly in bottom of baking dish to cover. Thaw, drain, and thoroughly squeeze spinach until dry. Spread out evenly over shallots in bottom of baking dish. Sprinkle Swiss cheese over shallots and spinach.

In a large bowl, beat eggs, cream, and all seasonings together and pour into the baking dish. Bake for 1 hour or until set completely. May be covered and kept overnight in the refrigerator.

Tips and variations: If baked in a water bath (in a shallow pan of water) your quiche will not form a brown crust. It will take longer to bake—as much as 30 additional minutes.

For muffins, if you want a time saver, we have found that Krusteaz Cranberry Orange Muffin Mix is absolutely delicious (and easy) with grated orange rind and chopped pecans added to it.

Cocoa Cottage B&B

Larry Robertson & Lisa Tallarico
223 S. Mears Avenue, Whitehall, MI 49461
231-893-0674 | 800-204-7596
www.cocoacottage.com | innkeeper@cocoacottage.com
3 Rooms, 1 Suite
Heaven for foodies and chocoholics in a lake resort town

This authentically restored, 1912 Arts & Crafts bungalow, offers you quiet refined character, world-class attention to detail and CHOCOLATE!

The philosophy of food at the Cocoa Cottage B&B is: If it's worth making, it's worth making a fuss over. Larry and Lisa both love to cook (and eat), and spending time in their beautiful kitchen is one of their favorite passions. Their creations are made from scratch using the freshest ingredients, (organic, whenever possible) with an extra pinch of creativity!

Enjoy your day relaxing by the cozy fireplace or on the sun-dappled porch. Their elegant gardens or Lake Michigan's sugar sand beaches invite you to unwind in a peaceful setting. The Cocoa Cottage is located just one block from a 50-mile paved bike trail, unique shopping, antiquing, and dining. The Cocoa Cottage is situated in the heart of a very walk-able community with the friend-liest proprietors.

Larry and Lisa, resident owners and innkeepers, have received numerous awards for their delicious breakfasts and warm hospitality, as well as restoration awards for the quality of design and restoration of their inn. Their guests' accolades are too many to mention here. These are just a few:

"Gracious hosts, beautiful accommodations, delicious food ... and chocolate!"—Guest

"This is a lovingly restored Craftsman bungalow with kind and considerate innkeepers. The breakfasts are delicious and the inclusion of chocolate zucchini bread and other chocolate treats is a special touch."—Guest

Panettone Pain Perdu,
Merlot Poached Pears & Lemon Curd

Yield: 4 generous servings

"Panettone is a type of sweet bread loaf originally from Milan, Italy, usually prepared and enjoyed for Christmas and New Years. It contains candied orange, citron, and lemon zest, as well as raisins, which are added dry and not soaked. The light bread texture in contrast to the sweet dried fruit bits is intoxicating—soaked in our custard and grilled to golden perfection. Our Christmas tradition can now be yours. Buon Natale, Enjoy!"

4 Bosc pears, peeled w/stems	1/8 tsp orange oil
2 cups Merlot, good quality	2 Tbsp Grand Marnier
1½ cups water	1 tsp cinnamon
¾ cup pear nectar	4 slices panettone
1 crushed cinnamon stick	(homemade is best)
6 peppercorns, crushed	generous amount of grated
1 Tbsp vanilla	fresh nutmeg
fresh lemon curd	powdered sugar, to garnish
(homemade is best)	fresh berries, to garnish
1 cup heavy cream	maple syrup, to garnish
4 large eggs	

Start by poaching the pears. Not-quite-ripe Bosc pears work best. (Bartlett pears are too hard, red pears are too soft). Peel pears—leave stems attached. Combine wine, water, nectar, cinnamon, peppercorns, and vanilla in a saucepan deep enough to hold 4 pears covered in poaching liquid. Cook uncovered for 40–50 minutes, until tender. Slice pears in half, core with melon-baller and fill space with fresh homemade lemon curd. Serve pears warm; add lemon curd just before serving.

In a bowl, whisk together heavy cream, eggs, orange oil, Grand Marnier, and cinnamon. Cut 4 (1-inch) thick slices of panettone. Place in large shallow dish and cover with custard mixture. Grate nutmeg over the top. Turn once to coat.

Heat a well-buttered frying pan and place bread slices in pan. Don't use cooking spray or margarine. Grill until both sides are browned and the center springs back when touched.

Arrange slices creatively on a plate and sprinkle with powdered sugar. Garnish with fresh berries. Arrange pear on the plate. Serve with country sausage patties or links and warmed pure Michigan maple syrup. We serve this dish year round. Enjoy!

Comstock House B&B

John & Jane Johansen
414 Maple Street, Big Rapids, MI 49307
231-796-475 | 877-796-4753
www.thecomstockhouse.com | info@thecomstockhouse.com
3 Rooms
Walk to historic downtown | Close to White Pine Rail-Trail

Enter the Comstock House and enjoy taking a step back in time. The inn is an elegant Eastlake brick-style home built by D.F. Comstock in 1896. The Comstock House is proud to be listed on the State of Michigan Historic Places. The décor in each room is accented with additional authentic, antique treasures found from around the world. Furnishings are elegant, yet comfortable. Enjoy sitting in the library looking through photos and memorabilia. All the luxuriant features combined with the ambiance of this historic, old world Victorian home awaits.

The Comstock House is located only a couple blocks from historic downtown Big Rapids. Enjoy shopping, dining, and antiquing all within walking distance. While here, take a stroll down the Riverwalk that starts directly across the street and leads through the park and along the river on a paved trail. Also for the biking enthusiasts, the B&B is located only a quarter-mile from the White Pine Rail-Trail.

Guests are welcome to enjoy a restful and luxurious night in comfort and wake up to a delicious, unique, gourmet breakfast. Breakfast is served on Blue Willow China in the dining room. The innkeepers love to start breakfast with cream cheese filled pastries. If smiling faces are an indication of happiness, these pastries do the trick. It's one of the many delicious recipes that the innkeeper learned from Michael Whitman, a cooking instructor at Grand Rapids Community College. Another favorite at the inn is the double chocolate chip muffins. Those who love chocolate will *love* these muffins.

Double Chocolate Chip Muffins

Yield: about 10 muffins

*"Lots of chocolate lovers stay at the Comstock House B&B.
This is a super simple recipe, and they're so delicious."*

½   cup orange juice
½   cup water
3   Tbsp oil
1   Tbsp vinegar
1   tsp vanilla
1½ cups flour (gluten-free flour may be used)
½   cup sugar
¼   cup cocoa
1   tsp baking soda
¼   tsp salt
⅓   cup chocolate chips

Preheat oven to 375°F.

In a medium bowl, mix orange juice, water, oil, vinegar, and vanilla. In another bowl, mix together flour, sugar, cocoa, baking soda, and salt. Stir dry mixture into wet mixture. Fold in the chips, being careful not to over mix.

Fill muffin cups ¾-full. Bake for 10–12 minutes.

Variations:

This filling may be added:

4   oz. cream cheese
¼   cup powdered sugar
2   drops almond extract
1   Tbsp cornstarch

Mix all ingredients and inject into the center of each muffin before baking using a pastry bag. Or partially fill muffin cup with muffin mixture, use a teaspoon to add filling and cover with more muffin mix.

This recipe has been adapted from Michael Whitman, chef at Grand Rapids Community College.

Country Chalet / Edelweiss Haus B&B

Carolyn & Ron Lutz
723 S. Meridian Road, Mount Pleasant, MI 48858
989-772-9259
www.countrychalet.net | RCL9259@earthlink.net
4 Rooms, 3-bedroom Chalet
Pastoral retreat | 17 minutes to city and casino

The Country Chalet and Edelweiss Haus have a European flair from the architecture and décor to the down-filled duvets. The two homes are set among rolling pastures, ponds, and gardens with a sunset view to the west. Each of the four guest rooms in the Edelweiss Haus has a private bath, a TV, and a door to the balcony brimming with flowers in season. The Country Chalet has a suite of three rooms. Guests are invited to enjoy tea, meet, read, or play cards or board games in the common areas of each house. A full breakfast is served including Carolyn's fresh baked goodies.

"My husband and I, my parents, and our three children all enjoyed a wonderful night at the Edelweiss Haus. My mother says it was simply the most enjoyable stay she has ever experienced, and my daughter is asking when we can visit again! Ron and Carolyn were the most terrific hosts imaginable, and we are very glad we found the Edelweiss Haus."—Guest

The Veggie Thing

"At the sight of so many vegetables at the breakfast table, many guests take only a sample the first time the dish is passed, although the colored peppers on top with the melted cheese are very attractive. When it comes around again, guests almost always take a larger portion. Using soy cheese makes this a satisfying entrée for vegans. In season, most of the veggies are from our own garden. Our guests affectionately call the dish, The Veggie Thing."

1	tsp extra virgin olive oil
½	large onion, diced
1	handful frozen peas
1	handful frozen corn kernels
1	red potato, eyes removed, scrubbed and shredded
	sea salt
	freshly ground black pepper
	additional seasoning, to taste (your preference)
1	small zucchini, sliced and diced
1	small summer squash, sliced and diced
1	blossom of broccoli, sliced and diced
1	blossom of cauliflower, sliced and diced
1–2	baby carrots, shredded
¼	each of a red, yellow, and orange sweet pepper, diced
	Jarlsberg or soy cheese, finely shredded, to garnish

Add oil to a large skillet over low heat. Add above ingredients to the skillet in the order listed above, saving the cheese for last. With low heat, stirring is not necessary.

When the vegetables are almost tender but still colorful, add the cheese. When the cheese melts, remove from heat and *slide* the contents of the skillet onto an oval serving dish. Serve warm.

Tips and variations: The *slide* is always touchy. First, tap the side of the skillet to see that the contents are free to slide, and then tip the skillet to about 45 degrees until it begins to slide. With the larger oval dish below the skillet, start the slide at one end and move to the other end, so the round shape in the skillet reforms to the oval shape of the dish. The melted cheese on top helps to hold the veggies together. It's spectacular when it works but when disaster happens, use a large spoon for a gentle reshaping.

Crimson Cottage Inn the Woods

Kathy & Michael Henry
2009 W Lakewood Boulevard, Holland, MI 49424
616-994-0922
www.crimsoncottageinn.com | kathy@crimsoncottageinn.com
3 Rooms
Wooded setting 1.5 miles to beach, 5 miles to city center

Crimson Cottage is nestled in a quiet wooded area, giving guests a feeling of seclusion and serenity although just minutes from restaurants, shopping, and activities. The cottage offers a casual, cozy, comfortable experience, while newer construction provides lots of light, views, larger bathrooms, plenty of hot water, and room to spread out!

Guests are welcome to bring in lunch or dinner and use the common areas to dine. In warmer weather, guests can enjoy sitting in the backyard surrounded by beach grass, birds, and a view of a neighboring pond. Guests might even catch a glimpse of other wildlife.

At Crimson Cottage Inn the Woods, the innkeepers know that breakfast is as important as bed, and appetites and food preferences are as varied as the guests. Kathy and Michael try to accommodate all requests, including special dietary needs. For very early risers, a coffee pot in each room allows guests to start the day with the first cup when desired. A buffet presentation in one of the main dining areas includes a hearty hot main entrée, pastry, fruit, juice, yogurt, and granola. This buffet-style allows guests to fill their own plates with their favorites and meet fellow travelers. To dine privately and quietly, at no extra charge, simply complete a menu the night before indicating your breakfast choices and it will be delivered to the room. The innkeepers' culinary roots are mid-western, with traces of German and Southern influences thrown in. They happily offer enough healthy choices for the "conscientious" eater, and are able to offer soy- and gluten-free options if given enough notice. Chocolate chip cookies are available 24/7. Kathy's interest in multiple seasonal china settings adds interest to the dining room, and Michael likes to see them put to good use.

German Apple Cake

Yield: 8–10 servings

"This has been in our family for years and in my recipe box for over 40 years so I am not sure who gets the credit! My sister, Judy, reminded me of it and began baking it for our B&B. It is now a staple on our menu rotation and a favorite of guests and my husband Michael."

3	eggs
1½	cups vegetable oil
2	cups sugar, plus ½ cup for topping
3	cups flour
½	tsp salt
1	tsp baking soda
2	tsp cinnamon, plus 1 tsp for topping
1	tsp vanilla
1	cup chopped nuts
3	cups sliced apples (Granny Smith work very well)

Preheat oven to 350°F.

In a large bowl, beat together eggs and oil until foamy. Add next 5 ingredients and mix well.

Ina separate bowl, mix vanilla, nuts, and apples until apples are well coated. Add apples to egg mixture and blend. Pour into a 9x13-inch pan.

For topping: Combine ½ cup sugar and 1 teaspoon cinnamon and sprinkle over the top.

Bake for 45–60 minutes. Cool completely and cut into desired squares.

Days Gone By B&B

Jane & Jack Poniatowski
201 N. High Street, Northport, MI 49670
231-432-0098
www.DaysGoneBybnb.com | jane@daysgonebybnb.com
4 Rooms
Resort town at the tip of Leelanau Peninsula

Michigan's "little finger," the Leelanau Peninsula, has much to offer, and at its tip is the quaint village of Northport and the Days Gone By B&B. Here you will find the relaxation and serenity that makes for a magical stay. Outside, beautiful gardens and a 9'x9' stone fireplace offer a perfect sitting area to gaze at the constellation of stars overhead. Inside, cozy rooms, alluring breakfast aromas, and conversation with newfound friends are all part of the day's adventure.

Northport defines charm—small in size, but huge on amenities. There is the picturesque marina on Grand Traverse Bay, a beach and playground, unique shops and restaurants, amazing views from Braman Hill, Friday night summer concerts in the park, the Northport Community Arts Center with world-renowned performances, and hiking and biking trails, all within walking distance.

A short drive away are Leelanau State Park, the Grand Traverse Lighthouse, Leelanau Sands Casino, the mesmerizing sunsets in Peterson Park on Lake Michigan, and Sleeping Bear Dunes National Park. Traverse City will ignite the palate with its rolling hills dotted with cherry orchards and wine vineyards with tasting rooms.

Coming from excellent home cooks on both sides of the family gave Jane the interest and the expertise to try to create menus that earn praises from the guests. While admittedly a "recipe follower," Jane almost always tweaks the ones she finds to please the palate of her and Jack, who is, himself, a sous chef extraordinaire.

Savory French Toast with Tomato Jam

Yield: 2 servings

*"I'm adding this recipe to our list of faves!
It's very easy, unique, and delicious."*

Tomato jam

½	Tbsp olive oil
½	cup onion, finely chopped
½	garlic clove, minced (optional)
1	(14-oz.) can diced tomatoes in juice (fire-roasted are preferable)
½	Tbsp sugar
¼	tsp dried thyme
¼	tsp coarse kosher salt
⅛	tsp black pepper

4	thick slices of day-old baguette, 2 per serving
½	cup milk
2	eggs
	kosher salt & freshly ground black pepper
2	tsp herbs de Provence (be generous)
2	tsp butter
2–4	poached eggs, 1–2 per serving

For jam: Heat oil in medium saucepan over medium heat. Add onion and garlic; cook until onion is soft and translucent, stirring often, about 4 minutes. Add diced tomatoes with juice, sugar, thyme, salt, and black pepper. Cook over medium-high heat until almost all liquid evaporates and mixture is reduced to about 1⅛ cups, stirring occasionally, about 8–10 minutes. Cool to room temperature.

For French toast: Soak bread in the milk on both sides to soften, about 5 minutes per side, depending on how hard the bread is. (If it is softer, it may need less time.) Beat the eggs with salt, pepper, and herbs de Provence in a flat or shallow dish. Gently melt the butter in a frying pan until foaming, but not colored. Pull the bread from the milk and turn it around in the egg mixture to coat. Fry on both sides until golden brown. Serve with a spoonful of tomato jam.

Tips and variations: Serve with a sprinkle of herbs such as parsley or chives for color. Jam may be made a day ahead and refrigerated. Leave out at room temperature before serving.

This recipe has been adapted from "Savory French Toast" by Laura Calder, Cooking Channel; and "Tomato Jam" by Amy Finley.

Dewey Lake Manor B&B

Joe & Barb Phillips
11811 Laird Road, Brooklyn, MI 49230
517-467-7122 | 800-815-5253
www. deweylakemanor.com | info@deweylakemanor.com
5 Rooms
On a lake amid many lakes | Near Michigan International Speedway

Dewey Lake Manor is nestled in the Irish Hills of southern Michigan; a jewel of blue sky, fresh air and sparkling lakes; an area of quaint towns, botanical gardens, and scenic drives. Dewey Lake Manor itself has paddleboats, a canoe, a picnic area with a bonfire pit, grills, picnic tables, and eighteen acres in which to wander. The Dewey family, who also named the lake, built the century-old historic home.

There are nearby wineries, the Pioneer Wine Trail, antique stores, shopping, and festivals.

At Dewey Lake Manor, a breakfast buffet is offered if there are more than four guests. With fewer guests the meal is served family-style, not plated. The menu consists of fresh fruit, a hot dish, meat, a variety of breads, juice, coffee/tea, and sometimes dessert, such as fruit crisp or bread pudding. The innkeepers have their own strawberry patch and are expanding their garden to include raspberries and blueberries.

"This was our first experience with a B&B and we could not have chosen a more perfect way for celebrating our anniversary. Upon our arrival, Barb greeted us at the door and showed us to our room where we were welcomed by a warm gas fireplace and a congratulatory rose in a vase."—Guest

Bread Pudding

Yield: 10 servings

"I am not Irish but I belong to a group called 'Oh These Irish Hills.' I was asked to bring a dessert to our St. Pat's Day celebration. I consulted my Irish friends who shared that bread pudding was a common signature dessert. I researched recipes and have developed our own Dewey Lake Bread Pudding, which we serve often on our breakfast buffet ... Enjoy!"

6	stale large croissants
1	cup dried cherries/cranberries/raisins or mix of all
5	extra large eggs, plus 2–3 egg yolks
5	cups half & half or milk or a mixture of both
1½	cups sugar
½	tsp vanilla

Preheat oven to 350°F. Spray a 9x13-inch or 10x15-inch pan with cooking oil.

Slice croissants in half and place bottoms in pan with cut side up. Sprinkle dried fruits on croissants and put tops back on so that the fruit is between layers. In a bowl, whisk together eggs, milk, sugar, and vanilla, and pour over the bread. Press down and soak 10–15 minutes. Place in pan of hot water; cover with tent of foil.

Bake for 45 minutes. Uncover and bake for an additional 40–45 minutes.

Tips and variations: Serve warm with whipped cream, or you may garnish with a drizzle of lemon or caramel sauce.

Dove Nest B&B
St. Joseph

Jitka & John Nelson
5000 Scottdale Road, St. Joseph, MI 49085
269-429-2211 | 269-921-2229 (cell)
www.dovenestbedandbreakfast.com
4 Rooms
Amid vineyards and orchards | Minutes to Lake Michigan

Relax in the small town atmosphere of St. Joseph, "Michigan's Most Romantic City." Cobblestone streets, quaint shops, a choice of restaurants and cafés, beautiful white sand beaches, and gorgeous sunsets make this town a "must see." Throughout the summer season there are plenty of activities to keep everyone entertained. Join in festivities such as the Blossomland Parade, Art Festival, Jazz Nights, or enjoy Antiques on the Bluff displays and sales. Tour the Michigan wineries and discover award-winning winemakers. Stay at the Dove Nest B&B and you are within minutes of enjoying more than a dozen wineries and tasting rooms.

Return in the evening and relax by the fire pit, read a favorite book by the pond, enjoy colorful gardens, or watch the doves and pigeons in their aviaries. The Dove Nest reflects one of John's life-long loves—a love for birds and nature. Enjoy the sight of beautiful birds in open aviaries or in artistic display cages at the back of the property. Jitka loves the wild doves and thinks that having wild doves is a sign of a "happy home." For something unique to mark a special anniversary, birthday, or other milestone, arrange for a White Dove Release.

The Dove Nest B&B is located on 2.5 acres that has been planted with hundreds of trees and shrubs. John and Jitka love the flowers, their blooms, and scents from early spring throughout the summer to the first frost in the fall. Garden chairs and benches can be found throughout the property, inviting guests to stop, relax, and enjoy the beauty of nature.

From their travels, the innkeepers have a collection of international art and delight in international cuisine. With the delicious breakfast, guests will have a taste of the local food fresh from the farm: sausages, eggs, vegetables, and seasonal fruit—much harvested from their own organic garden. Guests are invited to sample the high quality European condiments and Far East seasonings to complement the farm fresh meal.

Waffles with Hot Raspberry Sauce

Yield: 4 waffles, 2 cups sauce

*"Waffles are always welcome at the breakfast table.
At Dove Nest B&B in St. Joseph, we serve these with any
hot fruit sauce or Michigan maple syrup plus fresh fruit."*

Waffles
2   eggs
1½ cups milk
½   cup oil
1   tsp vanilla
2   Tbsp sugar
2   cups flour, sifted
2   tsp baking powder
2   egg whites, beaten

Raspberry Hot Waffle Sauce
2   cups fresh or frozen raspberries, divided
½   cup sugar
1   Tbsp cornstarch
½   cup water
1   Tbsp lemon juice
1   cup raspberries for garnishing (optional)
    whipped cream (optional)

Preheat waffle iron (7-inch). Lightly spray with oil.
In a large bowl, beat eggs, add milk, oil, vanilla, and sugar; mix well. Combine flour and baking powder in a bowl. Add to the batter ingredients, blending well. Slowly mix in beaten egg whites. Pour appropriate amount onto waffle iron and cook according to manufacturer's instructions.

Hot Raspberry Sauce: Purée 1 cup of raspberries in a blender. Combine sugar and cornstarch in a saucepan. Stir in water until mixture is smooth. Stir in the puréed berries and 1 cup of whole berries. Bring to a boil, stirring constantly for 1 minute. Remove from heat and stir in lemon juice.

Pour hot raspberry sauce over hot waffles. Top with whipped cream and more whole raspberries, if desired.

Tips and variations: Beaten egg whites and sifted flour add lightness to waffles.

Use raspberry sauce over hot cakes of all kinds, or over vanilla ice cream.

Dutch Colonial Inn

Bob & Pat Elenbaas
560 Central Avenue, Holland, MI 49423
616-396-3664
www.dutchcolonialinn.com | dutchcolonialinn@comcast.net
4 Rooms
A touch of Dutch in a town that celebrates its heritage

Built in 1928, the décor of this inn accentuates the era of the 1930s. Many lovely antiques of mahogany and cherry add to the beauty of the inn. While the décor is elegant, the inn has a very comfortable and homey feel. There are two-person Jacuzzi tubs and fireplaces to add to the warmth and cozy atmosphere. Hospitality at its best will enhance your stay. The inn's motto is, "Our home is your home." The inn is 15 blocks south of downtown Holland—a lovely walk on a beautiful summer day—and a short drive from some of the most beautiful beaches on the Lake Michigan shoreline.

Breakfast pampers guests with a healthy and hearty homemade feast. Awaken to fresh brewed coffee while the fragrance of homemade muffins, coffeecakes, and breads baking fills the air. Savory scents follow as sausages and ham and egg casseroles are baking in the oven. While these bake, the innkeeper patiently prepares the opener—a fresh fruit cup of tiny morsels of every possible fruit flavor, topped with a dollop of creamy vanilla yogurt and a wedge of kiwi, strawberry, or the fruit of choice. Each recipe provides flavor and nutrition, as most recipes are low-fat, yet tasty. As guests dine, they have the opportunity to get to know the other guests at the table.

Twelfth Night Scones

Yield: 12–15 scones

"Guests LOVE these scones, especially with homemade lemon curd."

1¾ cups flour
¼ cup sugar
2 tsp baking powder
¼ tsp baking soda
¼ tsp salt
¼ cup butter, softened
½ cup dried cranberries or cherries
½ cup white vanilla chips
1–2 tsp orange zest
½ cup vanilla low-fat yogurt
⅓ cup buttermilk

Topping
1–2 Tbsp buttermilk or milk
½–1 tsp orange zest
1 Tbsp sugar

Heat oven to 375°F. Spray a round pizza stone with cooking oil.

In a large bowl, stir together flour, sugar, baking powder, soda, and salt. Cut butter into mixture until it resembles coarse crumbs. Stir in cranberries, vanilla chips, and orange zest. Add yogurt and buttermilk; stir just until dry ingredients are moistened.

Shape dough into a ball; place on stone. With floured fingers, press dough into an 8-inch round circle, leaving the edges higher so the liquid topping stays on the dough. Brush dough with buttermilk or milk and sprinkle the sugar/orange zest mix over the top. Bake 20–30 minutes, or until edges are light brown. Cut into wedges. Serve lemon curd or berry preserves with these delicious scones.

Farmhouse Inn B&B

Jeffrey & June Hinkle
4927 28½ Mile Road, Homer, MI 49245
517-418-0014
www.thefarmhouseinnhomer.com
thefarmhouseinnhomer@gmail.com
3 Rooms
Country setting 9 miles south of I-94 at Albion

The Farmhouse Inn, a stately Italianate Victorian-style home built in 1850, nestled in Amish country, is awaiting your visit. The inn is completely restored and furnished with antiques throughout the home, including each guest room with its own European flavor. The innkeepers are committed to ensuring that each stay is memorable and invites return visits.

In the quaint village of Homer (circa early 1800s), visitors will find Daphne's Gift Shop, Cascarellis Pizza and Peanuts, and a wonderful new library, all of which are worth visiting.

Nearby, there is an Amish-owned bakery, a general store and other family-owned shops, a winery, brewery, and birding sites. Area activities include golfing, biking, swimming, canoeing, and kayaking, all within a short drive.

A gourmet, plated breakfast is served to guests in a comfortable dining room. There is also a deck where guests may eat while enjoying the quiet country surroundings. In the summer, the in-ground pool is open, as well as the hot tub.

June's Coffee Cake

Yield: 8–10 servings

*"Fabulous with morning, afternoon, or evening coffee.
Your guests will return for more."*

Filling
- ½ cup granulated sugar
- 1 tsp cinnamon
- ½ cup walnuts or pecans, chopped

Cake
- 3 cups all-purpose flour, sifted
- 1 tsp baking soda
- 3 tsp double-acting baking powder
- ½ cup butter
- 1 cup granulated sugar
- 3 eggs
- 1¼ cups sour cream (not low-fat)

Preheat oven to 375°F. Grease an angel food pan.

For filling, mix sugar, cinnamon, and nuts in a small bowl; set aside.

Sift together flour, baking soda, and baking powder in a bowl. At medium speed in a mixer bowl, cream butter until light. Gradually add sugar, beating well. Add eggs one at a time, beating well with each. Blend in flour mixture alternately with sour cream. Turn half of batter into pan and top with filling. Spread remaining batter evenly over filling.

Bake 1 hour. Cool for 10 minutes in the pan. Turn out of pan and finish cooling.

Frankenmuth B&B (Bender Haus)

Elden & Beverly J. Bender
337 Trinklein Street, Frankenmuth, MI 48734
989-652-8897
www.frankenmuth.org | benderjb@juno.com
4 Rooms
Walk to unique shops, festivals, and dining on Main Street

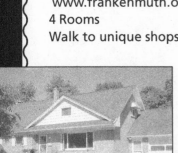

When traveling to a friendly, small town like Frankenmuth, why not stay at a friendly, small place like Frankenmuth B&B? This "homestay" B&B will offer a unique experience as one of Michigan's iconic travel destinations from the point of view of two people who call Frankenmuth home.

Guests have used adjectives like "spotless," "welcoming," and "homey" to describe Frankenmuth B&B, which also is known as Bender Haus. All of the rooms have a queen-size bed. One of those rooms also has two twin beds. The innkeepers raised three children here and opened their home as a B&B in 1980. After all these years, they still love welcoming families into their home.

Breakfast is served family-style, although early risers will find coffee and tea ready and waiting. Breakfast fare includes a choice of juices, fresh fruit, plus a hot entrée such as a savory egg dish and muffins or other treats from the oven. One of the signature dishes is Bender Haus Peach French Toast, the baking of which fills the house with the aroma of cinnamon, vanilla, and brown sugar.

Bender Surprise Muffins

Yield: 12 muffins

"This recipe started as a coffee cake we served with Cool Whip or ice cream. Guests loved it and never left a crumb behind. When I converted it to muffins, guests wouldn't take them and Elden always ended up eating the leftovers. So one day, I used the processor to cut the rhubarb very fine. We now call them "Bender Surprise Muffins" and ask our guests to guess the main ingredient. This past year, only two correctly guessed rhubarb. But everyone loved them."

1¼ cups brown sugar, packed
½ cup vegetable oil
2 tsp vanilla extract
1 egg
1 cup buttermilk
2½ cups all-purpose flour
½ tsp salt
1½ cups diced fresh or frozen (well-drained) rhubarb
1 tsp baking powder
1 tsp baking soda
½ cup nuts, chopped

Topping
1 tsp cinnamon
⅓ cup sugar

Preheat oven to 350°F. Grease a large muffin tin.

In a large bowl, combine the first five ingredients and mix well.

Stir in the remaining ingredients and combine. Pour batter into muffin cups.

In a small bowl, mix topping ingredients; sprinkle on top of muffins, pressing lightly into batter. Bake 15–18 minutes.

Gingerbread House B&B

Mary Gruler
1130 Bluff Street, Bay View, MI 49770
231-347-3538
www.gingerbreadbb.com | webmaster@gingerbreadbb.com
1 Room, 3 Suites
Area of Victorian cottages near Petoskey | Walk to beach

The Gingerbread House B&B is one of 400 Victorian cottages situated in the heart of the Bay View Association, a national historic landmark. The inn has accommodated summer guests since the early days of the twentieth century. The Gingerbread House is one of five homes clustered on Bluff Street, which provides direct private access to the beach and to the wide grassy walking path overlooking the water.

It has been lovingly restored and operated since 1988 by the current innkeeper, Mary Gruler, who after 40 years as a nurse and nurse educator, decided to make hospitality her next career. Be prepared to be pampered.

Guests may enjoy early morning coffee in their rooms or on the front porch, a favorite gathering place. Breakfast begins with fresh fruit, yogurt, Mary's own granola, and beverages, followed by her homemade specialties such as gingerbread pancakes or gourmet French toast. Friendly conversation is the norm at the table, and breakfast promises to provide an enjoyable start to each day.

Bay View's cultural, intellectual, spiritual, and recreational events offer summer residents and guests an atmosphere virtually unchanged since the turn of the last century. A stroll through the peaceful streets is often accompanied by the sound of music students practicing under the guidance of skilled instructors. Enjoy the Bay View Music Festival concerts that draw thousands of visitors each year.

Filled Lemon Crêpes with Lemon Sauce

Yield: 2–4 servings

Batter
- 1 egg, plus 2 egg whites
- 2 cups flour
- 2 cups milk
- ½ cup canola oil
- 1 Tbsp sugar
- 4 tsp baking powder
- 2 tsp lemon zest
- ¼ tsp salt

Sauce
- ¾ cup sugar
- 2 Tbsp cornstarch
- 1 cup water
- 1–2 tsp lemon zest
- 3 Tbsp lemon juice
- 2 egg yolks

Filling
- 4–6 tsp. softened cream cheese, to garnish, divided, and to taste
- 4–6 tsp. orange marmalade, to garnish, divided, and to taste
- 4–6 tsp. toasted chopped pecans, to garnish, divided, and to taste
- whipped cream (optional)

Heat a griddle or frying pan to high.

Combine all batter ingredients. Batter should be thin. Add milk if necessary.

Pour about ⅓ cup of batter onto hot griddle, spreading with the back of a spoon if necessary. Turn over when slightly browned. Remove when both sides are browned.

Keep crêpes warm in low-heat oven until all are prepared. Cover with damp towel to prevent drying.

To prepare sauce, combine all ingredients in a saucepan and stir over medium heat until thickened. Add water if too thick.

To serve, spread each crêpe with cream cheese and place a tablespoon of marmalade and some nuts in the center. Fold crêpe in thirds.

Serve two or three per person. Top with warm lemon sauce and an optional dollop of whipped cream.

Tips and variations: In the sauce, instead of cornstarch, you can use 3–4 teaspoons of arrowroot as a thickener. Note that no part of an egg is left over: The batter uses two whites (plus a whole egg), and the sauce uses two yolks.

Ginkgo Tree Inn

Jean Prout
309 N. Main Street, Mount Pleasant, MI 48858
989-773-8733
www.ginkgotreeinn.com | info@ginkgotreeinn.com
9 Rooms
Downtown setting on the Chippewa River | Restaurant on site

Guests who enjoy the charm and personality of B&B inns will love the Ginkgo Tree Inn. Upon entering the circular drive, there is a sense that this experience will be something special. The inn offers a level of luxury not always expected at a B&B. With a restaurant on site, guests are able to dine in for lunch and dinner.

Ease away tension on the back patio while watching the sun set over the Chippewa River. Two blocks away, downtown comes alive at night with the glitziest of shops and places to dine. Restaurants by the inn are trendy, plentiful, and most importantly, within walking distance. On Thursdays and Saturdays the park behind the inn is bustling with fruit, flower, and vegetable vendors at the Farmers' Market.

Inn breakfasts include delicious chef-made specialties of French toast, omelets, crêpes, quiche, farm fresh eggs, and jam made with the owner's homegrown fresh fruit. The dining room is a great place to meet with family or any friends made while roaming around the neighborhood.

Sara Russ' Blueberry-Buttermilk Pancakes

Yield: 6–8 servings

"We prepare these pancakes at Ginkgo Tree Inn when fresh blueberries are in season, from late spring through late summer."

2 eggs
2 cups all-purpose flour, sifted
3 Tbsp sugar
2 tsp baking powder
1 tsp baking soda
1 tsp salt
2¼ cups buttermilk
4 Tbsp unsalted butter, melted
1 tsp vanilla extract

1 cup fresh blueberries
confectioners' sugar for dusting
additional softened butter for serving (optional; we don't typically use the extra)
warm maple syrup for serving

Preheat oven to 200°F, if needed to keep pancakes warm until ready to serve.

In a bowl, using an electric mixer, beat the eggs on medium speed until frothy. Add the flour, sugar, baking powder, baking soda, salt, buttermilk, melted butter, and vanilla. Stir just until the batter is smooth and no lumps of flour remain; do not over mix.

Heat an electric griddle to medium-high heat until a few drops of water flicked onto the surface skitter across it. Lightly grease the griddle with oil or spray with nonstick cooking oil. Using a batter dispenser set on the large setting, dispense the batter onto the griddle. (Or, just use a spoon, as I do.) Alternatively, ladle about 1/3 cup batter onto the griddle for each pancake.

Scatter blueberries evenly over each pancake (about 1 tablespoon per pancake). Cook until bubbles form on top and the batter is set, 1–2 minutes. Using a spatula, flip the pancakes and cook until golden brown on the other side, 2–3 minutes. Transfer to a baking sheet and keep warm in the oven while cooking the remaining pancakes.

Dust the pancakes with confectioners' sugar and serve warm with butter (optional) and maple syrup.

Tips and variations: When making the batter, take care not to over mix it, as too much stirring will develop the gluten in the flour and result in tough pancakes.

Glen Arbor B&B and Cottages

Katie & Jeff Rabidoux
6548 Western Avenue, Glen Arbor, MI 49636
231-334-6789
www.glenarborlodging.com | innkeeper@glenarborbnb.com
6 Rooms and Suites, 2 Cottages
Surrounded by Sleeping Bear Dunes National Lakeshore

This nineteenth-century inn, up-dated with all the amenities, is in the heart of the village of Glen Arbor. Surrounded by the Sleeping Bear Dunes National Lakeshore, the inn is steps from Lake Michigan's sugar sand beaches, inland lakes, towering sand dunes, and country corners for exploring. Try all that is nearby: hiking, biking, golfing, swimming, antiquing, wineries, canoeing, fishing, boutique shopping, galleries, and much more.

A stay at the Glen Arbor B&B and Cottages is sure to make days spent on the Leelanau Peninsula unforgettable. Striking furnishings in every room, suite, and cottage, exceptional hospitality, delicious home-cooked breakfasts, and thoughtful amenities assure guests' comfort. As featured in *Midwest Living* and on *Good Morning America*, the inn and cottages await visitors.

A cozy living room with a large fireplace, striking dining room, sweeping front porch, and spacious yard are perfect for relaxed conversation, a quick card or board game, snuggling in to read a favorite book, or just soaking up the ambiance of Glen Arbor.

A delicious breakfast, made with the freshest local ingredients, is served each morning for guests in the house. Breakfasts include fresh-baked muffins or bread, a hot egg dish, seasonal fruit, yogurt, our special honey-vanilla signature granola, juices, tea, and custom-blend roast coffee. Cottage guests, of course, have kitchens to make their own special breakfasts.

Special honey-vanilla granola, fresh-baked muffins, juices, teas, and Leelanau Roasters' coffee are always offered.

Caramel Apple Strata

Yield: 8–10 servings

½	cup butter
¼	cup corn syrup
2	cups packed brown sugar
½	cup heavy cream
3	large Granny Smith apples, peeled and chopped
2	Tbsp lemon juice
2	Tbsp sugar
½	tsp cinnamon
½	tsp nutmeg
½	cup chopped pecans
1	loaf cinnamon bread (day old is best)
10	eggs
1	cup 2% milk
1	tsp salt
1	tsp vanilla extract

Grease a 9x13-inch glass-baking dish.

Using a deep saucepan combine butter, corn syrup, and brown sugar. Bring to a boil over medium-high heat, stirring constantly. Add heavy cream and whisk together. Bring back to boil over medium-high heat. Caramel sauce will boil violently. Stir constantly, remove from heat and set aside.

In a large bowl, toss apples with lemon juice, sugar, spices, and pecans.

Place whole slices of bread to cover bottom of baking dish, but not overlapping. Spoon the apple mixture over bread, drizzle about half of the caramel sauce over apples. Cube remaining bread and place on top of apples. Mix eggs, milk, salt, and vanilla well with whisk and pour over the casserole. Refrigerate overnight.

In the morning, preheat oven to 350°F.

Bake uncovered 50–55 minutes or until a knife inserted near the center comes out clean. Let stand 10 minutes.

Warm remaining caramel sauce, drizzle over top of the strata, slice and serve.

Grand Victorian B&B Inn

Ken & Linda Fedraw
402 N. Bridge Street, Bellaire, MI 49615
231-533-6111 | 877-438-6111
www.grandvictorian.com | innkeeper@grandvictorian.com
6 Rooms
Village charm in an area of lakes an hour from Traverse City

Located in beautiful Bellaire, the Grand Victorian B&B was selected as one of America's Top 10 Romantic Inns in 2006—certainly the right choice for a romantic getaway! This award-winning Queen Anne has graced the covers of travel magazines and the pictured icon for national B&B sweepstake promotions. Built in 1895, the home was placed on the National Register in 1978. Immediately upon entering, step back in time to incredible 100-year-old craftsmanship.

Breakfast at the Grand Victorian is an experience. Guests awaken to fresh brewed coffee and tea right at their door. Delightful kitchen aromas waft through the home, leading them to the ornate Victorian dining room with candle-lit place settings consisting of fine china and crystal. At this point many run back to their room to fetch their cameras before the delightful setting is disturbed. Once seated, guests are served a range of plated breakfast delights such as fresh fruit, pastries, coffeecakes, egg dishes, cereals, and breads. Entrées are made from the freshest ingredients and are locally produced whenever possible. Menus can be adjusted to meet individual dietary concerns. The kitchen becomes active again in the afternoon as Linda makes evening treats so good that guests make late afternoon trips back to the inn so as not to miss out.

Bagel Strata with Sausage & Spring Vegetables

Yield: 8–10 servings

"This is one of our guest favorites, as Linda has successfully combined key breakfast elements into one savory dish."

7 cups diced bagels (¾-inch cubed), reserve 1 cup for topping after baking

4 Tbsp (½-stick) butter, melted kosher salt and freshly ground pepper

3 Tbsp vegetable oil

6 oz. mushrooms, thinly sliced

1 cup diced asparagus (½-inch pieces)

½ cup frozen peas, thawed

6 oz. Italian sausage, crumbled and cooked

6 oz. white cheddar cheese, grated

8 eggs

2 cups half & half

Preheat oven to 350°F.

In a bowl, stir together bagel cubes, melted butter, salt, and pepper to coat well. Spread cubes on baking sheet. Bake, stirring several times while cooking, for 25 minutes until golden. Let cool.

In sauté pan over medium high heat, warm 1 tablespoon of oil. Add half of mushrooms. Cook, stirring occasionally, until tender, 5–6 minutes. Transfer to paper towel-lined plate. Repeat the process until all mushrooms are cooked. In same pan over medium heat, warm 1 tablespoon of oil. Add asparagus; cook, stirring occasionally until just tender, about 4 minutes. Transfer to paper towel-lined plate.

In a bowl, stir together 6 cups bagel cubes, mushrooms, asparagus, peas, sausage, and 4 ounces of cheese. Transfer to 2-quart baking dish. In bowl, beat together eggs and half & half, then pour over bagel mixture. Cover, refrigerate at least 1 hour or up to overnight.

Preheat the oven to 350 degrees F. In food processor, pulse remaining bagel cubes into coarse crumbs. Uncover strata. Bake for 50 minutes. Sprinkle with remaining 2 ounces of cheese and bagel crumbs. Bake an additional 10 minutes.

Tips and variations: On occasion, I have not roasted the bagel cubes but just used them as they are. Turns out just fine if you wish to skip the roasting part. Also, I use the mini bagels as they are nice and chewy. You can use a little less oil than called for when sautéing the mushrooms and asparagus.

Grey Hare Inn Vineyard B&B

Cindy & Jay Ruzak
West Rue de Carroll Road, Traverse City, MI 49685
231-947-2214 | 800-873-0652
www.greyhareinn.com | rabbit@greyhareinn.com
1 Room, 2 Suites
A working farm and vineyard on Old Mission Peninsula

The Grey Hare Inn Vineyard B&B is an elegant country vineyard estate located on Old Mission Peninsula in the heart of scenic northern Michigan's wine country. As a working farm and vineyard, the estate offers the experience of a hospitality style typical of a "mas" (farmhouse) in southern France. Take a tour of this boutique vineyard and enjoy the panoramic bay views and the beauty of this scenic and serene peninsula. The inn offers the experience of an "Old World Grape Harvest" where attendees can harvest grapes, then stomp them with their feet in a wooden vat. Grey Hare Inn is also unique in that it offers a Boat and Breakfast option on their 42-foot sailboat.

With Traverse City just seven miles from the inn, guests can enjoy all the activities offered in this premier vacation town. Enjoying wine-related cuisine and wine tastings will keep most visitors busy for days.

The Grey Hare Inn's gourmet breakfasts, as well as evening hors d'oeuvres and nightly room turndown treats, combine the cuisine of Provence and Tuscany with products of northern Michigan. Guests choose individual times for breakfasts and are served at bistro tables for two in the vineyard-themed dining area, or outdoors on the patios in full view of the vineyards, or under a grapevine-covered trellis. The multi-course plated meal includes such items as wine poached pears with mascarpone cheese and Up North Egg Crêpes that guests have frequently referred to as "awesome," "fantastic," or "amazing."

One guest admitted that the crêpes evoked a feeling that he creatively described as, "wanting to burst into song."

Grapes in Grappa

Yield: 6 servings

"When in season we use grapes straight off the vine for this dish, which adds a tremendous depth of flavor; however, store bought grapes are a tolerable substitute, but then I would use wine versus grappa to bring out more grape flavor. As part of an Italian-themed breakfast we serve this first course with homemade rosemary/thyme focaccia bread that is topped with fig jam, caramelized onions, bacon, and blue cheese."

1 bunch red seedless grapes (approx ¼ cup per person)

1 bunch green seedless grapes (approx ¼ cup per person)

⅓ cup grappa (distilled liquor made from grape skins, it's expensive but no substitute works as well—so splurge). You may substitute white wine.

1 lemon (the zest or peel), slivered with shredder

1 (8-oz.) container mascarpone cheese (can actually use about ⅔ of one for 6 servings)

⅓ cup grape juice, prepared or made fresh

mint sprigs for garnish

About 2 hours before serving (okay if longer, but alcohol taste increases with time), cut 3 cups of grapes, of varied colors, in half both lengthwise and widthwise and put into bowl. Toss with ⅓ cup white wine or grappa, mix in the lemon zest and place in the refrigerator. Toss periodically to redistribute fluids.

Place mascarpone in mixer bowl with a standard paddle or whisk attachment. Blend on low speed as grape juice is gradually added in a steady stream. It tends to separate when you add the grape juice. Scrape sides of bowl, then whip on medium-high speed for a minute or so until sauce appears well blended and is slightly thickened. Stop blending if it begins to separate (useable at this point as taste is the same but appearance rather grainy and volume is less—age and temperature of mascarpone appear to be factors.) Stir in ½ tablespoon of grappa, or skip this for non-alcohol version or when there's no grappa available.

Tips and variations: Keep mascarpone in refrigerator until ready to make sauce. The sauce can be done 1 day ahead. Shake to remix. Sauce, however, is best fresh.

You can use prepared grape juice or make it fresh by puréeing 1½ cups of grapes in food processor and straining mixture to get 1/3 cup intense juice.

Hankerd Inn B&B

Janet Rochefort
10350 Hankerd Road, Pleasant Lake, MI 49272
517-769-6153
www.hankerdinnresort.com | hankerd@voyager.net
16 Rooms
Rural lakes area northeast of Jackson | Ideal for groups, crafters

Come and enjoy cutting-edge country hospitality at the Hankerd Inn, a thoroughly renovated and modernized historic farmhouse, circa 1885, between Jackson and Ann Arbor and close to each. Amenities include lovely guest rooms, each decorated with period antiques, named after and reflecting the interests and occupations of the original family members.

Three unique buildings make up this B&B "estate" on four landscaped acres adjacent to a 27-hole golf course. One building is the original farmhouse, now a traditional B&B that is the perfect choice for an individual or couple. The second is a private, new-construction cottage—just the right size for a small family. The third is a three-story "faux barn" with its own state-of-the-art kitchen, large rooms with twin beds and nothing but space on the lower level. It easily accommodates large gatherings and family reunions with a spacious dining room that can seat 45 guests. It is a favorite spot for quilting and scrap-booking groups.

Breakfasts are exceptional and as varied as the storehouse of recipes collected by Janet over the years. Check the website to learn about cooking classes being held in the beautiful demonstration kitchen.

Jewish Apple Cake

Yield: 6–8 servings

*"Here is a great fall recipe I get lots of requests for.
Enjoy the aroma of your kitchen as it bakes."*

3	eggs
1½	cups sugar (you can use ½ brown and ½ white)
1	cup vegetable oil
½	tsp salt
2	cups flour
1	tsp baking soda
1	tsp cinnamon
½	tsp nutmeg
1	tsp vanilla
4–6	apples, peeled, cored, and cubed
½	cup walnuts

Preheat oven to 350°F. Grease a 9x13-inch baking pan.

In a large bowl, beat eggs, add sugar and oil, then the rest of ingredients.

Pour into pan and bake for 45 min.

Tips and variations: Serve with a dollop of whipped cream or vanilla ice cream.

Heritage Manor Inn

Ross & Diane Hunter
2253 Blue Star Highway, Fennville, MI 49408
269-543-4384
www.heritagemanorinn.com | rdhunter@heritagemanorinn
14 Rooms or Suites
Near Lake Michigan, Saugatuck, and South Haven

Country Style Bed & Breakfast

Heritage Manor Inn is located on three beautiful country acres near Lake Michigan, between Saugatuck and South Haven. Upon arrival at Heritage Manor Inn, guests will be greeted in the breathtaking two-story foyer with its marble floor and stone wall lining the stairway. Lighting the way to the second floor is a crystal chandelier.

The Heritage Manor Inn welcomes families with children who will enjoy the spacious yard, sand volleyball court, basketball hoop, picnic areas with barbecue grills, and the large children's play set. The heated indoor pool is a great place to unwind, cool off, or take an evening swim. Beaches, hiking and biking trails, tennis, horseback riding, golf, canoeing, and fishing are all nearby!

Winter brings a whole new set of outdoor activities. Beautiful cross-country ski trails are close by in the Allegan State Forest and Saugatuck State Park.

Each morning a delicious breakfast is served in the dining room with its flagstone fireplace, oak floors, pine beam ceiling, and long harvest tables. The delicious full buffet breakfast includes Belgian waffles, eggs, sausage, home baked breads, muffins, and sweet rolls, seasonal fresh fruit, cereal, juices, and of course plenty of hot coffee! A guest kitchen is available to keep snacks cold, and is stocked with microwave popcorn, fresh cookies, and hot beverages.

Fruit Crisp

Yield: 6 servings

"I don't really follow much in the way of written recipes, but here is one that's a favorite of guests. We frequently serve apple crisp or peach crisp with a half-cup of locally grown blueberries. We have even made mulberry crisp in early July when the mulberry trees have abundant fruit. While this dish is appropriate as a dessert, any kind of fruit dish also is wonderful for breakfast."

4 cups fruit, sliced and peeled, such as apples, peaches, blueberries or a combination

Topping
1 cup butter
2 cups brown sugar, packed
1½ cups flour
1½ cups rolled oats
1 tsp cinnamon
1 tsp nutmeg

Preheat oven to 375°F. Grease an 8x8-inch baking dish.

Place fruit in the baking dish. Mix topping ingredients with an electric mixer or pastry blender until crumbly. Sprinkle topping on fruit.

Bake for about 30 minutes or until fruit is bubbly and topping starts to turn golden.

Serve warm.

Tips and variations: Quick-cooking oats probably will work just as well if that's what you have. When served as a dessert, whipped cream is a great accompaniment.

Hexagon House B&B

Matt & Sandy Werner
760 Sixth St., Pentwater, MI 49449
231-869-4102
www.hexagonhouse.com | innkeepers@hexagonhouse.com
4 Rooms, 1 Cottage
Wide porches, expansive lawn, charming port town

The Hexagon House B&B was built in 1870 by S. E. Russell as a boarding house for lumbermen visiting Pentwater from Chicago and around the Great Lakes. Back then one could climb up into the cupola and see ships arriving from Lake Michigan. Today, of course, the trees have reached a height where the lake is no longer visible. The Hexagon House has only changed hands six times since its construction and was completely restored in 1996 by Curt and Jan Werner. Together, they transformed this jewel of Pentwater into one of the premier inns to experience during any west Michigan travels.

As visitors wind their way past Pentwater Lake and enter the village, the first sight they'll be greeted with is a peaceful, mast-filled harbor, reminiscent of the New England coast. Continuing through town, guests will find numerous boutique clothing stores, art galleries and antique shops, and delicious restaurants to sample. At the north end of town, the tour turns west to Pentwater State Park, one of Michigan's finest public beaches.

Guests of the Hexagon House Inn will be greeted each morning with the wonderful aroma of breakfast coming from the open kitchen. There they will find the innkeepers preparing favorite recipes, often ones that return guests have requested! Main courses are plated for each guest and always served with fresh fruit, sausage, or bacon. Breakfasts are homemade with farm fresh ingredients, including local Michigan farmers' market harvests whenever possible. Breakfast is served in the family room surrounded by beveled glass windows. In the summer, breakfast is served on the wraparound porch, where guests may enjoy a peaceful Pentwater morning with the birds singing.

Honey Puff Pancake with Triple Berry Sauce

Yield: 6 servings

"This often-requested favorite from return guests of Hexagon House is like nothing you've ever tasted."

3	Tbsp butter, divided	**Triple Berry Sauce:**
1	cup milk	
6	eggs	
3	Tbsp honey	
3	oz. cream cheese	
1	cup flour	
½	tsp salt	
½	tsp baking powder	

Triple Berry Sauce:

3 cups cold water
5 Tbsp cornstarch
¼ cup fresh lemon juice
2 cups sugar
8 cups fresh or frozen mixed berries, no sugar added
2 Tbsp Triple Sec or raspberry liqueur (optional)

Preheat oven to 400°F. Grease a 10-inch ovenproof skillet with 1 tablespoon of butter.

In blender, add milk, eggs, honey, cream cheese, flour, salt, and baking powder. Let stand while preparing skillet: add remaining 2 tablespoons of butter to skillet. Heat in oven just until butter sizzles, about 2 minutes. While skillet is in oven, blend ingredients in blender at a high speed for 1 minute. Scrape the sides of blender and blend at high speed for one more minute until smooth. Remove skillet from oven. Immediately pour batter into hot skillet.

Bake for 20–25 minutes or until puffed and dark golden brown.

In large heavy saucepan, mix the cold water, cornstarch, lemon juice, and sugar. Stirring constantly, bring to a boil. The mixture will thicken and become smooth and almost clear. Lower heat and add berries. If using frozen berries, cook until berries are defrosted and have released their juices (about 10 minutes). Add Triple Sec and raspberry liqueur, if desired, and keep warm until serving.

When Honey Puff Pancake is plated, drizzle Triple Berry Sauce over pancake. Serve immediately.

Tips and variations: Any leftover sauce freezes well and is delicious over ice cream, pound cakes, and pancakes.

Historic Webster House

Gail & Frank Partee
900 Fifth Street, Bay City, MI 48708
989-316-2552 | 877-229-9704
www.historicwebsterhouse.com
info@historicwebsterhouse.com
6 Rooms
On a street of elegant old homes | Walk to riverfront downtown

Escape for a romantic getaway. Have a glass of wine by the parlor fireplace or in the wine bar. Spend an evening outside sitting under the pergola stargazing. Enjoy long bubble baths by candlelight in the whirlpools then settle into a luxurious featherbed. Awaken to the aroma of gourmet delicacies being prepared for a sumptuous breakfast. Go home feeling pampered and fully rested.

The innkeepers, Gail and Frank, make a wonderful team. They share breakfast, cleaning, and laundry duties. Frank chooses the menus from an extensive recipe file that he and Gail have been collecting for years. Gail's personal favorite is an asparagus and zucchini frittata. Frank, ever the comedian, says that his favorite meal is one that someone else makes for him!

The Historic Webster House breakfast room features Asian-influenced Bradbury and Bradbury custom wallpaper, a beautiful, original fireplace, and luxurious furnishings that make for a comfortable, yet elegant experience. Private tables are available, or guests may choose to sit with one another. Breakfast can also be delivered to each room. Breakfast is individually plated using fine china, crystal and silverware. Three-course breakfasts begin with a choice of juices, coffee, teas, homemade granola and fresh fruit, followed by made-from-scratch breads, muffins or coffeecakes, and end with a scrumptious hot entrée. Special dietary needs are always accommodated.

Wild Mushroom & Gruyère Quiche

Yield: 6 servings

1   9-inch pie crust (preferably homemade)
1   cup Gruyère cheese, grated
2   Tbsp butter
½   cup onions, chopped
1   lb. assorted fresh wild mushrooms, chopped
1   cup Egg Beaters® or 4 eggs
1   cup cream
3   Tbsp sundried tomatoes
1   Tbsp fresh basil, coarsely chopped

Preheat oven to 450°F. Line pie crust with pie weights.

Bake pie crust for 6–8 minutes or until the edges are light golden brown. Remove the pie weights. Sprinkle bottom of crust with grated cheese.

Reduce oven to 375°F.

Melt 2 tablespoons butter in a large skillet over medium heat. Add onions and cook until soft. Add mushrooms and cook, stirring occasionally, until soft and lightly browned. Remove from heat. In a bowl, mix eggs (or Egg Beaters®), cream, sundried tomatoes, basil, and mushroom mixture. Pour into pie crust.

Bake 30–35 minutes or until a knife inserted in the center comes out clean.

This recipe has been adapted from Egg Beaters®.

House on the Hill B&B

Phillip & Marcia Palajac
9661 Lake Street, Ellsworth, MI 49729
231-588-6304
www.thehouseonthehill.com
innkeeper@thehouseonthehill.com
8 Rooms
Country village setting | 45 minutes to Traverse City

The House on the Hill is northern Michigan's premier B&B. From the beautiful rooms to the gourmet breakfast, come bask in the warmth of the hospitality, where guests always feel like family. Located in the quiet country village of Ellsworth in northwest lower Michigan, only 15 minutes from picturesque Charlevoix and 45 minutes from Traverse City, Phillip and Marcia Palajac have perfected the ideal traveler's combination of elegant country lodging, fine dining, and relaxation.

The House on the Hill B&B makes breakfast a culinary adventure with Michigan tastes and gourmet flair. The goal is to serve guests recipes they wouldn't typically make at home. Guests' breakfast experience should be just that, an experience! With homemade jams, butters, and breads to accompany each entrée, the innkeepers aim to please the palate. Breakfast is a social time of meeting new people and finding out what a small world it actually is, many going home with new friends. Breakfast is plated and served in three courses, starting with a fruit-based dish, then homemade breads, jams, and butters, followed by the entrée that could be savory or sweet.

"Sitting squarely between two of Michigan's most outstanding restaurants, this bed and breakfast is a vortex for food lovers. Visitors to the converted Ellsworth farmhouse also find the amiable hospitality ... and drop-jaw breakfasts."—Traverse Magazine

Very Berry Puffy Pancake

Yield: 2 servings

*"This dish is a different variation of pancake that
puffs up and then falls so you can fill it full of fruit."*

2	Tbsp butter
½	cup all-purpose flour
½	cup milk
2	eggs
½	tsp vanilla
1½	cups strawberries, quartered
½	cup blueberries
1	tsp sugar
	powdered sugar for garnish
	crème fraîche (optional)

Preheat oven to 425°F. Melt butter in a 9-inch glass pie pan in oven for
4–5 minutes. Brush melted butter over bottom of the pan.

Combine flour, milk, eggs, and vanilla in a medium bowl; beat with
a wire whisk until well mixed. Pour batter into hot pie pan. Bake for
14–17 minutes or until puffed and light golden brown.

Combine strawberries and blueberries in a medium bowl and sprinkle
with sugar to bring out the juices. Spoon berry mixture into puffed
pancake. Sprinkle with powdered sugar.

Top with a dollop of crème fraîche if desired.

Serve immediately.

Tips and variations: Substitute any fruit combination.

Inn at Old Orchard Road

Elizabeth DeWaard
1422 South Shore Drive, Holland, MI 49423
616-335-2525
www.theinnatoldorchardroad.com | orchardroad@chartermi.net
3 Rooms
One-time flower farm | Go everywhere on adjacent bike path

The Inn at Old Orchard Road is a 1906 Dutch farmhouse, which once sat surrounded by brilliantly blooming gladiola and mum plants. Flower farms were almost indigenous to the area and traces of the old foundation for the bulb and seed storage building are still in evidence today. Breathe in cool lake breezes from the quaint front porch while relaxing on antique wicker furniture or head for the spacious patio, rustic gazebo or refreshing fountain in the back yard where there is a choice of sun or shade.

Downtown Holland has many specialty shops with unique store-fronts and a fabulous variety of restaurants. Heated sidewalks make for easy wintertime shopping. The Greater Holland Area Dutch tour-ist attractions will keep visitors busy. There is Windmill Island, Dutch Village, and Hope College. The tulip displays are popular around the beginning of May marked by the world-famous Tulip-Time-In-Holland Festival. Holland and the greater area offer miles of bike paths (for walking, too) starting right in front of this B&B!

For breakfast, guests start with a frosty glass of juice and, perhaps, a frozen fruit compote or a berry and cream treat. Follow that with a crusty French toast and meat combination or a fluffy egg soufflé in its own ramekin. Add a double-sized muffin, and breakfast is all set. Plenty of coffee or tea to sip will help finish that breakfast conversation!

Dutch Apple Dumplings

Yield: 10 dumplings

2   cups shortening
4   cups flour
1   Tbsp sugar
1   tsp salt
1   tsp baking soda
1   egg, beaten
½   cup water
3   Tbsp lemon juice
10 large, firm, tart apples
¾   cup brown sugar mixed with 1 tsp cinnamon, divided
5   Tbsp butter divided

Sauce
2   cups water
1   cup sugar
2   Tbsp butter
2   Tbsp cinnamon

In a large mixing bowl, combine first 5 ingredients. Mix in next 3 ingredients with a pastry blender until mixture holds together. Divide dough into 10 equal balls.

Peel and core apples. On floured surface, roll out ball in a circle; place apple in center; fill apple with 2 teaspoons of sugar mixture and a dot of butter. Wrap dough evenly around apple. Pinch to seal. Place in gallon size freezer bags and freeze until ready to use.

In a saucepan, combine sauce ingredients and simmer for 3 minutes. Divide as you wish and freeze.

To bake: Preheat oven to 475°F. Place frozen dumplings in individual ramekins and bake for 10 minutes. Reduce heat to 350°F. Bake for an additional 50 minutes. Heat sauce and pour over dumplings before serving.

J. Paule's Fenn Inn

Paulette Clouse
2254 S 58th Street, Fennville, MI 49408
269-561-2836 | 877-561-2836
www.jpaulesfenninn.com | jpaules@accn.org
5 Rooms, 2 Suites
Pastoral setting minutes from Lake Michigan beaches

Guests say the J. Paule's Fenn Inn is the best-kept secret in southwest Michigan. Just minutes from Lake Michigan, there are many places and activities to entertain, including wineries, orchards, rivers, horseback riding/sleighing in the winter, downhill and cross-country skiing, hiking, biking, and so much more, including lighthouses. The inn is very centrally located to Holland, South Haven, Allegan, and just minutes from Saugatuck and Douglas. Good prices, great specials.

The inn is close to Hutchens Lake, where guests can take a leisurely walk down the side road to the lake and play in the water at the boat launch. There is a small swimming area, and it is also a very good lake for fishing.

Share in the relaxing B&B's amenities. Come partake and enjoy the area's many activities for an excellent getaway, romantic or otherwise. Or just stay at the inn and read a book, or have some popcorn and watch a movie from the inn's collection.

Breakfast brings out Paulette's treasure trove of recipes, some borrowed but many created by herself. For the most part, they are simple to prepare, and she is happy to share the recipes with her guests. Some of her guests' favorites are Pecan French Toast, Apple Puff Pancakes and Stuffed French Toast with Strawberry Sauce. Fresh coffee, teas, and a variety of chocolates, and endless cookies are always available.

Apple Puff Pancakes

Yield: 8–12 servings

"Always a 'wow!' at J. Paule's Fenn Inn."

- ¼ cup butter plus additional for sautéing apples
- 4 eggs
- ¾ cup all-purpose flour
- ¾ cup milk
- ½ tsp salt
- ¼ cup sugar
- ¼ tsp ground cinnamon
- 2 medium apples, thinly sliced

Preheat oven to 400°F.

Place two 8- or 9-inch pans in oven with butter divided between the pans. Take out when butter has melted and coat bottom and sides of pans with pastry brush. Also add a spray of cooking oil.

In a large bowl, beat eggs; add flour and beat for 1 minute; add milk and salt, beating for 1 additional minute on medium speed.

Mix sugar and cinnamon together in a small bowl.

In a saucepan, sauté apples in butter and a little of the sugar-cinnamon mixture until semi-firm. Arrange apples in the two pans and top with batter. Sprinkle remaining cinnamon-sugar mix on top.

Bake uncovered until puffed and golden brown, or about 20–25 minutes.

Kalamazoo House B&B

Laurel & Terry Parrott
447 W South Street, Kalamazoo, MI 49007
269-382-0880
www.thekalamazoohouse.com | thekalamazoohouse@msn.
10 Rooms
Walk to eateries, theater, parks, brewpubs, galleries, and more

Kalamazoo is a city of never-ending special events, and the Kalamazoo House B&B is in the perfect location to enjoy them all. Guests love the pampering, amenities, and service of this popular B&B. The inn's convenient downtown location puts guests within blocks of all the fine restaurants, theaters, museums, brewpubs, festivals, art venues, and shopping that make Kalamazoo such a vibrant small city.

The Kalamazoo House B&B offers warm hospitality in a carefully restored 1878 Victorian. The beautiful public areas and restful guest rooms mix fine antiques with more modern furnishings selected with comfort in mind. Some rooms have romantic jetted tubs (some for two) and electric fireplaces. All rooms have high-speed WiFi, temperature control, flat-screen TVs & DVDs, and private baths.

At the Kalamazoo House, the word for breakfast is "choice." Guests choose when to eat. Let the innkeepers know approximately the desired time for breakfast, and they make sure the selected entrée is prepped and ready at the given time. Guests choose what to eat. All breakfasts begin with a generous fruit course accompanied by muffins or other baked goods, juices, coffee and tea. For the main entrée, select from a daily menu of five or six savory and sweet items. The varied menu means that special diets are quite easy to accommodate.

While community tables are found in many B&Bs, there isn't one here. Instead, there are smaller, individual tables. Traveling alone and want to eat alone? Not a problem. Or you've come with friends, or you've made friends with other guests, and you have decided you'd like to eat together? That can happily be arranged.

Cajun Corned Beef Hash

Yield: 4 servings

"This savory dish has quickly become a favorite at the Kalamazoo House!
Terry says he puts some 'giddy-up' in it, and our guests agree.
This is NOT your grandfather's corned beef hash."

canola oil for sautéing
3 cups or so bagged frozen Western-style hash browns
1 medium onion, chopped
¾ cup green peppers, diced
¾ cup red, orange or yellow peppers (or a mixture), diced
3 Tbsp Cajun seasoning, to taste
1½ cups good-quality thin-sliced corned beef, chopped
8 eggs
hollandaise sauce, store bought or homemade
paprika
chopped tomato and chives for garnish

Coat the bottom of a 9-inch skillet with canola oil and heat over medium heat.

Add frozen hash browns, onion, peppers, Cajun seasoning, and corned beef.

Stir together; sauté until vegetables are cooked through; then add more oil and turn up the heat a bit to crisp the potatoes. Poach the eggs and prepare the hollandaise sauce.

Divide the hash between 4 shallow serving dishes. Place 2 poached eggs on each serving, and top with hollandaise sauce. Sprinkle with paprika and garnish with tomatoes and chives. Serve with toast.

Tips and variations: This hash is plenty hot for most of our guests, but we offer hot sauce on the side for those who like their spicy dishes even spicier! You'll find that the poached eggs and hollandaise sauce mellow the heat, so don't be timid in using the Cajun seasoning.

Kingsley House
B&B Inn

Dave Drees
626 West Main Street, Fennville, MI 49408
866-561-6425 |269-561-6425
www.kingsleyhouse.com
romanticgetaways@kingsleyhouse.com
6 Rooms
Small-town setting | Just minutes to Lake Michigan and Saugatuck

The Kingsley House Inn is within minutes of the resort towns of Saugatuck, Holland and South Haven. Experience all that these resort towns have to offer: sunsets over Lake Michigan, beaches strewn with seashells, antique shops, and numerous boutiques with unique gifts. For the more athletically inclined, there is downhill and cross-country skiing, hiking the Saugatuck Dunes State Park or biking through the vineyards and orchards.

Breakfast is always an event at the inn, no matter what day of the week. Breakfasts are homemade with farm fresh ingredients and local Michigan farmers' harvests whenever possible. A typical breakfast starts with Peaches in a Cloud, fresh seasonal fruits, blueberry coffee cake, lemon poppy seed muffins and more. The main course includes numerous guest favorites such as Apple-Cherry Crisp French Toast, Egg Strata Soufflé, Belgian waffles, fluffy omelets, sweet-tangy kielbasa sausage, cheesy basil potatoes and more. Dietary restrictions are no problem. The innkeepers go out of their way to accommodate guests' needs.

Dave has numerous years in the restaurant industry and appreciates great cuisine and understands the importance of presenting outstanding flavor enhancements in his cooking. The Olive Cart, a shop opened by Dave, is a wonderful extension of this passion. Olive Cart products include high quality extra virgin olive oils and aged balsamic vinegars, all available in the South Haven store and online. The store has a tasting room with tapenades, glazes, stuffed olives, fresh-baked breads, pastas, pestos, and unique gourmet gifts featuring Michigan made pottery.

The Olive Cart, 424 Phoenix Road, South Haven, MI 49090, Phone: 269-637-4754, E-Mail Address: olivecart@yahoo.com

Basil Olive Oil Fried Eggs with Salsa Romesco

Yield: 2 servings

"For this recipe our innkeeper incorporates extra-virgin olive oil, red wine vinegar, and aged balsamic vinegar from his own store, the Olive Cart."

1 small tomato, cut in half
1¼ cups Olive Cart Basil Leaf Extra Virgin Olive Oil, divided
1 tsp kosher salt
3 cloves garlic, unpeeled
1 Tbsp almonds, blanched, toasted
1 Tbsp hazelnuts, toasted, skins removed
¼ slice bread, toasted
1 medium red bell pepper, roasted, coarsely chopped
1 Tbsp Olive Cart Red Wine Vinegar
⅛ tsp cayenne pepper
salt, to taste
4 medium eggs
4 small slices of sourdough batard, toasted
Olive Cart's Premium 25 year White Balsamic Vinegar, for drizzle
fresh chives, for garnish, optional

Preheat the oven to 350°F. Drizzle tomato halves with a tablespoon of the basil leaf extra virgin olive oil and a pinch of salt. Place the tomatoes, cut side down on a baking sheet. Roast 45–60 minutes or until they are soft and the skin has wrinkled and blackened slightly. Allow to cool, and then peel.

Place garlic in a very small, ovenproof skillet, and cover halfway with a portion of extra virgin olive oil. Roast about 20 minutes or until the garlic is soft and malleable. Cool and separate pulp from the skin. Reserve the garlic-infused oil and set aside.

Place nuts in bowl of food processor and pulse twice. Add toast to processor and pulse until the mixture forms a coarse paste. Add the tomatoes, roasted garlic with the reserved garlic-infused oil, red bell pepper, vinegar, and cayenne pepper. Add salt, to taste. Pulse until mixture is smooth. Add another ¼ cup of extra virgin olive oil slowly and pulse until well blended. Taste and adjust seasonings.

For the eggs, pour enough of the remaining basil leaf olive oil into a large skillet to cover the bottom with ¼ inch of oil. Heat until hot. Gently crack egg and add one at a time to hot oil, frying to desired yolk hardness. Place one fried egg on one slice of toasted sourdough, top with a spoonful of the sauce mixture. Drizzle white balsamic vinegar over the egg. Garnish with fresh, chopped chives if desired. Serve immediately.

LogHaven B&B & Barn

Gail & Paul Gotter
1550 McGregor Road, West Branch, MI 48661
989-685-3527
www.loghavenbb.com | gotter@m33access.com
Inquire about rooms
Surrounded by Huron National Forest | Bring your horse and ride

LogHaven B&B and Barn is nestled in the heart of the Huron National Forest. Hiking, snowmobile, and cross-country skiing trails are right outside the door. The "barn" invites guests to bring their horses and ride the trails. Attractions and activities for everyone are within a 15-mile drive: swimming, river rafting, golfing, canoeing, boating, and fishing. There is plenty of shopping in Victorian West Branch and the Tanger Outlet Mall. Not to be missed is Amish country for quilts, furniture, bakery goods, and craftwork.

The LogHaven B&B provides lovely rooms, private baths, and a friendly atmosphere.

Knowing that LogHaven is completely off the power grid and generates its own electricity via wind and solar makes guests savor the warmth and coziness of this inn all the more. Many guests have said that sitting on the front or back deck with a beverage of choice is the best choice of all!

LogHaven offers a complete country breakfast prepared by innkeeper Paul. Enjoy baked goods, fresh fruit, and perhaps a strata, skillet dish, or French toast served with homemade jams and locally produced maple syrup. Coffee is available any time of day. A variety of complimentary beverages are offered in each guest room. Enjoy cookies hot and fresh from the oven every day.

Glazed Carrots & Parsnips

Yield: 6–8 servings

"Carrots are a wonderful complement to parsnips, an often-overlooked root vegetable that achieves its greatest sweetness when it stays in the ground until after the first frost."

1½	lbs. parsnips and carrots, mixed in any proportion
2	Tbsp olive oil
2	Tbsp balsamic vinegar
½	cup brown sugar
1	tsp cornstarch
	salt and pepper

Peel and "coin" vegetables. Place vegetables in boiling water for 7–9 minutes. They will still be crisp. Drain. Combine olive oil, vinegar, and sugar in a saucepan over medium heat. Thicken with cornstarch. Stir in vegetables to glaze. Cook to desired tenderness.

Add salt and pepper to taste.

Tips and variations: Choose parsnips that are firm and white, with no soft spots or discoloration. If the tops are attached, make sure they're fresh and green. Avoid parsnips that have lots of hairy secondary roots. Some cooks remove the center core at the wide end of a larger parsnip.

Munro House B&B & Spa

Lori & Mike Venturini
202 Maumee Street, Jonesville, MI 49250
517-849-9292 | 800-320-3792
www.munrohouse.com | themunrohouse@gmail.com
7 Rooms
Small town minutes from Hillsdale College | Spa on premises

"The Best Place to Stay in Southern Michigan" is at the Munro House B&B in downtown Jonesville. It is the oldest house and the first brick building in Hillsdale County. This Greek Revival mansion was once used as a station on the Underground Railroad and is the oldest southern Michigan B&B that was originally built as a private residence. The pre-Civil War home is located along the Old Sauk Trail (U.S. Highway 12) in downtown Jonesville. Relax in one of seven unique guest rooms, enjoy on-site massage and spa services, or make yourself at home in the large common area.

The innkeepers serve as ambassadors to the world as guests from 65 countries on 6 continents have enjoyed small town American hospitality at their inn since 1985. Great rates and comfortable accommodations have led interesting people from across America and from around the globe to share breakfast in this great old house.

Munro House specializes in weekend getaway packages for couples, weekday corporate rates for business travelers, plus anytime lodging for parents and alumni of nearby Hillsdale College. Modern amenities keep guests satisfied in this great old house in this great small town. Convenient location to a dozen nearby restaurants and a friendly atmosphere make the Munro House B&B a short-term home away from home.

A hot made-to-order breakfast is offered 7 days a week with a low-carb option available every day. Start with coffee, tea, and "James Bond" orange juice. Spread homemade jam on your muffin and enjoy a blend of fresh cut fruits as a starter. Waffles, French toast, and/or an egg entrée follows. Because everything is made-to-order, breakfast is not over until our guests are full.

Seafood Nachos

Yield: 6–8 servings

"Chef Night Cooking Parties for Amateurs is a popular event at the Munro House. Up to 14 cooks invade the kitchen to prepare a feast for all to enjoy. The seafood nachos are an unusual combination that has always been a hit for these cooking parties or any special event gathering."

8	oz. shredded imitation crabmeat
8	oz. cooked shrimp (chopped)
½	cup sour cream (regular or low-fat)
1	(4.5-oz.) can green chilies, diced
1	tsp chili powder
½	tsp ground cumin
¼	tsp salt
1	cup chunky salsa
1	cup Monterey Jack or a Mexican-mix cheese, shredded
½	cup black olives, sliced
2	scallions, sliced
1	(14-oz.) bag tortilla chips

Preheat oven to 350°F.

Mix crab, shrimp, sour cream, chilies, chili powder, cumin, and salt in a large bowl.

Cover bottom and sides of a 9x13-inch dish with tortilla chips. (Save some chips for dipping.) Cover chips with seafood mixture and top with salsa, cheese, olives, and scallions. Bake 16 minutes or until heated through and cheese is melted.

Serve hot.

National House Inn

Barbara Bradley
102 S Parkview, Marshall, MI 49068
269-781-7374
www.nationalhouseinn.com | frontdesk@nationalhouseinn.
14 Rooms, 2 Suites
History meets modern comfort | Small-town charm

Visit National House Inn and enjoy every aspect of this "home" with its heritage and tradition that has welcomed guests for 170 years. Simple pleasures abound at the inn. Read a good book on the porch, warm yourself by a crackling fire, or treasure some quiet time alone or with friends in one of the three parlors.

The guest rooms offer all the luxuries of today with the same gracious hospitality first enjoyed by stagecoach travelers years ago. Nineteenth-century flavor is tastefully blended with modern conveniences.

National House Inn overlooks Fountain Circle in the middle of picturesque Marshall and is within easy walking distance of shopping and dining. Discover why the National Trust of Historic Preservation named Marshall as one of their "Dozen Distinctive Destinations" in the country! Marshall is one of the most beautiful cities in Michigan and a storehouse of nineteenth-century architecture with 850 structures that helped the town to earn its National Historic Landmark District designation.

Enjoy a complimentary home-cooked breakfast each morning. Begin your day with a variety of delicious items including waffles, fruit, pastries, eggs, juice and coffee. Enjoy an afternoon tea with sweets and a variety of teas in the parlor adjacent to the dining room. Freshly popped popcorn is available each evening.

Almond Torte

Yield: 6–8 servings

"What's a breakfast or brunch buffet table without something so yummy it could also be considered a dessert? Here's a guest favorite at National House."

1	cup	flour
1½	Tbsp	sugar
¾	stick	butter
2		egg yolks

Topping

1   cup cream
1   cup sugar
1   cup almonds, sliced
¼   tsp almond extract

Preheat oven to 325°F.

In a bowl, combine flour, sugar, butter, and yolks. Press into tart pan. Bake for 10 minutes. Remove from oven.

Raise oven temperature to 375°F.

Mix cream and sugar in saucepan. Bring to boil over medium heat. Stir in almonds and extract. Pour onto crust. Bake for 25 minutes.

Oviatt House B&B

Fanny Bluhm
244 East 8th Street, Traverse City, MI 49684
231-675-6709
www.oviatthouse.com | franny@oviatthouse.com
Located in Old Town

There are six beautifully furnished guest rooms in this classic historic home built in 1900, and only two blocks from downtown Traverse City. It's furnished with beautiful Early American furniture from the Federalist Period of 1750–1850. There's a comfortable living room to relax in, along with a small kitchen and garden deck, with Wi-Fi available in all rooms. House guests are furnished keys to come and go as they please and are allowed the utmost privacy.

A fun breakfast with lots of specialties is included, made with local fresh organic foods. A glass of local wine from one of our peninsulas will welcome you in the evening. Hot and cold beverages are available all day. We offer lodging that is centrally located to enjoy your biking, hiking, skiing, and golf, as well as trips to local wineries and cherry orchards of the Grand Traverse Bay area. 2013 Member Traverse City Chamber of Commerce.

Quinoa Fruit Salad with Zesty Ginger Dressing

Yield: 2 servings

This is a delicious and really nutritious grain dish for breakfast or lunch. Fruit and grains combined together with a zesty ginger-honey dressing—a great leap from hot oatmeal!

Quinoa Salad

1½	cups water
1	cup uncooked quinoa, RINSED
¼	tsp salt
½	cup dried apricots, sliced very thin
½	cup almonds or cashews, slightly toasted
1	cup fresh cherries or grapes (¼ cup dried cherries substitute)
¼	cup very thinly sliced onion—red onion, chives, wild leeks ... vary it
⅓	cup Zesty Ginger Dressing
	baby greens for plate decoration

Zesty Ginger Dressing

2	Tbsp grated fresh ginger
¼	cup honey (agave nectar is okay, too)
2	Tbsp wine vinegar (light colored)
2	Tbsp fresh lime juice
1	clove garlic
¼	cup olive oil

Rinse quinoa to remove the natural coating from it. Place water and quinoa in a saucepan and bring to a boil, add salt then cover and simmer quinoa for 10 minutes. Remove quinoa from heat and cool. Fluff quinoa and combine with apricots, nuts, cherries or grapes, and onion. Toss again with the Zesty Ginger Dressing; add more to taste if needed. Season with salt and pepper if desired. Save the balance of the dressing up to a week.

To make the dressing: Whisk first 5 ingredients, and slowly drizzle in olive oil to thicken.

Tips and variations: Both quinoa and couscous are healthy ancient grains and can be substituted for one another, so cook the same way. Soaking the grains for as long as you can while preparing other ingredients releases more nutrition by giving them a chance to swell and "sprout." Substitute grapes for cherries when one is out of season.

The Painted Turtle Inn

Christine Shull
3205 Lakeshore Drive, Saint Joseph, MI 49085
269-982-9463
http://paintedturtleinn.com | Christine@paintedturtleinn.com
Small town charm with cobblestone streets and quaint shops

St. Joseph, Michigan

A distinctive B&B in Saint Joseph, situated on Lakeshore Drive overlooking the bluff, with each room offering vantage points highlighting the lake, The Painted Turtle Inn is known for its location, luxurious accommodations, and gourmet breakfasts. The mid-century home features a completely redesigned interior to ensure a clean, quiet, and comfortable experience for our guests, along with adding modern conveniences including fully updated private baths for each of our five guest rooms.

Once you've enjoyed your relaxing evening and slept soundly in your room, a gourmet breakfast awaits you, always featuring the best produce in season and as many fresh, local ingredients as available. After breakfast, you will be ready to head to one of the breathtaking beaches southwest Michigan has to offer, go antiquing, wine tasting, or create your own adventure in Pure Michigan.

Pear, Gorgonzola and Caramelized Onion Galette

Yield: 4–6 servings

This is an easy dish that looks like it took hours of slaving in the kitchen to make. It is always a hit at parties and looks very fancy. I get requests for the recipe every time I make it. Works well as an appetizer or paired with a green salad for a light meal. Can be served warm or at room temperature.

2   large sweet onions, thinly sliced
1   Tbsp butter
¼   tsp salt
¼   tsp pepper
½   (15 oz. pkg.) refrigerated pie crust dough
2   pears (Bartlet, Bosc, D'Anjou)
1   Tbsp flour
½   cup chopped pecans
3   oz. crumbled gorgonzola
1   egg for egg wash

Preheat oven to 425°F. Cook butter and onions in a skillet over medium-low heat 20–30 minutes or until onion is caramelized, stirring often. Season with salt and pepper when done cooking and set aside. Unfold pie crust onto parchment or Silpat mat and roll into a 14-inch circle. Slice pears thinly (with a mandolin if available) and toss with flour to coat in a small bowl. Spread half of the onions over pie crust leaving a 4-inch border. Arrange pears over onions; top with remaining onions, pecans, and cheese. Fold the 4-inch borders of the dough toward the center, pressing gently. You will have a rustic tart with filling exposed in the center. Carefully transfer parchment or Silpat with tart onto baking sheet. Brush dough with beaten egg. Bake for 20–25 minutes or until golden. Cool at least 5 minutes before cutting wedges to serve.

Park House Inn

Toni Trudell & Melissa Raywood
888 Holland Street, Saugatuck, MI 49453
269-857-4535
www.parkhouseinn.com | info@parkhouseinn.com
10 Rooms
Stroll to galleries and restaurants along tree-lined streets

Although Park House Inn is over 150 years old, amenities are continually being added for guests' comfort and enjoyment. All the guest rooms have private full baths and fireplaces. The spirit of the lumberman's past will always be present. History buffs should ask about Mooreville and the lumber milling operation in the early days of Park House.

Here at Park House Inn the aromas of a home-cooked breakfast linger in the dining room inviting guests to enjoy another cup of coffee before heading out for the day. Take a walk along the tree-lined streets and boardwalk into downtown. Saugatuck and Douglas both offer shops, galleries, and parks to explore. There are no fast food restaurants, gas stations, or the usual chain stores. Every shop is unique and charming. Dine at one of the many restaurants in Saugatuck and Douglas, all with menu items to please any palate.

Visit Lake Michigan dune shores with its daily changing vistas. Explore the Saugatuck Harbor Natural Area with its marked trails through the inter-dunal wetlands—alone or on a guided tour. The open dunes are home to the endangered Prairie Warbler, migrating monarchs, and other birds and wildflowers.

Return to the inn to relax and feel the stresses of the day fall away. Teapots are out for brewing a choice of teas to enjoy with homemade cookies or brownies.

Park House Inn serves a full breakfast daily, buffet style. Always included are fresh fruit, yogurts, and an alternating main entrée. Specialties include decadent French toast, fabulous frittatas, and freshly baked scones. Winter guests enjoy the community table fireside in the dining room or, in warmer seasons, on the porch at tables for two. The inn is always open to repeat guests' requests for their favorite breakfast or goodies!

Bludacious Blueberry French Toast

Yield: 8–12 servings

"We are located in western Michigan surrounded by amazing blueberry farms. We use the fresh berries in season and freeze about 50–80 pounds for use in the off-season. It's a wonderfully decadent breakfast dish, not for calorie counters, but definitely for blueberry lovers!"

2¼	cups 2% milk
1	cup brown sugar, divided
¾	cup fat free half & half
1	tsp vanilla
6	eggs
½	tsp nutmeg
1	loaf multigrain or regular French bread, sliced 1" thick
2	cups blueberries, fresh or frozen (unthawed)
¼	cup unsalted butter, melted
1	cup chopped pecans (optional)
	warmed blueberry syrup
	whipped cream (optional)

The day or night before serving: Spray or grease a 9x13-inch glass baking pan. In a large mixing bowl combine milk, ½ cup brown sugar, half & half, vanilla, eggs, and nutmeg. Layer bread slices on bottom of baking pan. Pour egg milk mixture over bread layer. Cover with plastic wrap and refrigerate overnight or for at least 6 hours.

Day of serving: Remove plastic wrap from baking pan, preheat oven to 350°F. Pour blueberries (fresh or unthawed frozen) over bread layer. Sprinkle remaining ½ cup brown sugar over blueberries; pour melted butter over brown sugar. If you have guests with nut concerns, set aside the nuts as an optional add-on when serving. If there are no nut concerns, sprinkle chopped pecans over top of the entire prepared casserole. Increase oven temperature to 400 degrees F., place uncovered casserole in oven. Bake 25–28 minutes until bubbly. Watch closely for over browning of top. Serve with warmed blueberry syrup, optional whipped cream and pecans.

This recipe has been adapted from bedandbreakfast.com (recipe source: *Place in Time B&B, Texas*).

Pentwater Abbey B&B

Sandy & Matt Werner
760 Sixth Street, Box 778, Pentwater, MI 49449
231-869-4094
www.pentwaterabbey.com | karensabbey@gmail.com
3 Rooms
Stroll to shops and eateries | Walk to Lake Michigan beaches

The Abbey was built in 1868 for Thomas Collister. He was a prominent businessman and lived in the house until the turn of the century. He was active in the furniture factory and designed the village water system. The innkeeper's love of antiques and Victorian ambiance is seen throughout the common areas and in each guest room with floral rugs, carved fireplaces, claw-foot bathtubs, lace, and antiques.

The Abbey starts the morning with coffee brewing early. Many guests come to the kitchen for a cup to take upstairs, outside to sit at a table, a walk to the beach (3 blocks away), or maybe to just watch the cook and find out what is for breakfast! The aroma of coffee and food filters into the rooms and wakes guests up. After 26 years of running the Abbey, many guests remember what they had for breakfast the last time they were here and request it again. Living in an area where so many fruits and vegetables are grown, the fruit in season is often on the menu. A lot of recipes are made with apples and blueberries. The oven pancakes are a favorite.

Abbey guests love having homemade cookies when they arrive. There is always something yummy being baked here.

Activities around Pentwater are too numerous to list. A few of the favorites are: hiking, biking, boating, fishing, and golfing. For those looking for more sedate activities there is shopping, dining, and leisurely sightseeing.

"We visited Pentwater Abbey at the end of September. The innkeeper was very warm and welcoming and very informative about the local area. The B&B is centrally located. The breakfast was superb, with sensational blueberry muffins every morning!"—Guest

Fruited Buttermilk Oven Pancakes

Yield: 4–6 servings

"This is one of the Abbey's favorite recipes. This is requested time after time when guests return. I have made a few changes to the recipe. I make these often when blueberries are in season."

1½ cups all-purpose flour
2½ Tbsp sugar
1 tsp baking soda
1 tsp baking powder
¼ tsp salt
1 egg, beaten
1½ cups buttermilk
3 Tbsp cooking oil
1 cup blueberries
2 Tbsp sugar
½ tsp ground cinnamon

Orange butter
½ cup butter, softened
1 tsp finely shredded orange peel
1 Tbsp orange juice

maple syrup

Preheat oven to 350°F. Grease and flour a 15x10x1-inch baking pan.

In a mixing bowl combine flour, sugar, baking soda, baking powder, and salt.

In another mixing bowl combine egg, buttermilk, and cooking oil. Add all at once to dry ingredients. Stir just until mixed but still slightly lumpy. Spread batter evenly in pan. Sprinkle fruit over top of the batter. In a small bowl, combine sugar and cinnamon and sprinkle over the fruit.

Bake for 10–15 minutes or until top springs back when lightly touched and top is lightly brown around the edges. Cut into squares. Serve with orange butter and maple syrup.

Orange Butter: Beat softened butter, orange peel, and orange juice until combined; chill.

This recipe has been adapted from *Better Homes and Gardens Brunch and Breakfast Cookbook*.

Prairieside Suites Luxury B&B

Cheri & Paul Antozak
3180 Washington Avenue SW, Grandville, MI 49418
616-538-9442
www.prairieside.com | cheri@prairiesidesuite.com
7 Rooms
Suburban setting | Minutes to downtown Grand Rapids

Prairieside Suites Luxury B&B is an award-winning romantic Michigan destination. The goal at Prairieside is to create an "experience" not just a "stay." The beautiful guest rooms are the heart of this nurturing environment. They're each individually themed after a different part of the world. Come experience the dedicated Couples Massage Room. Prairieside Suites is located only minutes from downtown Grand Rapids and Rivertown Crossings Mall.

Every day a full hot candle-lit breakfast is served in the dining room where guests can come together, enjoy conversation and great food. Breakfast might consist of fresh fruit, juice, and a scone, followed by the famous quiche alongside an English muffin topped with Canadian bacon, provolone and a slice of tomato, plus a choice of coffee, tea, or homemade hot cocoa. Each morning is a delight!

The same wonderful breakfast that is served in the dining room can be delivered right to your room for guests to enjoy at their "table for two." The in-room refrigerator can also be packed with a deluxe continental breakfast of juice, yogurt, muffins, fruit, plus granola and milk so guests can snuggle, sleep late, and eat whenever they like—on their own schedule in the privacy of their room.

Cheri's Egg Strata

Yield: 16 servings

"With this recipe you can sleep late and still be Queen of Everything in the kitchen. I have been tweaking this recipe since we opened in 2002. Our guests love it and our family still requests it for Christmas morning. It's the perfect holiday breakfast because you can make it the day before and it'll hold in the refrigerator overnight. Or you can make and store it unbaked in the freezer until you need it. What could be easier?"

20	eggs, lightly beaten	5	cups Italian-style garlic croutons
1	can cream of mushroom soup	2	cups sharp cheddar cheese, shredded
3	cups milk	3	cups hash brown potatoes
2	Tbsp prepared mustard		onions, green/red peppers, mushrooms (whatever you like)
1	tsp salt		
½	tsp black pepper		shredded cheese, to garnish
1	lb. Purnell's "Old Folks" Spicy-Medium Country Sausage, cooked and cooled		

Spray two 9x13-inch glass casserole dishes with cooking oil.

In a very large bowl, whisk together eggs, soup, milk, and spices. Add all remaining ingredients (except the cheese for garnishing); blend well. Divide mixture equally into the casserole dishes.

Refrigerate overnight or up to 4 days. It can also be frozen. If you are not refrigerating overnight, allow the dish to set at least a couple of hours in the refrigerator for croutons to absorb the egg mixture.

When you are ready to bake, preheat the oven to 350°F. Bake uncovered for 50 minutes. Pull out of oven and add cheese on top as a garnish.

Let rest for 10 minutes before cutting into 8–10 pieces. The cheese will melt during the resting time.

Tips and variations: Serve with diced fresh tomatoes mixed with mild salsa served on the side or canned diced garlic/basil/oregano tomatoes. Add a couple of crescent-wrapped sausages. We use Jones Heat and Serve.

If adding mushrooms to the dish, microwave them for one minute to keep the brown from running while they sit in the refrigerator overnight.

Presque Isle Lodge

Robin & Laurie Spencer
8211 E Grand Lake Road, Presque Isle, MI 49777
231-929-4684
www.presqueislelodge.com | innkeeper@presqueislelodge.c
7 Rooms, 1 Suite
About 40 minutes to Alpena or Rogers City

The Presque Isle Lodge is a National Registered Historical Landmark. The lodge is located midway between Alpena and Rogers City on Michigan's "Sunrise Side." Nestled in a scenic wooded setting and across from gorgeous Grand Lake, the lodge offers an unrivaled experience in relaxation and enjoyment.

The Presque Isle Lodge is a particularly intact example of the rustic resort properties constructed during the "golden age" of rustic architecture of the 1920s to 1940s in Michigan. Newell A. Eddy, Jr. built Presque Isle Lodge in 1920.

Presque Isle Lodge was purchased by Robin and Laurie Spencer in 1986. They operated the lodge for 26 years. It is currently owned by their son, Shandy and his wife Penny and managed by Shandy's brother, Steven. The entire Spencer family as well as friends and relatives have helped with the restoration project. Many people, including guests, have contributed to the cause by providing historical documents, pictures and stories. The Spencer's are enjoying the restoration of the buildings and grounds for future generations. It is hoped that the atmosphere created will allow history to come alive for guests as well as providing many fond memories of time spent at the Presque Isle Lodge.

"Our ceremony was held on the Lodge grounds with Lotus Pond in the background. Robin, his staff and the facility were just outstanding! What a glorious weekend. A party and setting to remember for a lifetime!"—Guest

Overnight Egg Brunch

Yield: 12 servings

"This recipe is a common one but one that brings back memories of my mother and a special breakfast at Easter."

- 8   eggs, beaten
- 2   cups milk
- 1   tsp salt & pepper
- 1   tsp dry mustard
- 8   slices white bread (cubed)
- 1   cup ham, cubed
- 2   cups cheddar, grated

In a bowl, mix eggs, milk, salt, pepper, and mustard. Layer bread, ham, and cheese alternatively in the bottom of a 9x13-inch shallow baking dish. Pour egg mixture over all; cover with plastic wrap and refrigerate overnight.

In the morning, preheat oven to 375°F. Bake for 1 hour.

Tips and variations: Substitute longhorn cheese (sharp) for cheddar or sausage for ham.

Sauté a green or red onion, or scallions to add a little color to the egg mixture.

Sand Castle Inn

Charles & Mary Jane Kindred
203 Dyckman Ave., South Haven, MI 49090
269-639-1110
www.thesandcastleinn.com | innkeeper@thesandcastleinn.c
7 Rooms, 3 Suites
Overlooks park | 1 block from Lake Michigan

Experience a truly relaxing getaway with lodging on Lake Michigan at the Sand Castle Inn. In 1996, this historic resort hotel in South Haven was completely restored. All of the rooms are new and offer a range of amenities for comfort and enjoyment. The common areas include a designer-decorated living room with fireplace and a large Victorian front porch overlooking beautiful Stanley Johnson Park across the street. There is also an outdoor heated pool for summer use. The Sand Castle Inn is conveniently located within easy walking distance to all of the shops, restaurants, and entertainment in South Haven harbor.

Friendly, pampering guest service and a full gourmet breakfast are included. At the Sand Castle Inn, a continental breakfast is available for the early risers who are headed out for the day. A buffet breakfast is served from 9:00-10:00 a.m. with three homemade baked goods every morning. There are fresh local fruits, an egg dish or baked French toast, and a side dish of meats or potatoes. Guests welcome the homemade breakfast smoothies in the summer months and hot apple cider in the winter months.

Egg & Cheese Soufflé Casserole

Yield: 20 servings

"This is the signature breakfast entrée at Sand Castle Inn. Many returning guests request this dish. We always have copies of the recipe ready to hand out after breakfast."

1	cup butter
1	cup all-purpose flour
12	large eggs
2	cups milk
2	lbs. Monterey Jack cheese, cubed
6	oz. cream cheese, softened
4	cups cottage cheese
2	tsp baking powder (1 tsp baking powder for high altitude)
1	tsp salt
2	tsp sugar
¼	tsp cream of tartar
4	green onions, chopped
	chopped parsley or more chopped green onions, for garnish

Preheat oven to 350°F. Generously grease two 9x13-inch pans.

Melt butter in a saucepan. Add the flour and cook until smooth. In a large bowl, beat the eggs. Add the milk, cheeses, baking powder, salt, sugar, cream of tartar, and onions. Combine with the butter-flour mixture. Stir until blended.

Pour into baking pans. Bake uncovered for 45–60 minutes. Garnish with parsley or onions.

Tips and variations: I like to serve fresh salsa on the side. You can add cooked bacon after baking—just crumble and sprinkle on top. This dish can be prepared the previous day and then baked in the morning. Reduce ingredient quantities by half for a smaller group and use only one pan.

Sandtown Farmhouse B&B

Tom & Caroll Harper
W14142 Sandtown Road, Engadine, MI 49827
906-477-6163
www.sandtownfarmhouse.com | tom@sandtownfarmhouse.com
3 Rooms
80 rolling acres offer year-round outdoor pursuits

At Sandtown Farmhouse in Engadine the world slows down for guests to enjoy the 1920 farmhouse B&B, which was originally built from a Sears' house kit. The inn is located on 80 acres of rolling fields and woodlands. Hike the trails, watch wildlife, relax in the porch swing, and reminisce about the old days. Look at the antique farm equipment, tour the gardens, or lift the lid on the cookie jar. All this awaits at Sandtown Farmhouse B&B. Best of all, it is open year-round.

The farm offers great hunting, spring wildflowers, fall colors, snowmobile access, cross-country skiing and snowshoeing, woodland walking, and hiking trails. Guests can also watch birds or wildlife, or just enjoy the beauty of nature.

Nearby attractions include sandy Lake Michigan, Tahquamenon Falls, Lake Superior, Whitefish Point, Seul Choix Lighthouse, Seney Wildlife Refuge, Pictured Rocks, and great fishing lakes.

Early risers sip coffee or tea and chat with Caroll as she cooks breakfast the way great-grandmother did—on the wood-fired cook stove! The hearty morning meal is served family style in the dining room. Home baked rolls, coffee cakes, pancakes, bacon, waffles, sausage, and potatoes are among the treats that change daily.

Whole grains, farm fresh eggs, berries and herbs from the garden, cast iron skillets, and wood fired cooking—oh what fun to be had in the farmhouse kitchen! Guests are welcome to chat, nibble, and relax as traditional favorites are cooked from scratch.

Soupe de l'Ile d'Orlean (French Canadian Secret)

Yield: 6–8 servings

*"This is a terrific soup recipe from my older brother's recipe file.
He received it from Michelle Johnson of Quebec City, Canada.
I've added my own touch: rutabaga. I like to prepare this soup on a
cold winter day. The soup simmers gently on the wood-burning
cook stove while we take a tromp on the snowshoes."*

6	onions, coarsely chopped
4	Tbsp butter
4	small turnips, medium dice
6	fresh carrots, peeled and sliced
½	rutabaga, peeled, medium dice
2	green onions, coarsely chopped
28	oz. crushed tomatoes
2	Tbsp sugar
4	Tbsp fresh parsley or 2 Tbsp dried parsley
2	tsp beef base concentrate
1	tsp black pepper
1	quart water
2	Tbsp fresh chervil or 1 Tbsp dried chervil

Begin with a large pot. Sauté the chopped onion in the butter until it becomes translucent and tender. Add all the other ingredients except chervil. Cover and simmer 1 hour or more. Add the chervil near the end of the cooking time as it is a delicate herb and the flavor easily dissipates.

Tips and variations: Serve it with crusty bread and fresh cheese curds.

Saravilla B&B

Linda & Jon Darrow
633 N State Street, Alma, MI 48801
989-463-4078
www.saravilla.com | ljdarrow@saravilla.com
6 Rooms, 1 Suite
Tree-lined street in college town | 20 minutes to Mount Pleasant

Saravilla is a three-story 11,000-square-foot Dutch Colonial home built in 1894 by a local lumber baron as a summer cottage for his newlywed daughter. Listed on the Michigan Historic Register, Saravilla boasts imported period woodwork, original wall coverings, period light fixtures, leaded glasswork, and magnificent craftsmanship throughout. With its landscaped grounds, inviting front porch, landmark turret, seven very spacious welcoming guest rooms, and 1200-square-foot ballroom, Saravilla delights guests with the grace and charm of an era gone by. Saravilla offers a delightful taste of the B&B experience for everyone from first-timers to seasoned travelers.

Located right in the middle of Michigan's lower peninsula, the inn is near Mt. Pleasant, Central Michigan University, Soaring Eagle Casino, and an easy drive to numerous golf courses and other recreational and cultural attractions.

Breakfast is served at the Saravilla B&B in a variety of ways depending on the guests and their needs. The innkeepers are quite willing to accommodate guests' individual schedules and dietary requirements. They are able to serve entrées plated for small groups or buffets for larger groups, and there is an option for a family-style serving arrangement. Whichever the serving style, there are always one or two hot entrées, fresh fruit, several kinds of baked pastry items, choices of juice and other beverages, cereals and oatmeal, plus bagels, English muffins, and wheat bread for toast. Locally produced fruits, vegetables, jams and jellies are used whenever possible.

A fully supplied kitchenette is available to guests. Beverages and snacks are available for a nominal charge or guests may bring their own.

Cheesy Potato Oven Omelets

Yield: 12–15 servings

"This is one of the first recipes I tried when we opened Saravilla as a B&B in 1991, and I have used it regularly ever since. It uses potatoes instead of bread and is easy to make. It should be prepared at least the evening before. It can be divided up into various size dishes to serve smaller or larger groups. It can be prepared without meat for vegetarians. It reheats very well. Leftovers freeze well."

1	lb. ground sausage, cooked and drained
1½	cups French-fried onions, crumbled, plus more for topping
2	cups Monterey Jack cheese, shredded
2	cups frozen hash brown potatoes, thawed
1	Tbsp minced fresh (or dried) parsley
10	eggs
2	cups milk
1	tsp salt (optional)
½	tsp pepper
1½	tsp crushed rosemary

Grease a 9x13-inch baking dish.

In a large bowl, combine sausage, onions, cheese, potatoes, and parsley. Blend together the eggs, milk, salt, pepper, and rosemary in a separate bowl. Pour liquid ingredients over dry ingredients and mix together. Pour into the baking dish. Cover with plastic wrap or foil and refrigerate overnight.

The next morning, preheat oven to 350°F. Uncover before baking and sprinkle additional crumbled fried onion rings on top of the casserole. Bake for 1 hour.

Tips and variations: Any breakfast meat or cheese can be used. The parsley and rosemary seasonings are what make this dish different.

Seymour House B&B

Mike & Patty Kirsch
1248 Blue Star Highway, South Haven, MI 49090
269-227-3918 | 866-568-0202
www.seymourhouse.com | info@seymourhouse.com
5 Rooms, 1 Cabin
Halfway between South Haven and Saugatuck

The Seymour House is a beautiful brick Italianate-style mansion built by William H. Seymour in 1862 and remains one of the finest homes in the area. The Seymours were prominent lumber barons as well as prosperous peach farmers and bankers. The estate was once a commercial peony farm and one can still see peonies blooming in vacant woods beyond the present property.

The inn is perfectly located halfway between South Haven and Saugatuck, so spend days in one or both towns, and then come back to quiet in the country. The eleven-acre grounds are complete with maintained nature trails and a stocked one-acre pond.

A full gourmet breakfast is served each morning. A typical breakfast might begin with broiled grapefruit, Blueberry Swirl coffee cake, and a sausage soufflé. Enjoy the special house blend of excellent coffee and fresh produce from the finest farm markets in western Michigan. Lighter fare is always available upon request. With advance notice, special dietary needs can be accommodated.

Sausage Soufflé

Yield: 6–8 servings

"This is an old family favorite. We like it so much because it is prepared the night before, such as Christmas Eve, and pop it in the oven Christmas morning. It bakes while you are opening presents and enjoying each other!"

16	slices white bread
1	lb. shredded cheddar cheese
1	lb. pork sausage
6	eggs
2	cups milk
	salt, to taste

Remove the crust from the bread and cut into 1-inch squares. In a 9x13-inch baking dish, layer the bread and cheese in alternating layers. Fry the sausage in a fry pan and use as the final layer over the bread and cheese. In a bowl, beat the eggs, milk, and salt. Pour the egg mixture over the bread, cheese, and sausage layers. Cover and refrigerate the mixture overnight.

In the morning: preheat the oven to 350°F. Place a water bath on the lower shelf of the oven. Bake the dish for 45–50 minutes. If you forget the water bath, your soufflé will burn.

A knife should come away clean when the soufflé is done. Let rest for 10 minutes before slicing.

Sheridan House

Louis & Paula Meeuwenberg
7300 W Lake Drive, Fremont, MI 49412
231-924-5652
www.thesheridanhouse.com | paula@thesheridanhouse.com
2 Rooms
Quiet retreat on a lake 25 miles from Lake Michigan

The Sheridan House is a perfect quiet getaway for individuals, couples, or small groups. This elegant inn, built in 2001, sits on the shore of a beautiful 800-acre lake. Just 100 feet from the water's edge, guests may enjoy evening hors d'oeuvres and beverages. It is also just blocks from downtown Fremont, home of Nestlé® and Gerber® products.

To explain breakfast, it is best to begin the evening before. Guests most usually gather in front of the fireplace and enjoy the views of the lake while sipping their favorite beverages and snacking on ever-present cashews. The innkeepers pride themselves in their hors d'oeuvre offerings (well over two dozen), and as guests gather to acquaint themselves with their fellow travelers and their hosts, they are treated to good food and fun conversation. Following hors d'oeuvres, the guests are offered an extensive menu from which they can individually choose their desired breakfast for the following morning. This menu consists of a large variety of breads, including Hilda's Banana Bread (Hilda is Paula's mother), and Paula's Prune Bread. Eggs can be prepared as the guest desires. There is a choice of bacon, sausage or ham, waffles, fruits, and juices. A guest favorite is English Scramble. Special dietary requests can be accommodated with some advance notice.

To finish off the evening, a chocolate awaits each guest in their room.

Paula's Prune Bread

Yield: 7–8 small round loaves

"This moist, delicious prune bread is a favorite of guests who often ask to have some to eat later or to take with them."

¼	cup vegetable oil
2	cups sugar
2	large eggs
8	(2.5 oz.) jars strained Gerber® baby food prunes
½	cup milk, plus 2 Tbsp of milk
3	cups flour
2	tsp baking soda
1½	tsp salt
1	cup chopped walnuts

Preheat oven to 350°F. Grease 7–8 fruit cans (cleaned, of course, with top cut off).

In a large bowl, cream together the oil, sugar, and eggs. Add prunes and milk. In a separate bowl, mix the dry ingredients together. Add the dry ingredients to the prune mixture; mix together with a rubber spatula. Add the nuts and mix again.

Divide the batter into the fruit cans. Set the cans on 2 cookie sheets. Bake for 38 minutes or until a knife comes out clean. Remove from oven and let the loaves sit in the cans for 5 minutes, then invert and place loaves on a wire rack.

Sherwood Forest B&B

Keith & Susan Charak
938 Center Street, Douglas, MI 49406
269-857-1246 | 800-838-1246
www.sherwoodforestbandb.com
sf@sherwoodforestbandb.com
3 Rooms, 2 Suites, 1 Cottage
Saugatuck sister city | Walk to Lake Michigan

This beautiful Victorian home offers inviting elegance in a wooded setting. Hardwood floors, leaded-glass windows, an oak-paneled staircase, and a wraparound porch add to serene relaxation in ideal surroundings.

During the summer, guests can swim in the heated pool adorned with a giant mural of a sunken ship half-embedded in a coral reef surrounded by a couple of hundred fish, not to mention a mermaid or two, or walk half a block to a Lake Michigan public beach to enjoy spectacular sunsets. Bicycles are available for exploring the scenic lakeshore. In the winter, cross-country ski or snowshoeing along wooded paths is a favorite of the guests. For a shopping outing try the charming boutiques in Saugatuck and Douglas.

Sherwood Forest B&B is THE stopping-off place for foodies. During a stay here guests are treated to some of the most delightfully unique dishes and very quirky and fun-loving culinary musings. Hands-on cooking classes, a Culinary Mancation Marathon, and Sherwood Forest Gourmet Dinners are among the offerings. If food is your focus, don't miss this inn.

Soutine's Cinnamon Rolls

Yield: 8 servings

"This is a great Sunday morning delight. We've named it after a very young Siren of Sherwood, whose mother is a full-fledged member, and someday we're sure she'll also be a fantastic chefette."

3½	cups flour
4	tsp baking powder
1	tsp salt
½	cup cold butter, cut into small pieces
2	eggs, beaten
¾–1	cup milk

Filling

¼	cup butter, softened
½	cup brown sugar
1½	tsp ground cinnamon

Glaze

1½	Tbsp sugar
1½	Tbsp water
1½	tsp unflavored gelatin

Preheat oven to 400°F. Grease a cookie sheet.

In a large bowl, combine flour, baking powder, and salt. Cut in the cold butter until mixture resembles coarse meal. In a separate bowl, combine eggs and milk; add to flour mix to make a soft dough.

Roll out dough on lightly floured surface to make a 12x12-inch square about ¼-inch thick. Spread with the softened butter; sprinkle with brown sugar and cinnamon. Roll up and cut into 8 pieces about 1½-inches long. Place on cookie sheet swirl sides up. Bake for 20–25 minutes.

In a saucepan on medium heat dissolve sugar, water and gelatin. Whisk until blended and warmed through. Drizzle on rolls when they are done baking.

State Street Inn B&B

Bill & Janice Duerr
646 State Street, Harbor Beach, MI 48441
989-479-3388
www.thestatestreetinn.com | janice@thestatestreetinn.com
4 Rooms

Harbor town | Walk to shops, dining | Near canoe and kayak trail

Victorian charm beckons visitors to State Street Inn in Harbor Beach. Enjoy exploring this quaint lakeside community on the sunrise side of Lake Huron. The century-old Victorian farmhouse is perfect for all lodging needs. Enjoy old-fashioned warmth and grace, refreshing surroundings, and the simple joys of a traditional B&B where hospitality is the specialty and personal attention is given to each guest's every need.

Harbor Beach on Lake Huron has beaches, marinas, fishing, beautiful parks and a lovely flower-filled bicycle/pedestrian path. There are good restaurants, unique shops, museums, and terrific golfing. See for yourself how small town life—while peaceful, friendly and quaint—is never boring.

Breakfast is a special time at State Street Inn. Served daily, it always includes a freshly baked treat, a main hot entrée, and a fresh fruit platter. Coffee is on the table very early in the morning for any pre-dawn risers. If the entrée of the morning is sweet instead of savory, such as a cream cheese stuffed French toast or pumpkin pancakes, the meal will also include some locally made sausage and fresh fruit.

So many guests have asked for Janice's recipes over the years, that she decided to publish her own cookbook. With over 200 great recipes *Simply Delicious: The State Street Inn Cookbook* will be a great addition to your collection. It is available at their gift ship or go their website for more information.

Banana Chocolate Chip Muffins

Yield: 18–24 muffins

*"These are always a big hit at breakfast. I like to serve them
with a fresh fruit platter and one of our egg casserole dishes.
They also reheat nicely in the microwave for about 20–30 seconds."*

2	cups all-purpose flour
1	Tbsp baking powder
½	cup white sugar
½	cup brown sugar
2	eggs
2	bananas, very ripe, mashed
1	tsp vanilla
½	cup canola oil
½	cup buttermilk
½–¾	cup semi-sweet chocolate chips

Preheat oven to 350°F. Line muffin tins with paper cups.

In a bowl, combine flour, baking powder, and sugars; blend thoroughly.
In a separate bowl, combine eggs, bananas, vanilla, oil, and buttermilk.
With an electric mixer, blend until creamy. Pour wet ingredients into flour
mixture and add chocolate chips; mix until just combined.

Fill muffin cups about ⅔-full and bake for 20 minutes, or until golden
brown on top.

Tip: These are best served warm, when the chocolate chips are still gooey.

Torch Lake B&B

Debbie Cannon
4417 Trillium Ridge Road, Central Lake, MI 49622
231-599-3400
www.torchlakebb.com | torchlakebedandbreakfast@gmail.com
3 Suites
On hill overlooking lake | Scenic 45-minute drive to Traverse City

Relax and be pampered! Enjoy Torch Lake the way an inn should be enjoyed. This spacious and charming B&B provides spectacular views. This majestic Queen sits high above beautiful Torch Lake, listed by National Geographic as being the third most beautiful lake in the world. The aqua-colored waters of Torch Lake are crystal clear and many people say that this is where the rainbow stores its color.

Centrally located between Traverse City and Elk Rapids, Petoskey and Charlevoix, Central Lake, Bellaire and Alden, guests to the area have countless opportunities for shopping and antiquing, boating, swimming, sailing, wind surfing, canoeing, fishing, kayaking, biking, hiking, or resting and relaxing. Torch Lake B&B is open year-round and every season holds its unique promise of fun and adventure. For the "wilder side"—serious to not-so-serious gamblers can indulge themselves at the Odawa casino in Petoskey and Turtle Creek Casino in Traverse City, both just minutes away.

Come and experience this piece of paradise. In the morning, guests are awakened to the aroma of freshly baked pastries or Grandma's Famous Apple Torte Cake. Coffee is always ready early so guests may sip a cup of freshly brewed java and enjoy the sound of waves lapping on Torch Lake's shoreline. While a scrumptious breakfast is being prepared, guests are lulled by a peaceful and tranquil setting and spectacular views. Breakfast is always prepared with the finest and freshest locally grown products available. To cap off a busy day, enjoy the evening with a little stargazing into the spectacular northern Michigan sky.

Grandma's Famous Apple Torte Cake

Yield: 8–10 servings

"This delicious Apple Torte Cake was one of Grandma's many treats that our family enjoyed through the years. We always looked forward to Grandma making this delightful morsel for special family gatherings and holidays. Many guests of Torch Lake B&B ask for the recipe and I am always happy to share it with everyone."

3	eggs
1¾	cups sugar
1	tsp baking soda
1	tsp cinnamon
1	tsp vanilla
½	tsp salt
2	cups flour
1	cup oil
4	apples, tart or a variety, sliced thin
½	cup nuts (optional)

Preheat oven to 350°F. Grease and flour a 9x13-inch baking pan.

In a large bowl, mix eggs and sugar. Add soda, cinnamon, vanilla, salt, and flour. Mix well. Add oil; blend well. Fold apples into batter. (Grandma used tart and I use a variety.) Add nuts if desired.

Pour into baking pan and bake for about 1 hour.

Twin Oaks Inn

Willa Lemken
227 Griffiths Street, Saugatuck, MI 49453
269-857-1600 | 800-788-6188
www.bbonline.com/mi/twinoaks | twinoaks@sirus.com
6 Rooms
Central location in chic, artsy resort village on Lake Michigan

What was once a nineteenth-century lumbermen's boarding house is now an elegant and charming Olde English B&B. The inn is nestled at the foot of Hoffman Street Hill in a quiet area of downtown Saugatuck, with easy access to shopping, restaurants, art galleries, and all the town's activities.

Relax in the warmth and charm of antiques and modern amenities at Twin Oaks Inn.

While open year-round, it is during the off-season that guests most especially enjoy their evening refreshments in front of a peaceful and cozy fireplace.

"Just went here for a weekend getaway with my husband. We had such a delightful stay! Not only was this bed and breakfast a stone's throw away from downtown Saugatuck, but in the mornings we received an amazing homemade breakfast prepared by the innkeeper, Willa. During our stay, we sampled homemade French toast, coffeecakes, quiche, sausage, and muffins, as well as coffee and juices. It was served on a long table in an elegant dining room."—Guest recommendation on Yelp!

Greek Quiche

Yield: 6–8 servings

"This unique, light and fluffy quiche melts in your mouth!"

6	eggs
3	Tbsp flour
1/8	tsp nutmeg
2	cups milk
1	pkg. frozen spinach (squeezed dry)
½	cup tomatoes, chopped and deseeded
¼	cup feta cheese
1	ready-made pie crust (pierced and prebaked)

Preheat oven to 350°F.

In a medium bowl, beat 3 eggs with the flour and nutmeg. Add the remaining eggs, beat again and add milk. Blend well. Set aside.

Arrange spinach, tomatoes and feta cheese in the prepared pie crust. Pour egg mixture into pie crust. Bake 45–50 minutes until a knife inserted in the center comes out clean. Let quiche rest for 10 minutes before cutting and serving.

Tips and variations: Other delicious combinations are asparagus and feta, ham and Swiss, or broccoli and cheddar.

Victoria Resort B&B

Jan Leksich
241 Oak Street, South Haven, MI 49090
269-637-6414 | 800-473-7376
www.victoriaresort.com | jantheinnkeeper@yahoo.com
9 Rooms, Cottages
In the heart of a quaint Lake Michigan harbor town

Just steps from Lake Michigan, the Victoria Resort B&B reflects its historic beginnings while providing modest to luxurious rooms with fireplaces and whirlpool tubs. The Victoria has the perfect combination of the friendly ambiance expected from a B&B with the right amount of privacy for a getaway.

A stay at the Victoria Resort B&B will bring reminders of a time when resorts flourished in the quaint lakeside town of South Haven. At the end of the street are the sandy beaches of Lake Michigan, where visitors can catch a glimpse of a spectacular sunset any time of year. The downtown area is just a short walk along tree-lined streets. When the weather is warm, borrow bikes for a ride around town or stay at the resort to play a game of tennis!

Guests of the B&B enjoy a full homemade breakfast of muffins, breads, fruit, and one of the Victoria's signature hot entrées. Classic blueberry pancakes made with local South Haven blueberries is a special treat.

Apple Baked French Toast

Yield: 10–12 servings

"Guests of Victoria Resort almost always ask for the recipe every time we serve this. Granny Smith apples are ideal for this dish."

1	loaf cinnamon bread, roughly cut into cubes, crust included
12	eggs
2	cups half & half
½	tsp cinnamon
½	tsp nutmeg
1	Tbsp vanilla extract
¾	cup brown sugar, divided
1	stick butter, melted
2	Tbsp molasses
2–3	firm, tart, crisp apples, cored, peeled, chopped

Liberally coat inside of 9x13-inch glass pan with cooking oil. Fill up to the edge with cinnamon bread cubes.

In a bowl, mix together eggs, half & half, cinnamon, nutmeg, and vanilla. Pour egg mixture over the bread. Sprinkle ¼ cup brown sugar on bread mixture.

In a small bowl, combine melted butter and molasses. Drizzle a third of the butter-molasses mix over the bread mixture. Sprinkle another ¼ cup brown sugar and another third of the butter-molasses mix. Layer chopped apple on bread mixture. Sprinkle with last ¼ cup brown sugar and pour the last of butter/molasses mixture on top. Cover with foil; refrigerate overnight.

In the morning, preheat oven to 350°F. Bake for 40 minutes with foil cover.

Reduce heat to 325°F., remove foil, and bake another 20 minutes.

Tips and variations: You may substitute corn syrup for the molasses.

Gordon Food Service sells a cinnamon bread that works well for this dish. Freeze it to use as needed. Use a sharp knife to cube the bread while still frozen.

If you're planning to serve this for a crowd, you can make the entire dish ahead and freeze it. Thaw the day before and let it rest in the refridgerator overnight.

Vitosha Guest Haus Inn

Kei J Constantinov
1917 Washtenaw Avenue, Ann Arbor, MI 48194
734-741-4969
www.a2vitosha.com | info@a2vitosha.com
10 rooms
Leafy residential area on a main street leading to campus

Channel your
inner gargoyle

Vitosha
GUEST hAUS INN

Vitosha Guest Haus Inn is found within a historic castle stone complex on the edge of the University of Michigan, Ann Arbor campus. It boasts lodging for 32 in English period surroundings. Vitosha Guest Haus is the third incarnation of Dr. Dean Meyer's historic home (1917), restored and refurbished by the Constantinovs fifteen years ago. Following the tenure of the Unitarians, who added two buildings to the complex, it now serves as a sophisticated lodging, retreat, cultural, wedding, and event venue. For guests' enjoyment it features outer gardens with quince, grape, English roses, and period furnishings—while maintaining a cyber-savvy environment for scholars and business people.

Vitosha Guest Haus Inn is noted for its accommodating breakfasts (kosher, vegan, gluten- and lactose-free diets).

Guests at the inn enjoy all that Ann Arbor has to offer. The historic area of downtown Ann Arbor offers a unique setting for shops, markets, and restaurants. Summer brings the local growers to the Farmers' Market, and artisans from far and wide show their work at the many art fairs. Autumn heralds football season and the youthful excitement of collegiate sports. The walk from Vitosha across Burns Park to the stadium takes only twenty minutes. Whatever the reason for your visit, there are any number of additional distractions to keep you interested in this great Midwest college town.

Wild Rice Croquettes

Yield: 12–15 servings

*"This recipe could be a vegetarian breakfast entrée
or served for lunch or dinner."*

1   cup wild rice
3   garlic cloves, peeled
1   cup basmati rice
5   eggs
3   scallions, minced, saving some greens as garnish
1   small yellow onion, minced
¼   cup cilantro, chopped
    Tamari soy sauce
    salt and pepper, to taste
4   Tbsp sesame seeds
½   cup Asiago cheese, shredded
½   cup carrots, shredded
¼   cup walnut pieces

In large saucepan, boil wild rice for 20 minutes with garlic. Add basmati rice. Cover and cook until fluffy (al dente, not mushy!), approximately 15 minutes. Turn off heat. Do not lift lid for 15 minutes. Let cool.

Whisk eggs in a small bowl and add to cooled rice. Add scallions, onions, and cilantro. Season with soy sauce, salt, and pepper. Add sesame seeds. Mix cheese, carrots, and nuts into rice.

Form into small patties or into larger/flatter veggie burgers, and drop by spoonfuls into hot peanut or corn oil. Adorn with scallion leaves. Serve with Sambal Indonesian hot sauce.

Voyager's Inn B&B

Caryn Wilson
210 East Street, Three Rivers, MI 49093
269-279-9260
www.voyagers-inn.com | reservations@voyagers-inn.com
3 Rooms
Walk to downtown shops | 40 minutes south of Kalamazoo

Voyager's Inn B&B is the place to visit for a fabulous southwest Michigan getaway! Whether looking for a place to kick back and relax, or a place with opportunities for boating, fishing, great antiquing, fabulous farmers' markets, hiking and biking trails, skiing, wineries, and more, visitors will find it here in Three Rivers.

Voyager's Inn is a showcase of the Victorian era's fine craftsmanship: massive oak and cherry pocket doors, hardwood floors, gingerbread scrollwork, and a grand staircase. Common areas include a beautiful parlor with a brilliant blue-tiled fireplace, a music room with a piano, the library, a fabulous front porch, beautiful backyard gardens with sitting areas.

The inn is a strong supporter of community supported agriculture. They use eggs from local Amish farms, and the milk for their home-made yogurt comes from a local chemical free, family-run farm in Three Rivers. Bacon, ham and breakfast sausage come from local farms whenever possible and zucchini, pumpkin, tomatoes, corn and other seasonal vegetables are purchased at the Three Rivers Farmers' Market. Apples, strawberries and other fruits come from near-by orchards or fruit farms.

As you can imagine, with all these fresh ingredients, breakfast is a delicious treat. Descriptive names for breakfast menus include The Lumberjack, Amish Ambiance, or The Queen Anne. Coffee, tea, and other beverages are available around the clock and look for sweet treats in the parlor each evening. Accommodations can happily be made for vegetarian and/or gluten-free meals upon request.

Maybelle's Delicious Rum Balls

Yield: 2 dozen

"Maybelle was a long-time family friend who enjoyed an evening sip of rum. These tasty treats are named for her, and it's hard to eat just one!"

2   cups vanilla wafers, finely crushed
1   cup confectioners' sugar, plus more for rolling dough
1   cup walnuts, finely chopped
3   Tbsp cocoa powder
3   Tbsp maple syrup
½   cup rum

In a large bowl, mix dry ingredients. Add maple syrup and rum. Roll dough into balls. Roll balls in confectioners' sugar. Serve at room temperature.

Tips and variations: Dough may be chilled before rolling. A bit more or less rum may be needed to achieve proper rolling consistency.

Waterloo Gardens B&B

Gary & Lourdean Offenbacher
7600 Werkner Road, Chelsea, MI 48118
877-433-1612 | 734-502-6195
www.waterloogardensbb.com | info@waterloogardensbb.co
1 Room, 1 Suite
Short drive from vibrant Main Street

Explore Chelsea Village while staying in this elegant country ranch. Chelsea is the home of Jiffy Mix, a fun tour for the whole family—as is the Chelsea Teddy Bear Factory.

There are three large playgrounds in town, including an Indoor Playscape and Timbertown. The kids (and adults) can stroll through town enjoying the many sculptures and grab a cone from one of three ice cream parlors. For more eating opportunities, there is the Common Grill, the Chelsea Grill and Las Fuentes.

Silver Lake Beach and Waterloo and Pinkney Recreation Areas are just a few minutes away, offering wonderful hiking, biking, and wildlife viewing opportunities. The Discovery Center in the Waterloo Recreation Area is great fun for the kids.

Chelsea is the perfect base for visiting the southeast Michigan wine country. Bring a bottle back to the inn and enjoy it in the bar or parlor; or after a soak in the hot tub.

Stroll around the gardens and fruit trees or hang out on the huge furnished outdoor deck, surrounded by flowers!

Enjoy a hot breakfast in the morning with the hosts. Fresh fruit and Peach French Toast are favorites.

Blueberry German Pancakes

Yield: 8–12 servings

"This recipe tastes wonderful and is a snap to make. We created it when we had a large crowd to feed. We had the idea to bake our pancakes in the oven. The result has been a favorite ever since."

2½	cups flour
2	tsp baking powder
1	tsp baking soda
2	tsp ground cinnamon
2	Tbsp granulated sugar, optional
2²/3	cups buttermilk
1	tsp vanilla extract
2	Tbsp vegetable oil
2	eggs
¾	cup fresh or frozen blueberries
¾	cup brown sugar
1	Tbsp ground cinnamon, for topping

Preheat oven to 350°F. Spray a 9x13-inch baking dish with nonstick cooking oil; set aside.

In a large bowl, combine flour, baking powder, baking soda, cinnamon, and sugar. In a separate bowl, combine buttermilk, vanilla, oil, and eggs. Add to dry mixture; stir until well blended with no lumps.

Stir in blueberries. Pour mixture into prepared baking dish; top with brown sugar and cinnamon. Bake 35 minutes, or until a wooden pick inserted in the center comes out clean.

Tips and variations: Add more buttermilk if mixture is too thick. Mixture should run off a spoon in a consistent stream, but not drip. Serve hot with butter and warm maple syrup.

White Rabbit Inn

A.J. and Jan Boggio
14634 Red Arrow Highway, Lakeside, MI 49116
800-967-2224 | 269-469-5843 fax
www.whiterabbitinn.com | info@whiterabbitinn.com
6 Rooms, 2 Cabins
Near wineries, Lake Michigan beaches and trails

The White Rabbit Inn is located in the lovely little village of Lakeside, Michigan, only 90 minutes from the hustle and bustle of downtown Chicago, or less than 3.5 hours from Detroit or Indianapolis. It is surrounded by sophisticated antique stores, exquisite art galleries, highly acclaimed gourmet restaurants, and only a short drive from nearby award-winning Michigan wineries like Round Barn Winery, St. Julian, Domaine Berrien Cellars, and Tabor Hill. Best of all, the inn is only a few blocks from the nearest public beach access. Less than five miles away rests majestic Warren Dunes State Park with its sugar sand beaches, wooded trails, and Lake Michigan. For fans of the fine arts, nearby Three Oaks is home to both the Vickers Film Theatre as well as the Acorn Performing Arts Theater. Guests will find plenty to do year-round in Harbor Country.

Guests are welcome in the lodge at any time to catch up on some reading, pick out a favorite movie, or enjoy a late night snack. Since a visit to the inn is for relaxation, there are no phones in the rooms.

Breakfast is served in the lodge, an airy building with large picture windows overlooking the woods. Enjoy the "hearty" continental buffet while watching for deer, colorful wild birds, or the inn's favorite pair of chipmunks.

Strawberry Cream Cheese Bread

Yield: 12 servings

"This rich and creamy fruit bread is a regular hit at the White Rabbit Inn. It tastes great with strawberry jam for breakfast, or with a scoop of strawberry sherbet on top for dessert."

½	cup butter, softened
1	cup sugar
1	(3-oz.) pkg. cream cheese, softened
2	eggs
1	tsp vanilla extract
2	cups flour
2	tsp baking powder
½	tsp baking soda
½	tsp salt
½	cup milk or half & half
1½	cups strawberries, chopped
½	cup finely chopped pecans (optional)

Preheat oven to 350°F. Grease and flour a 9x5-inch loaf pan.

With an electric mixer, cream butter, sugar, and cream cheese until fluffy.

Add eggs one at a time. Mix in vanilla. In separate bowl, mix flour, baking powder, baking soda, and salt. Combine flour mixture with butter mixture until just blended.

Add half & half and stir just to blend. Do not over mix!

Drain chopped strawberries and blot dry. Carefully fold in strawberries and nuts. (Dough mixture will be thick.)

Pour into prepared loaf pan and bake for 50–60 minutes.

Let bread mellow for one day before serving.

White Swan Inn

Cathy & Ron Russell
303 S. Mears Avenue, Whitehall, MI 49461
231-894-5169 | 888-948-7926
www.whiteswaninn.com | stay@whiteswaninn.com
3 Rooms, 1 Suite, 1 Cottage
Walk to theater, shops, dining, and lake in a resort town

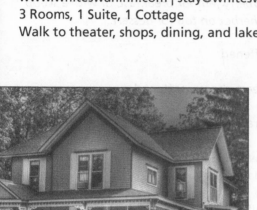

White Swan Inn B&B is located in the charming resort community of White Lake along the shores of Lake Michigan, halfway between Chicago and Mackinac Island. The beauty of Lake Michigan with its sunsets and unspoiled beaches enhances the area. Every season offers a variety of outdoor activities as well as theater, concerts, and museums. The White Swan Inn is within walking distance of shops and dining. The lake and a paved bike trail are only a block away. Open year-round, White Swan Inn has been greeting guests since 1995. Gracious hospitality in a relaxing setting is the hallmark of this award-winning B&B.

Incorporating local ingredients from the farmers' market and farm stands brings the freshest taste to the table. Fresh ingredients paired with loving attention create tempting treats. Each season offers a variety of fresh produce. Savory or sweet breakfasts and snacks at the B&B are an essential part of the travel experience. If you have an early morning tee time, need to attend a business meeting, or want to sleep in a little longer—flexibility is the key at White Swan Inn. Breakfast can be arranged to accommodate your schedule.

This B&B has something additional and very different to offer guests. Docked on White Lake is their Nova 40 twin diesel motor yacht, christened the *Third Swan*. This on-the-water B&B experience is exceptionally unique. There is ample room aboard for six passengers, with an open-air flying bridge, enclosed aft deck, and plenty of room for catching some sun. *Third Swan* and her crew can offer memorable experiences such as sunset cruises, historic water tours, and overnight dockside accommodations. Join USCG-licensed Captain Ron Russell aboard *Third Swan* for some fun in the sun!

Multi-Grain Waffles

Yield: 6–8 servings

"A waffle for breakfast is nice; a multi-grain waffle is even better. With this recipe, adding more fiber to your morning meal is easy, tasty, and healthy. Enjoy your waffles with pure Michigan maple syrup for a delicious start to your morning."

¾	cup all-purpose flour
¾	cup whole-wheat flour
½	cup old-fashioned rolled oats
2	Tbsp milled flax seed
2	Tbsp sugar
4	tsp baking powder
1	tsp salt
1¼	cups soy milk
¼	cups canola oil
2	eggs
1	tsp vanilla

Mix all dry ingredients together in a large bowl. In a small bowl, whisk together soy milk, oil, eggs, and vanilla. Pour wet ingredients into dry ingredients and gently stir together until fully incorporated. Batter will be lumpy.

Let batter rest 10–15 minutes. Heat waffle iron. When hot, spray iron surfaces lightly with cooking spray. Cook waffles according to manufacturer's instructions.

Wind in the Pines B&B

Deitmar & Marion Stollenwerk
13573 S Gallagher Road, Traverse City, MI 49684
231-932-8608
www.windinthepinesbb.com | windinthepines@hughes.net
3 Rooms
Peaceful setting in the pines | 15 minutes from downtown

A true "up north" experience awaits at Wind in the Pines B&B. This beautiful log home, built in 2004–05, is nestled among acres of pines offering peaceful, quiet relaxation. The three spacious guest rooms reflect the beauty of the north woods with their pine cone, bear, and moose themes. The innkeepers have incorporated all the lodging needs of the discriminating traveler.

Unique shops, water sports, golf, art, over 30 wineries, and a vast array of excellent dining experiences are available in the Grand Traverse region. Explore Sleeping Bear Dunes, hear a concert at Interlochen Arts Academy, or visit the wineries of Leelanau and Old Mission Peninsulas. Wind in the Pines is located at the base of the Leelanau Peninsula—ideally situated to provide easy access to the beautiful Grand Traverse region and just five miles from Traverse City.

Wind in the Pines B&B is certified by the National Wildlife Federation as a wildlife habitat. This certification recognizes the efforts of the property owners to "plan, landscape, and do sustainable gardening so that wildlife may find quality habitat—food, water, cover, and places to raise their young." Relax on the patio or glance out any window and enjoy the wide variety of birds, wild turkeys, ruffed grouse, or even the occasional deer or coyote.

Apple-Bacon Egg Bake

Yield: 4 servings

"We would like to give credit to the former innkeepers for this wonderful recipe."

- 1½   cups hash browns, frozen
- ½   cup onions, chopped
- ½   tsp seasoned pepper, plus a pinch for the egg mixture
- 2   small apples, diced
- 1   cup cheddar cheese, divided
- 8   Tbsp bacon pieces, divided
- 6   eggs
- ⅔   cup milk
- ⅔   cup sour cream

Preheat oven to 350°F. Grease four 2-cup baking dishes.

Brown potatoes and onions in a frying pan. Add pepper. Add apples and brown slightly. Put mixture in a bowl and mix in ¾ cup of the cheese and 4 tablespoons of bacon pieces.

Fill each baking dish with approximately ½ cup of the hash brown mixture. You may have extra mixture left over. You will need to leave room in each baking dish for the egg mixture to rise.

Beat eggs, milk, sour cream, and a pinch of pepper in a bowl. Pour over mixture already in each baking dish. Sprinkle 1 tablespoon of cheese and then 1 tablespoon of bacon pieces on top of each.

Bake uncovered for 35–40 minutes.

Tips and variations: Let the dish sit for about 10 minutes before serving. It will be hot!

Just Baked

Breads, Muffins, Scones & Coffee Cakes

Of all the appealing aromas you could wake up to, what's more delightful than some crumbly temptation in the final stage of baking in a hot oven? This is a frequent occurrence at a Michigan bed and breakfast, one of the many reasons to choose a B&B stay. Each of our innkeepers have their own specialties, including muffins, coffee cakes, yeast breads, pastries, popovers, scones, biscuits, and more. So many miraculous tastes can result from the transformation of flour, eggs, and a few other ingredients.

Recipes in the Featured Recipes chapter

In this chapter

Banana Nut Bread

Yield: 2 loaves

- 2 eggs
- 1 cup brown sugar
- 1 stick margarine
- 1 tsp vanilla
- 2 cups mashed bananas (3–4)
- ½ cup milk
- 1 Tbsp lemon juice
- 2 cups flour
- 1 tsp baking powder
- 1 tsp baking soda
- 1 tsp cinnamon
- 1 cup chopped walnuts
- 1 cup raisins

Preheat oven to 350°F. Grease two loaf pans.

In a large bowl, cream together eggs, brown sugar, margarine, and vanilla. Add bananas, milk, and lemon juice, combining well.

In a separate bowl, sift together flour, baking powder, baking soda, and cinnamon. Slowly mix flour mixture into soft mixture. Stir in nuts and raisins.

Pour into loaf pans and bake 45 to 55 minutes.

Frankenmuth B&B (Bender House)

Banana Bread

Yield: 1 loaf

"The addition of hickory nuts in our banana bread is a pleasant surprise to our guests."

3–4	ripe bananas, mashed
⅓	cup melted butter
1	cup sugar (can easily be reduced to ¾ cup)
1	egg, beaten
1	tsp vanilla
1	tsp baking soda
	pinch of salt
1½	cups all-purpose flour
½–1	cup walnuts or hickory nuts (optional)

Preheat oven to 350°F. Spray or butter a 4x8-inch loaf pan.

With a wooden spoon, mix butter into the mashed bananas in a large mixing bowl.

Mix in sugar, egg, and vanilla. Sprinkle the baking soda and salt over the mixture and mix in. Add the flour and mix well. Add nuts if desired. Pour mixture into pan.

Bake for 1 hour. Cool on a rack.

Remove from pan.

Tips and variations: It is easier to slice this banana bread if placed in the refrigerator after it is cooled.

Kalamazoo House B&B

Super-Moist Banana Bread

Yield: 1 loaf

"I've been using this recipe since I was in college. I adapted it from
Sunset's Easy Basics for Good Cooking Cookbook *by changing the*
all-white sugar and flours to half brown sugar and half whole-wheat
flour. It's moist and dense, the way I think banana bread should be!"

3	large very ripe bananas
½	cup brown sugar, packed hard
½	cup white sugar
1	large egg
4	Tbsp butter, melted and cooled
¾	cup all-purpose flour
¾	cup whole-wheat flour
1	tsp salt
1	tsp baking soda

Preheat oven to 325°F. Lightly grease 9x5-inch loaf pan.

Mash bananas (about 1 cup total or a bit more). Beat in sugars. Add
egg and cooled melted butter; stir until well mixed. In a separate
bowl, mix together flours, salt, and baking soda. Add dry ingredients
to wet ingredients; stir only until flour is moistened. (A few lumps are
expected.) Put batter in prepared pan.

Bake 55–60 minutes (less in a convection oven) until toothpick comes
out clean.

Cool in pan 5–10 minutes, then turn out on rack to cool. Cover well so
that it does not dry out.

Serve at room temperature.

Tips and variations: I like to use the blackest, mushiest bananas for
this—the riper the better. And if you have ripe bananas but you're not
ready to make banana bread, you can stick them in the freezer. Simply
pull out, thaw on a plate (they'll leak), cut off the end and squeeze
into your bowl.

Dove Nest B&B St. Joseph

Blueberry Bread

Yield: 15 servings

"Dove Nest Bed and Breakfast in St. Joseph serves quick breads to guests as a snack upon their arrival to make them feel welcome and appreciated."

1½	cups sugar
3	cups flour
1½	tsp baking soda
1¼	Tbsp cinnamon
1	tsp salt
4	eggs, beaten
1¼	cups oil
2	(10-oz.) pkgs. blueberries

Preheat oven to 350°F. Grease and flour or spray two 4x8-inch loaf pans.

Mix sugar, flour, baking soda, cinnamon, and salt together.

Add beaten eggs and oil to dry mixture. Mix by hand. Gently fold in blueberries. Pour into greased pans. Bake for one hour.

Michigan is the number one state in high bush blueberry production, with growers producing over 100 million pounds of blueberries every year. Most of Michigan's commercial blueberry production is located in southwest Michigan where sandy glacial soils and high water tables result in excellent blueberry soils. Over 20 blueberry varieties are grown in Michigan. The Michigan harvest season normally runs from late June through October.
—Michigan State University Extension and AgBio Research

Sandtown Farmhouse B&B

Golden Compromise Bread

Yield: 1 loaf

"This bread is the perfect compromise for guests who have a preference for whole-wheat or white bread. This recipe gives whole-wheat the softness found in breads baked only with white flour."

Sponge	Dough
2 cups whole-wheat flour	1 tsp salt
1 pkg. active dry yeast	¼ cup vegetable oil
½ cup warm water (105–110°)	2 Tbsp honey
2 cups warm buttermilk (105–110°)	1 large egg, fresh from my flock
2 Tbsp sugar	2 Tbsp ground flaxseed (meal)
	2–2¼ cups bread flour

Combine "sponge" ingredients in a large bowl and stir well. Cover with plastic wrap or a damp linen cloth and let sit for 1 hour (or more.) Using a sponge develops great flavor.

Add remaining ingredients using an electric mixer with a dough hook or by hand. Knead until smooth and elastic, 8–10 minutes. Shape into a ball.

Place dough in an oiled bowl, turning to coat the top of the ball. Cover with plastic wrap or the damp linen cloth. Let rise in a warm place (85°) for one hour or until doubled in bulk.

Grease an 8½ x 4½-inch loaf pan.

Punch dough down, turn out onto a lightly floured surface and knead lightly four or five times to deflate. Divide dough in half. Roll each portion of the dough into a 14x7–inch rectangle. Roll up jellyroll style, starting at the short side, pressing firmly to avoid air pockets. Place each loaf, seam side down, in the loaf pan. Cover and let rise in a warm place, free from drafts, 45 minutes or until doubled in bulk.

Preheat oven to 350°F. Bake for 25 minutes or until loaves sound hollow when tapped. Remove bread from pans immediately; cool on a rack.

Cherry Chip Muffins

Yield: 12 muffins

These muffins get their "lift" from sour cream, their "sweet" from white chocolate chips, and their "Michigan" from dried cherries.

- 1½ cups all-purpose flour
- ⅔ cup sugar
- ¾ tsp baking powder
- ¾ tsp baking soda
- ¼ tsp salt
- 1 egg
- 1 cup (8 oz.) sour cream
- 5 Tbsp butter, melted and slightly cooled
- 1 tsp real vanilla extract
- ¾ cup (or more) white chocolate chips
- ¾ cup (or more) dried Michigan cherries
     raw sugar for sprinkling on top

Preheat oven to 350°F. Grease or paper-line standard muffin cups.

In a large bowl, combine the flour, sugar, baking powder, baking soda and salt.

In another bowl, mix together the egg, sour cream, melted butter and vanilla.

Stir wet ingredients into dry ingredients just until moistened. Fold in chips and cherries.

Fill muffin cups ¾ full. Sprinkle with raw sugar. Bake for 18–20 minutes or until a toothpick comes out clean. Cool for 5 minutes before removing from pan to a wire rack.

Tips and variations: Variations are, of course, endless. The original Taste of Home recipe called for mint chocolate chips and no fruit.

This recipe has been adapted from Stephanie Moon's Sour Cream Chip Muffins recipe taken from *The Taste of Home Cookbook*.

Frankenmuth B&B (Bender House)

Orange Breakfast Muffins

Yield: 12 muffins

2	cups all-purpose flour
1/3	cup sugar
1	tsp baking powder
3/4	tsp salt
1/2	tsp baking soda
2	eggs, beaten
1	Tbsp grated orange peel
1	cup orange juice
1/3	cup oil
1/4	cup orange marmalade

Preheat oven to 400°F. Grease a muffin pan.

In a large bowl, thoroughly combine the flour, sugar, baking powder, salt and baking soda. Add eggs, orange peel, orange juice and oil; mix well.

Fill greased muffin pans 2/3 full. Bake for 20–25 minutes.

Heat marmalade until melted, brush over tops of hot baked muffins.

Marmalade is a fruit preserve made from the juice and peel of citrus fruits boiled with sugar and water. It can be produced from lemons, limes, grapefruits, mandarins, sweet oranges, and other citrus fruits, or any combination thereof. The benchmark citrus fruit for marmalade production in Britain is the Spanish Seville orange, prized for its high pectin content, which gives a good set. The peel has a distinctive bitter taste, which it imparts to the marmalade.—Wikipedia

Banana Buttermilk Muffins

Yield: 12 muffins

"Buttermilk is low in fat, making these muffins light and tender in texture, and healthier, too. This is also a great way to use overripe bananas. These muffins are a favorite with our guests."

- 1 cup unbleached all-purpose flour
- ¾ cup whole-wheat flour
- ½ cup sugar
- 2 tsp baking powder
- 1 tsp baking soda
- 1 cup low-fat buttermilk
- 1 cup well-mashed ripe bananas
- 2 Tbsp canola oil
- 1 egg
- 1 tsp vanilla extract
- ½ cup walnuts, chopped

Preheat oven to 375°F. Grease a standard 12-count muffin tin with canola oil cooking spray or use paper liners.

In a large bowl, stir together the all-purpose and whole-wheat flours, sugar, baking powder and baking soda. In another bowl or a large glass measuring pitcher, whisk together the buttermilk, bananas, oil, egg and vanilla. Pour the wet ingredients over the dry ingredients; stir until just blended. Do not over mix.

Spoon the batter into the prepared muffin cups, filling each about three-quarters full.

Sprinkle the tops evenly with the walnuts. Bake 15–20 minutes until muffins are lightly browned and a toothpick inserted in the center comes out clean. Let cool in the pan on a wire rack for 15 minutes, then turn out onto the rack and let cool completely.

Tips and variations: The muffins will keep in a zippered plastic bag at room temperature for 2 or 3 days or in the freezer for up to 2 months.

Store ripe bananas in the freezer and use as needed.

This recipe has been adapted from *Williams Sonoma Essentials of Healthy Cooking* by Dana Jacobi, Mary Abbot Hess, and Marie Simmons.

Just Baked

Historic Webster House

Gluten-Free Apple Muffins

Yield: 12 muffins

"We don't use 'mixes' at Historic Webster House and prefer to make everything from scratch. Many gluten-free recipes have very unusual ingredients that rarely get used. They also seem to fall apart—nothing to bind them. These muffins use simple ingredients, are moist, tasty, and they stay together!"

1	cup rice flour
½	tsp baking soda
1	tsp baking powder
½	tsp nutmeg
1	tsp cinnamon
¾	tsp salt
3	Tbsp canola oil
⅓	cup sugar
2	eggs
1	tsp vanilla
1	apple, grated

Preheat oven to 350°F. Grease a muffin pan.

Mix together rice flour, baking soda, baking powder, nutmeg, cinnamon, and salt. In a separate bowl, combine oil, sugar, eggs, and vanilla. Add wet ingredients and apple to dry ingredients.

Divide dough among muffin cups. Bake until brown or firm to the touch, approximately 14–16 minutes.

Blueberry Buckle or Muffins

Yield: 12 servings

"I got this recipe from my sister-in-law Doris. She had gotten it from her mother. I make these a lot when blueberries are in season."

¾ cup sugar
¼ cup butter
½ cup milk
1 egg
2 cups flour
2 tsp baking powder
½ tsp salt
2 cups blueberries

Topping

½ cup sugar
⅓ cup flour
1 tsp cinnamon
¼ cup soft butter

Preheat oven to 350°F. Grease a 9x13-inch pan or a muffin tin.

Cream together sugar and butter; stir in milk and egg. Sift flour with baking powder and salt and stir into wet ingredients. Add blueberries. In a small bowl, combine topping ingredients. Fill pan or muffin tins ¾ full; sprinkle with topping.

The muffin bake time is 20–30 minutes.

The buckle bake time is 45–55 minutes.

Pumpkin Cranberry Muffins

Yield: 12 muffins

*"A healthy start to your morning at White Swan Inn
or in your own kitchen."*

2	eggs
½	cup brown sugar
½	cup vegetable oil
⅔	cup pumpkin (not pie filling)
⅔	cup low-fat sour cream
5	Tbsp granulated sugar
½	tsp powdered ginger
¾	cup dried cranberries
2¼	cups all-purpose flour
1	Tbsp cinnamon
1	tsp milled flax seed
1	tsp baking powder
½	tsp baking soda
½	tsp salt
¼	tsp ground nutmeg

Preheat oven to 375°F. Grease muffin tins or use paper liners.

Whisk together the eggs, brown sugar, oil, pumpkin, sour cream, granulated sugar, and ginger in a large bowl. Stir in cranberries.

Sift the flour, cinnamon, flax seed, baking powder, baking soda, salt, and nutmeg together in a large bowl. Add dry ingredients into pumpkin mixture. Stir together until dry ingredients are moistened.

Divide the batter among the muffin cups.

Bake for 20–25 minutes or until lightly browned on top and a skewer inserted into the center of a muffin comes out clean. Cool on a wire rack.

Tips and variations: Instead of full-size muffins, divide batter into greased 24 mini-muffin cups. Bake for 15 minutes or until tested done. There will be additional batter for additional mini muffins or 2 mini-loaves. Mini loaves need to bake for approximately 35–40 minutes.

Lotta Lemon Muffins

Yield: 6 large or 12 small muffins

"These muffins are very moist and flavorful, especially with the addition of a tangy lemon glaze."

- 1¾ cups all-purpose flour
- ¾ cup sugar
- 1 Tbsp grated lemon peel
- 1 tsp baking powder
- ¾ tsp baking soda
- ¼ tsp salt
- 8 oz. lemon yogurt
- 6 Tbsp (¾ stick) butter, melted & cooled
- 1 egg, room temperature
- 1 Tbsp fresh lemon juice

Glaze
- ⅓ cup fresh lemon juice
- ¼ cup sugar
- 2 tsp grated lemon peel

Preheat oven to 400°F. Spray muffin tins with non-stick cooking spray.

Mix first 6 ingredients in large bowl; make well in center. In a separate bowl, whisk together yogurt, butter, egg, and lemon juice. Add to well; stir into dry ingredients until just blended. Spoon batter into prepared muffin cups, filling each ¾-full.

Bake until golden brown and tester inserted in center comes out clean, about 18–20 minutes for large or 12–15 minutes for small.

Meanwhile, prepare glaze: Cook all ingredients in small saucepan over low heat until sugar dissolves.

Remove muffins from pan. Transfer to wire rack. Pierce 6–8 holes in each muffin with skewer or fork. Drizzle hot glaze over tops, coating well.

Serve at room temperature.

Just Baked

Antiquities' Wellington Inn

Blueberry Citrus Muffins

Yield: 12 muffins

½ cup butter
½ cup sugar
2 eggs
2 cups flour
3 tsp baking powder
¼ tsp salt
⅓ cup milk
1 cup blueberries
  rind of one lemon or lime, finely grated

Preheat oven to 350°F. Spray muffin cups with nonstick cooking spray.

Cream butter, sugar and eggs in a small bowl. In large bowl, combine flour, baking powder and salt. Add creamed mixture alternately with milk until mixed. Fold in blueberries and lemon or lime rind.

Fill muffin cups ⅔ full. Bake for 25–30 minutes.

Blueberries are a great source of anti-oxidants, which lowers energy radicals in your body. They also contain trace amounts of vitamin C, which helps your immune system. Blueberries are often thought of as citrus fruits because of the citrus acid they contain, but they are an alkaline fruit.—Wiki Answers

Candlewyck House B&B

JJ's Banana Muffins

Yield: 10–12 muffins

"My son JJ loves bananas and we always keep them on hand. When he comes home, I make these special muffins for him. It's a recipe we worked out together back when I owned a gift shop/tea room."

1¾ cups flour
½ tsp salt
1 tsp baking soda
1 tsp cinnamon
1/3 cup softened butter
1 cup sugar, half brown, half white
2 eggs beaten
3 tsp vanilla
3 large ripe bananas, mashed

Preheat oven to 375°F. Grease a muffin tin.

Sift together flour, salt, baking soda, and cinnamon and set aside.

In a separate bowl, cream butter and sugars until fluffy. Add eggs, vanilla, and bananas, mixing well. Stir in dry ingredients. Fill muffin tins ¾-full. Bake for 22 minutes.

Tip: To speed up the ripening of a banana, place it in a paper bag or rolled up in a newspaper and leave out at room temperature.

J. Paule's Fenn Inn

Cranberry Orange Scones

Yield: 10 scones

2	cups flour
⅓	cup butter
1	Tbsp grated orange peel
2	tsp baking powder
½	tsp salt
¼	tsp baking soda
1	cup cranberries
¼	cup orange juice
¾	cup cream
1	egg
1	Tbsp milk
10	tsp sugar, divided

Glaze (optional)

½	cup confectioners' sugar
1	Tbsp orange juice

Preheat oven to 400°F.

In a bowl, combine flour and butter. Blend until mixture resembles coarse crumbs.

Add orange peel, baking powder, salt and baking soda. Set aside.

In a small bowl, combine cranberries, orange juice, cream and egg. Add to flour mixture and stir until a soft dough forms. Turn out onto a floured surface and gently knead 6–8 times. Pat dough into an 8-inch circle. Cut into 10 wedges. Separate wedges and place on an ungreased cookie sheet. Brush with milk and then sprinkle with remaining sugar.

Bake for 12–15 minutes until lightly browned.

Combine glaze ingredients if desired and drizzle over scones.

Grand Floridian Raisin Scones

Yield: 24 scones

"While enjoying afternoon tea at the Grand Floridian Hotel at Disney World, I asked the waitress if the chef would share his wonderful scone recipe. As you can see, the answer was yes. Now I am sharing it with you. It's one of our most-requested breakfast items."

4	cups all-purpose flour
3	Tbsp baking powder
½	cup sugar
1	tsp salt
2	Tbsp margarine
2	Tbsp shortening
3	eggs, beaten
1¼	cup milk
1	cup golden raisins

Preheat oven to 425°F. Lightly grease a baking sheet.

Sift the flour, baking powder, sugar, and salt into a large mixing bowl. Rub the margarine and shortening into the flour with your fingertips until the mixture resembles coarse meal.

In a bowl, combine the eggs and milk; stir into the flour mixture, just until the dough comes together. Fold in the raisins.

Roll the dough out to about ½-inch thickness on a lightly floured surface. With a 2-inch round cutter, stamp out 24 scones and transfer them to baking sheet. Bake the scones for 10–15 minutes or until they are light brown.

Serve at once with Devonshire cream or butter and jam. These scones should be crisp and brown on the outside and soft and white when you split them open.

Just Baked

Sand Castle Inn

Cherry Almond Scones

Yield: 8 large or 16 small scones

"I like to make these scones small because they bake faster and our guests can try all three of the baked bread assortments we put out each morning. If there are any of these delicious scones left over, we put them out in the afternoon and within minutes they are gone!"

2	cups all-purpose flour
1/3	cup sugar
2	tsp baking powder
1/4	tsp salt
1/3	cup chilled butter, cut into pieces
1	large egg
2/3	cup whipping cream
1	tsp vanilla extract
1	tsp almond extract
1	cup dried cherries
	egg wash (1 egg and 1 tsp water, beaten)
	sugar, for topping
	sliced almonds, for topping

Preheat oven to 325°F. Grease a baking sheet.

Combine flour, sugar, baking powder, and salt. Cut in butter with pastry blender. In a separate bowl, combine egg, whipping cream, and extracts. Add wet ingredients to dry ingredients just until moistened. Add cherries. Mixture will be very sticky.

Turn onto floured surface and knead 4–5 times with floured hands. Pat out to ½-inch thick and cut into circles. Or divide dough in half and pat out each half to ½-thick circle; cut each into 8–12 wedges.

Brush tops with egg wash. Sprinkle tops with sugar and sliced almonds. Place on baking sheet. Bake for 15–18 minutes.

Saravilla B&B

Michigan Cherry Chip Scones

Yield: 8–10 servings

"What's better than a baked item fresh out of the oven? This can be prepared the day before and baked fresh in the a.m. without getting up much earlier than needed. As scones go, these are very moist. Everyone always enjoys them. We use Michigan dried cherries, of course."

3	cups all-purpose flour
½	cup white sugar
2½	tsp baking powder
½	tsp baking soda
6	Tbsp cold butter (no substitutes)
1	cup vanilla yogurt
¼	cup, plus 2 Tbsp milk, divided
1⅓	cups dried cherries
⅔	cup white chocolate chips

Preheat oven to 400°F. Grease a baking sheet (or line it with parchment paper).

In a large bowl, combine flour, sugar, baking powder, and baking soda. Cut in butter until the mixture resembles coarse crumbs. In a separate bowl, combine yogurt and ¼ cup milk. Stir into dry mixture just until moistened. Knead in the cherries and chocolate chips.

Pat dough into a 9-inch circle. Cut into 8–10 wedges. Brush with the remaining milk.

Bake for 20–25 minutes or until golden brown. Serve warm.

Tips and variations: Try cranberries instead of cherries.

Using margarine will not give a good result.

For smaller scones, divide dough in half, making two circles on each end of the baking sheet. Cut each half into 6–8 wedges.

If dough is refrigerated overnight, bring to room temperature before baking.

This recipe has been adapted from *Taste of Home Magazine* (April/May 2003).

~~~~~~

Cherry, White Chocolate & Walnut Scones

~~~~~~

Yield: 16 large scones

"This recipe, originally made with cranberries, has been adapted using cherries, which are plentiful in the Leelanau Peninsula."

3	cups flour
½	cup sugar
2	Tbsp baking powder
½	tsp salt
¾	cup butter
¾	cup cream (coffee or whipping)
1	large egg
¾	cup walnuts, toasted and chopped
¾	cup dried cherries or dried cranberries
½	cup white chocolate chips, cut in half

Preheat oven to 350°F. Line a baking sheet with parchment paper.

In a large bowl, stir together the flour, sugar, baking powder, and salt. Cut the butter into small cubes and distribute them over the flour mixture. With a pastry blender, cut in the butter until the mixture resembles coarse crumbs. In a small bowl, stir together the cream and egg. Add the cream mixture to the flour mixture and stir to combine. Stir in the nuts, cherries, and chocolate chips.

On a lightly floured surface, cut dough into rounds using a cookie cutter. Place on baking sheet and bake for approximately 15 minutes, or until the top is lightly browned and a toothpick inserted into the center of a scone comes out clean. Remove from baking sheet to a wire rack and cool for 5 minutes.

Tips and variations: Sprinkle scones lightly with granulated sugar before baking.

Rather than cutting the scones on a floured surface using a cookie cutter, you may spoon the mixture directly onto the parchment-lined baking sheet.

This recipe has been adapted from a recipe used at Iris Garden Country Manor, Victoria, BC.

Glen Arbor B&B

Katie's Favorite Scones with Orange Glaze

Yield: 12–16 scones

"These are so rich and buttery, you won't believe how easy they are to make."

2 Tbsp sugar
2 cups all-purpose flour
1 Tbsp baking powder
5 Tbsp cold butter
1¼ cups heavy cream plus 2 Tbsp, divided
1 cup unsweetened frozen fruit
2 Tbsp sugar, for topping

Glaze
2 cups powdered sugar
3 Tbsp orange juice
1 Tbsp butter, melted
1 Tbsp 2% milk

Preheat oven to 400°F. Grease a baking sheet.

In large bowl, combine all dry ingredients with the chilled butter. Cut in butter with a pastry blender or two forks until the mixture resembles course crumbs. Stir in the cream until just moistened, then fold in the frozen fruit. (Use whatever fruit is in season.)

Turn dough onto floured surface and divide into 2 equal parts. Knead each portion of dough about 10 times. Press into two rounds about ¾ inch thick, then cut each round into 6 to 8 pie slices. Brush with the reserved cream and lightly dust with granulated sugar.

Separate and place the scones on the baking sheet. Bake for 20–25 minutes until golden brown. Cool on a wire rack about 5 minutes.

To make the glaze, whisk all 4 ingredients together in a small bowl. Drizzle the glaze over the warm scones and serve.

Apple Coffee Cake

Yield: 2 cakes, 6 servings each

*"A moist, scrumptious coffee cake perfect with a gourmet cup of coffee.
We serve it at the Hexagon House with a main breakfast entrée."*

1	cup canola oil
2	cups sugar
3	eggs
3	cups flour
1	tsp baking soda
1	cup walnuts, chopped
½	tsp salt
1	tsp vanilla
1	tsp cinnamon
3	cups apples, peeled, cored, and diced

Preheat oven to 350°F. Grease two round cake pans.

In a large bowl, mix together oil, sugar, and eggs. Add flour, baking soda, nuts, salt, vanilla, and cinnamon. Add apples last.

Divide the batter between two cake pans.

Bake 30–35 minutes.

Tip: This coffee cake freezes very well.

This recipe has been adapted from Gera Witte, sister of Hexagon House owners.

Peach Coffee Cake with Pecans

Yield: 6–8 servings

"One of our favorite coffee cakes. This mixture of fruit and nuts creates a delightful taste sensation, particularly when served with freshly brewed coffee or tea."

3	cups canned or frozen peaches
2	tsp cinnamon
3	cups all-purpose flour
3	tsp baking powder
1	tsp salt
½	cup butter, softened
1	cup sugar
1½	cups milk
3	eggs

Topping

½	cup pecans, finely chopped
½	cup packed brown sugar
2	Tbsp butter, melted

Preheat oven to 350°F. Grease a 9x13-inch baking dish.

If using frozen peaches, do not completely thaw before chopping. For canned peaches, drain before using. Chop peaches and mix with the cinnamon in a bowl. Set aside. Mix flour, baking powder, and salt in a bowl; set aside. In a separate bowl, cream butter and sugar together until fluffy. Add milk. Add eggs one at a time, mixing after each one. Add egg mixture to dry mixture and mix until well blended. Fold in chopped peaches. Pour mixture into baking dish.

In a small bowl, mix chopped pecans and brown sugar together and sprinkle over coffee cake. Drizzle the melted butter over the top. Bake for 50 minutes, or until a toothpick inserted into center comes out clean. Place baking dish on a wire rack and let cool for about an hour.

Variation: Substitute Granny Smith apples for the peaches to make a wonderful apple coffee cake.

Saravilla B&B

Gooey Lemon Coffee Cake

Yield: 10–12 servings

"I have used this recipe ever since 1991, when we opened Saravilla Bed and Breakfast. I don't remember where it came from. It's very easy to make. It always receives raves. It isn't too sweet."

1 lemon cake mix
2 eggs, beaten
½ cup margarine or butter, melted

Topping
8 oz. cream cheese (not low-fat)
2 eggs
2 cups powdered sugar

Preheat oven to 350°F. Grease a 9x13-inch baking pan.

With a wooden spoon, beat together the cake mix, eggs, and melted butter or margarine.

Pour into the baking pan.

For the topping: using a mixer, beat together the cream cheese and eggs until well blended. Add powdered sugar and beat until smooth. Pour over top of cake batter.

Bake for 35 minutes.

Tips and variations: Using butter is better. Use regular cream cheese. After cake is cooled, drizzle a thin powdered sugar frosting across the top of cake.

Katie's Sour Cream Coffee Cake

Yield: 8–10 servings

- 1   cup butter
- 2   cups sugar
- 2   eggs
- 1   cup sour cream
- ½   tsp vanilla
- 2   cups less 4 Tbsp flour
- 1   tsp baking powder
- ¼   tsp salt (use only if you use unsalted butter)

Topping

- ½   cup brown sugar
- ½   tsp cinnamon
- ½   cup pecans, chopped

Preheat oven to 350°F. Grease and flour a tube pan.

Cream together first 3 ingredients in a mixer. Add sour cream and vanilla; blend on lowest speed. Fold in dry ingredients by hand.

Combine topping ingredients in a small bowl.

Place half the batter in the tube pan. Sprinkle with half the topping. Pour in remaining batter and sprinkle with the rest of the topping. Bake for 55 minutes.

Seymour House

Lemon Walnut Danish

Yield: 8 Danish

Filling
- 1 Tbsp lemon juice
   zest of 1 lemon
- 1 (8-oz.) pkg. cream cheese, at room temperature
- 1/3 cup confectioners' sugar

- 1 sheet puff pastry cut into 2x2-inch squares
- 1/4 cup walnuts, finely chopped, for topping
   confectioners' sugar, for topping

In a bowl, combine all ingredients for the filling. Position each square of puff pastry on a cookie sheet. Turn the square so that it is orientated as a diamond. Place 1 tablespoon of filling into the center of each diamond. Brush the right and left corners of each diamond with water. Fold the right and left corners into the center until they just overlap. Freeze the filled pastry on the cookie sheet. This is an important step in making the pastry rise properly.

When ready to bake: preheat oven to 375°F. Line another cookie sheet with parchment paper and transfer frozen pastry puffs onto sheet. Brush with an egg wash (1 egg and 2 tablespoons water whisked together). Sprinkle with walnuts.

Bake for 20 minutes or until the puff pastry is lightly browned. Let cool before removing from the cookie sheet. Sprinkle with confectioners' sugar. Serve.

Dutch Colonial Inn

~~~~~~~~~~

Lemon Pull-Aparts

~~~~~~~~~~

Yield: 12 servings

"'Cute' little lemon rolls that are yummy!"

- 12 Rhodes™ dinner rolls, frozen
- 6 tsp lemon rind (zest of 2 lemons)
- ½ cup sugar
- ¼ cup butter, melted

Citrus glaze
- 1 cup powdered sugar
- 1 Tbsp butter, melted
- 2 Tbsp fresh lemon juice

Spray baking dish the night before and set frozen dinner rolls inside. Cover with plastic wrap and put in refrigerator overnight. Three hours before baking, pull out of refrigerator and cut rolls in half. Mix lemon rind and sugar. Drizzle butter over rolls then top with lemon/sugar mixture (reserve half the mixture for just before baking). Cover with plastic wrap and set in warm place so they can rise until they're double in size.

Preheat oven to 350°F.

Sprinkle remaining mixture over top and bake for 20–25 minutes. Remove immediately from pan and place on cooling rack. Combine glaze ingredients and drizzle over pull-aparts.

Tips and variations: You can also prepare these little rolls the night before. Make them as listed, cover with plastic wrap and store in the refrigerator overnight. A couple of hours before you want to bake them, take them out of the refrigerator and let them rise. Bake as directed.

Adrounie House B&B

Sticky Quickies

Yield: 8-10 servings

"My best friend, Edith, shared this recipe with me years ago. It was her family favorite. For many years our Christmas mornings included "sticky quickies" and a cup of coffee while opening Christmas gifts!"

3¼ cups unbleached flour, divided
2 pkgs. dry yeast
¾ cup milk
½ cup water
¼ cup sugar
1 tsp salt
1 egg

Topping
¾ cup butter
1 cup brown sugar, packed
1 tsp cinnamon
¾ cup walnuts or pecans, chopped
1 Tbsp corn syrup
1 Tbsp water

Put 1½ cups flour and yeast into mixing bowl. Heat milk, water, sugar, and salt until warm. Add to yeast mixture. Add egg. Beat on high speed for 3 minutes. By hand add remaining flour and mix. Cover and let rise 30 minutes, or place in refrigerator overnight (then let rise 30 minutes in the morning).

Preheat oven to 375°F.

For topping, combine all topping ingredients in small saucepan and heat until melted. (The longer this is cooked, the more "gooey" it will be, cook's choice.) Pour this mixture into a 9x13-inch baking pan. Stir the dough down and drop by tablespoons on top.

Bake for 12–15 minutes. When done, flip the pan over onto aluminum foil covered with a piece of wax paper. Separate pieces and place on serving platter or individual plates.

Buttonville Inn

Overnight Bubble Bread

Yield: 8–10 servings

"One of the easiest and best-tasting recipes for breakfast!
When planning to make these, remember that they must rise overnight."

½ cup pecan halves
18 frozen dinner rolls
1 (3.5-oz.) pkg. instant butterscotch pudding mix
½ cup butter
½ cup brown sugar
2 Tbsp Karo® syrup

Generously grease a standard Bundt pan.

Sprinkle pecans in bottom of pan. Place frozen dinner rolls on top of pecans. Sprinkle dry pudding mix over the top.

Combine butter, brown sugar and Karo® syrup in a small saucepan. Heat until boiling, then pour over rolls.

Cover with plastic wrap or wax paper and allow to stand overnight.

In the morning, preheat oven to 350°F. Bake for 20–30 minutes, until golden brown.

Tips: You can use walnuts in place of pecans. You can use only a half-package of the pudding or substitute vanilla pudding.

Castle in the Country B&B Inn

Apple-Filled Croissants

Yield: 2 dozen croissants

"The key to successful croissants is to keep the butter from melting while working the dough. In this "quick" recipe, we cut a massive amount of butter into dry flour instead of softening it and spreading it over the rolled out flour. This allows us to immediately roll and fold instead of chilling the dough first."

5 cups all-purpose flour, plus flour for work surface

1 lb. butter, cut into ½-inch cubes

1¾ cups milk, warmed

3 Tbsp sugar

1½ Tbsp yeast, instant active

2 tsp salt

2 tart apples, diced

2 Tbsp sugar

1 tsp cinnamon

1 egg for egg wash plus 1 Tbsp water

Cut butter into 3½ cups flour with a pastry blender, food processor or stand mixer until largest pieces of butter are the size of lima beans and flour has taken on a yellowed, cornmeal-like appearance. (Watch closely. Do not allow butter to melt.)

Put the mixture in plastic bag and place in cooler or freezer.

In a large bowl, mix remaining flour with milk, sugar, and yeast. Allow to rise 20–30 minutes. It should begin to foam. Add flour/butter mixture and salt to the yeast mixture. Combine to make a sticky mixture with butter particles.

Turn onto floured work surface and roll out to a large rectangle about ½-inch thick. Tri-fold twice, book-fold twice. Do not allow butter pieces to melt. (A tri-fold is what you would do to a sheet of paper before inserting into an envelope, a book fold is simply folding in half, then in half again.). Cut into 4 equal blocks. Refrigerate dough for 1–24 hours.

In a small bowl, combine diced apples with sugar and cinnamon. Set aside. If refrigerating overnight, prepare the apples just before baking.

When ready to bake: Preheat oven to 400°F. and line a cookie sheet with parchment paper. Roll out each block of dough into a 10-inch diameter disc. Cut into 6 wedges. Place an equal amount of apple filling on each wedge and roll from edge to point. Allow to rise until doubled in volume (about 1 hour).

Brush with egg wash and bake for 16 minutes.

Grandma's Buttermilk Biscuits

Yield: 8–10 biscuits

"I remember our family going over to Grandma's for Sunday morning breakfast. Grandma would always make buttermilk biscuits. If you asked Grandma for the recipe she would always say, 'Oh, just take three handfuls of flour and this much butter, a pinch of salt and a pinch of baking soda, then just add as much buttermilk as you think you need.' Grandma never used a recipe because she did not need them. Her baking and cooking were perfect without the aid of recipes. This is how I prefer to cook creatively every day."

- 2 cups all-purpose flour, plus a little extra
- ¼ tsp baking soda
- 1 tsp baking powder
- 1 tsp salt
- 6 Tbsp unsalted butter
- 1 cup buttermilk

Heat oven to 450°F. Flour a kneading board.

Combine dry ingredients in a food processor or bowl. Cut butter into small pieces and add to flour or pulse a few times with food processor. Add buttermilk and mix until it is combined. If it looks too dry add a bit more milk. (It should look wet.) Turn the dough out onto the floured board. Pat the dough gently down to ½-inch thick (do not use rolling pin to roll). Fold the dough gently about 5 or 6 times. Pat the dough gently to make 1-inch-high biscuits. Limit handling of the dough to make them lighter. Put biscuits on a baking sheet and bake for 12 minutes or until golden brown.

Tips and variations: You can freeze the dough and they can be baked without thawing for 20 minutes at 450°degrees F. These are just delicious, fast and easy.

Strawberry-Rhubarb Jam

Yield: 4–5 jars

"This is the only jam we serve at our inn. It is the quickest, easiest and tastiest jam you'll ever make. I love this recipe because it can be made with sugar free Jell-O and Splenda, so our diabetic and dieting guests can enjoy a treat right along with everyone else."

5   cups rhubarb, diced (can use a food processor)
4   cups sugar or Splenda
2   small boxes sugar free (or regular) Strawberry Jell-O

Combine rhubarb and sugar in a large pan. Cook on stovetop; bring to rolling boil for 10 minutes to dissolve sugar. Add Jell-O and mix well until dissolved.

Put into freezer containers. Cool and freeze.

Tips and variations: Our guests love to spread cream cheese on their toast first and then add a layer of this signature jam. Yummy!

This recipe has been adapted from an Amish woman I met at a farmers' market.

Cocoa Cottage B&B

Lemon Curd

Yields: 2 cups

"Lemon curd is a British teatime favorite. This velvety spread is heavenly on freshly baked scones, muffins, and tea breads. Another favorite is serving lemon curd on gingerbread or used as a filling for tarts and elegant cakes. Paired with a piece of thick Scottish shortbread you'll appreciate how lemon curd can transform a simple, somewhat homely cookie into something wonderful. We have paired it with our Merlot-poached pears."

1²/³	Tbsp cornstarch
½	cup cold water
2	large egg yolks
¾	cup sugar
¼	cup fresh lemon juice
1	tsp finely grated lemon zest

In a small bowl dissolve cornstarch in water.

In medium saucepan, whisk to combine yolks, sugar and lemon juice. Whisk in cornstarch mixture. Whisk gently over medium heat until sugar is dissolved and lemon mixture is hot, about 6 minutes. Boil over moderate-high heat for an additional 4 minutes, whisking constantly until the mixture is thick and glossy.

Strain lemon mixture into a heatproof bowl and stir in lemon zest. Let cool and serve. May be stored in refrigerator for up to 2 weeks.

Sweet Mornings

French Toast, Pancakes, Crepês & Cereals

Michigan bed and breakfast innkeepers typically have a breakfast repertoire that includes a variety of sweet entrées. What are your favorites? Pancakes, waffles, French toast, stuffed French toast, maybe a bread pudding or some delightfully close cousin to pie? Some dishes served at Michigan B&Bs are griddle favorites, others are from the oven. Some use the Michigan maple syrup, for which our state is famous. Others incorporate locally produced honey or preserves. Next time a decadent breakfast comes to mind, check out these favorite sweet entrées from Michigan bed and breakfast innkeepers.

Recipes in the Featured Recipes chapter

In this chapter

Sweet Mornings

Peaches & Cream French Toast

Yield: 12 servings

1	cup brown sugar, packed
½	cup butter, cubed
2	Tbsp corn syrup
1	(29-oz.) can sliced peaches, drained
1	(1-lb.) loaf day-old French bread, cubed
1	(8-oz.) pkg. cream cheese, cubed
12	eggs
1½	cups half & half
1	tsp vanilla extract

Grease a 9x13-inch baking dish.

In a small saucepan, combine the brown sugar, butter, and corn syrup. Cook and stir over medium heat until sugar is dissolved; pour into baking dish. Arrange peaches in baking dish. Place half of the bread cubes over peaches.

Layer with cream cheese and remaining bread.

Place the eggs, cream, and vanilla in a blender. Cover and process until smooth.

Pour over top of peaches and bread mixture. Cover and refrigerate overnight.

Remove from the refrigerator 30 minutes before baking.

Preheat oven to 350°F. Bake uncovered for 50–60 minutes or until a knife inserted near the center comes out clean.

This recipe has been adapted from *Taste of Home Magazine*.

Apple Raisin Pie French Toast

Yield: 8–10 servings

3	cups frozen apples. Do not thaw. We use Ida Red.
¼	cup raisins, dried cherries, or cranberries
1	stick unsalted butter, melted
½	cup brown sugar
6	eggs
1½	cups 2% milk
1	Tbsp vanilla
2	tsp cinnamon
1	loaf multigrain or regular French bread sliced 1-inch thick
	warmed maple syrup
	whipped cream (optional)
	chopped walnuts (optional)

The day or night before serving: Grease a 9x13-inch glass baking dish.

Layer apple and raisins in the bottom of the baking dish. In a small bowl, combine butter and brown sugar; pour over the apples and raisins. Mix eggs, milk, vanilla, and cinnamon in a large bowl. Place bread slices two at a time in egg milk mixture, remove quickly and make a layer over the fruit layer in the baking pan. Pour remaining milk and egg mixture over all. Cover with plastic wrap. Refrigerate at least 6 hours or overnight.

Day of serving: Preheat oven to 375°F. Take dish out of refrigerator and remove plastic wrap. Cover pan tightly with foil sprayed with cooking oil. Bake covered for 40 minutes, and then uncovered for 5 additional minutes, or until lightly browned. Let stand out of the oven 5 minutes before serving. Serve with warmed maple syrup, whipped cream, and chopped walnuts.

Tips and variations: Spraying the foil with non-stick spray prevents the foil from sticking to the bread slices.

Orange Pecan Baked French Toast with Peach-Orange Sauce

Yield: 6–8 servings

4 eggs
2/3 cup orange juice
1/3 cup milk
1/4 cup sugar
1/4 tsp nutmeg
1/2 tsp vanilla
1 loaf French bread, cut on a
    diagonal in 1-inch slices
1/2 cup butter, melted
1/2 cup pecan pieces
    powdered sugar, to garnish

Sauce
1 cup sugar
2 Tbsp cornstarch
1/4 tsp nutmeg
1/2 cup orange juice
1/2 cup peach juice reserved
    from the can of peaches
1 (15-oz.) can sliced peaches,
    drained and finely
    chopped
1 Tbsp butter, melted
1 tsp orange extract
1 orange, thinly sliced

In a large shallow bowl, beat together the eggs, orange juice, milk, sugar, nutmeg, and vanilla. Dip pieces of bread in this mixture and place slices in a 9x13-inch casserole dish. Pieces can be placed on top of others to form a double layer. Pour remaining mixture over bread slices. Cover with plastic wrap and refrigerate overnight.

In the morning, preheat oven to 375°F. Pour the melted butter into a large jelly-roll pan. Sprinkle the pecan pieces over the butter. Arrange the soaked bread slices on the jellyroll pan in a single layer. Bake for 20–25 minutes or until golden brown.

Turn slices over and keep warm in the oven until ready to serve. Place 2 slices on serving plate and sprinkle with powdered sugar, serve with Peach-Orange Sauce.

Peach-Orange Sauce: Combine sugar, cornstarch, and nutmeg in a medium saucepan. Add orange and peach juice. Stir well to eliminate lumps. Turn on heat to medium-high and add chopped peaches. Stir mixture and bring to a boil. Turn down heat to medium, stirring con-stantly, until mixture thickens. Remove from heat and add the butter and extract.

Spoon sauce over plated French toast. Add a twisted orange slice on top for decoration.

Sweet Mornings

Banana Nut French Toast

Yield: 4 servings

"Guests of Chesny's Keswick Manor love this classic French toast with its delicious buttery banana topping."

 4 Tbsp butter
 3 Tbsp brown sugar, packed
 ⅓ cup pecans or walnuts, chopped
 4 bananas, sliced diagonally
 4 large eggs, lightly beaten
 ½ cup half & half
 ½ tsp cinnamon
 ¼ tsp nutmeg
 ½ tsp vanilla extract
 1 pinch salt
 6 1-inch-thick diagonal slices French bread (may be a day old)
   butter for grilling
   powdered sugar, to garnish
   maple syrup (optional)

Melt butter over low heat in a sauté pan large enough to hold bananas. When melted, add brown sugar and nuts. Mix well. Heat until sugar has melted and is well blended. Add bananas. Continue cooking on low heat, stirring gently and only occasionally so as not to break up the bananas. In a small mixing bowl whisk eggs, half & half, and spices until smooth. Pour half the egg mixture into a pie plate or other shallow dish.

One at a time, add the slices of French bread and quickly coat both sides with the egg mixture. When completely coated, remove to a piece of wax paper or aluminum foil. Repeat, coating all the bread and placing on foil. Let the bread stand two minutes then recoat all the slices until the batter is gone, allowing bread to absorb between coatings.

Grill the battered bread on both sides over medium heat in a buttered frying pan or griddle until golden brown.

Plate three half pieces of French toast per person, topping each plate with ¼ of the banana nut sauce. Dust with powdered sugar. Serve with warm maple syrup.

Tips and variations: Maple sausage is a wonderful accompaniment.

Raspberry Almond Stuffed French Toast

Yield: 6 servings, 2 slices each

1	(8 oz.) pkg. cream cheese, softened
¼	cup powdered sugar
¼	tsp almond extract
12	slices day-old brioche, challah, or other egg bread (about one-pound loaf), ¾-inch thick slices
1	cup fresh raspberries
3	eggs, beaten
¾	cup half & half, light cream, or milk
3	Tbsp sugar
½	tsp vanilla
	dash salt
	fresh fruit slices of your choice, to garnish
	pure maple syrup or maple-flavored syrup

Preheat oven to 425°F. Grease a 15x10x1-inch baking pan.

In a large bowl, beat together the cream cheese, powdered sugar and almond extract. Spread the cream cheese mixture evenly over one side of each slice of bread.

Top half of the slices with raspberries. Top with remaining bread slices, cream cheese side down to create "sandwiches." Combine beaten eggs, half & half, sugar, vanilla and salt in a shallow bowl. Dip each sandwich in egg mixture, turning carefully to coat both sides.

Place sandwiches in the baking pan. Bake 15 minutes or until golden brown, flipping once after approximately 8 minutes.

Garnish with fresh fruit and sprinkle with powdered sugar. Serve with warm maple syrup, if desired.

Sweet Mornings

Pat Fliestra's Oven French Toast

Yield: 4–6 servings

8–10	slices your bread of choice
8	eggs
2	cups milk
2	cups half & half
2	tsp vanilla
½	tsp nutmeg
½	tsp cinnamon

Topping

¾	cup softened butter
1½	cups brown sugar
3	Tbsp real maple syrup
1½	cups nuts, chopped

Heavily butter a 9x13x2-inch baking dish.

Fill pan with bread slices to within ½ inch from the top. In a blender mix eggs, milk, half & half, vanilla, nutmeg, and cinnamon. Pour over bread. Cover and refrigerate overnight.

In the morning, preheat oven to 350°F.

In a small bowl, mix together topping ingredients and spread over bread mixture. Bake for about one hour, or until bread is puffed and toasted. Shield bread with foil if it is browning too quickly.

Sweet Mornings

Hawaiian French Toast with Coconut Milk

Yield: 4 servings

"This is a treat we serve in the winter. I use Hawaiian sweet bread. One of our guests told me she used banana bread and her family loved it. So, experiment a little and you might create your own family favorite."

- ⅔ cup canned coconut milk
- 2 eggs, lightly beaten
- 2 Tbsp superfine sugar
- ½ vanilla bean (I use 1 tsp vanilla essence)
- ¼ Tbsp ground cardamom
- 4 Tbsp unsalted butter, divided
- 8 slices Hawaiian sweet bread

Toppings
> confectioners' sugar, to dust
> blueberries
> whipped cream
> lemon rind
> cinnamon powder

In a bowl, mix well the coconut milk, eggs, sugar, vanilla, and cardamom. Pour the mixture into a shallow dish. Heat half the butter in a large skillet.

Dip 2 slices of bread into the egg mixture and sauté until golden on both sides, about 2 minutes for each side. Repeat with the remaining slices, adding remaining butter as necessary.

Serve dusted with the confectioners' sugar and topped with blueberries and whipped cream. I add a little bit of lemon rind and cinnamon powder for more flavor.

Banana Nut Crunch French Toast

Yield: 1–2 servings

"We inherited this dish from the previous owners of the Kalamazoo House, and over the years we've made a few alterations that we think make it better than ever. This is not a recipe that requires careful measures, so don't sweat it—if you dump these things together in approximately the amounts we give you here, it will work. And feel free to embellish!"

- 2 large eggs
- ½ cup milk
- 1 Tbsp sugar (more or less to taste)
  several good shakes of real vanilla
- ½ tsp Saigon cinnamon (or maybe more?)
- 3 1" slices whole-grain French bread, sliced diagonally
  Pam (or butter)
  Ground or sliced almonds
- 1 medium banana
  maple syrup
  powdered sugar

With a fork, mix eggs, milk, sugar, vanilla, and cinnamon in a pie plate or shallow bowl until fairly well mixed. Lay the slices of bread in the wet mixture to soak for 3–5 minutes. Turn over and continue soaking.

Heat a skillet over medium heat and spray with cooking spray (or use butter if you prefer). Sprinkle the bread slices generously with the almonds, and pat them into the bread a bit. Put the bread slices in the pan, nut side down, and then sprinkle the other side with almonds. Cook for several minutes until golden brown, and then flip and continue cooking. Meanwhile, slice the banana into a small pan of maple syrup and heat over low heat until well warmed.

Place the toast slices on a warm plate in a pinwheel fashion and scoop the bananas into a loose pile in the middle. Spoon the syrup over the bread slices.

Garnish with more nuts, and sprinkle with powdered sugar.

Enjoy!

Tips and variations: Serve bacon on the side as desired.

Apple-Cinnamon French Toast

Yield: 6–8 servings

*"A guest sent me this recipe. I like making this the day before
and having it ready to stick in the oven in the morning.
The aroma from the baking apples is heavenly!"*

3   large baking apples
6   Tbsp butter
1   cup firmly packed dark brown sugar
2   Tbsp dark corn syrup
1   tsp cinnamon
1   loaf baguette bread sliced 1-inch thick
3   large eggs
1   cup milk
1   tsp vanilla extract

The day before: Grease a 9x13-inch baking pan.

Peel, core, and slice apples. In a large, heavy skillet, melt butter over medium heat. Add apples and cook, stirring occasionally, until tender. Add brown sugar, corn syrup, and cinnamon. Cook, stirring until the sugar dissolves. Pour the mixture into the baking pan and spread to an even layer, arranging apple slices in concentric circles. Arrange bread slices in a layer on top. In a medium bowl beat eggs, milk, and vanilla with a fork until combined and pour over bread. Cover and chill overnight.

Before serving: preheat oven to 375°F. Remove the cover from the baking pan and bake for 30–35 minutes until the mixture is firm and the bread is golden. Let it cool for 5 minutes. Invert a serving tray over the baking pan and carefully flip both so that the apple layer is on top. Spoon any apple slices or syrup that remain in the pan over the top.

Tips and variations: I always use granny smith apples. Most will not want any maple syrup.

French Toast Casserole

Yield: 4–6 servings

*"The elegantly spiraled croissants combined with
maple cream make this a sinfully rich casserole."*

Syrup

1	cup sugar
½	cup butter
½	cup pure maple syrup
¼	cup milk or cream

6	large (6-inch) day-old croissants
3	large eggs
1	cup milk
½	tsp salt
1	tsp vanilla

Grease a 2½-quart Bundt pan.

For maple cream syrup, bring all ingredients to a simmer in a sauce-pan. Continue simmering until sugar is dissolved and syrup is slightly thickened. Pour half of the maple cream syrup into bottom of the pan.

Tear croissants in half width-wise so that each piece has a curved, horn-shaped end.

Overlap croissants around the side of pan like a fan, with the pointed ends facing down in the center of the pan. Pour remaining syrup over croissants.

In a bowl, whisk together the eggs, milk, salt, and vanilla and pour over top.

Cover and refrigerate overnight.

Preheat oven to 350°F. Remove pan from refrigerator and let come to room temperature, about 30 minutes. Bake uncovered 45–50 minutes or until browned and liquid is absorbed.

This recipe has been adapted from Donna Kelly.

Sweet Mornings

Peachy Blueberry Stuffed French Toast with Blueberry Sauce

Yield: 9–12 servings

"The Adrounie House serves this great French toast, which can be prepared the night before. Even the sauce can be made ahead of time and reheated. The blueberry sauce can be made with local berries, fresh, or frozen."

14 slices "Texas Toast" bread, crusts removed and cubed
1 (8-oz.) pkg. cream cheese
1 cup blueberries
1 cup canned sliced peaches, chopped
12 eggs
⅓ cup maple syrup
1 cup milk
1 cup orange juice
¼ tsp nutmeg

¼ cup pecan pieces

Topping
1 cup orange juice
1 cup granulated sugar
¼ tsp nutmeg
2 Tbsp cornstarch
2 cups blueberries
1 Tbsp butter, melted
1 Tbsp lemon juice

Spray a 9x13-inch or 10x12-inch glass baking dish with nonstick cooking spray and place half of the bread cubes in the bottom. Evenly place dollops of cream cheese over the bread and scatter blueberries and chopped peaches over all. Place the remaining bread cubes over the fruit and cheese.

In a large mixing bowl, beat together eggs, syrup, milk, orange juice, and nutmeg. Pour the egg mixture over the bread, fruit, and cheese. Sprinkle pecan pieces over all. Cover with plastic wrap and chill overnight in refrigerator.

In the morning, preheat oven to 325 degrees F. Remove plastic wrap and cover with aluminum foil. Bake for 30 minutes, then remove aluminum foil. Bake for an additional 30 minutes. When lightly browned, remove from oven and let set for about 10 minutes before cutting into serving pieces. Place cut French toast on serving plates and dust with powdered sugar.

Topping: In a medium saucepan, combine the orange juice, sugar, nutmeg, and cornstarch. Stir until mixed well. Add the blueberries and cook until the sauce thickens; stirring frequently. Remove from heat, and stir in the butter and lemon juice. Spoon warm sauce over plated pieces of French toast and serve.

Cinnamon Raspberry French Toast

Yield: 6–8 servings

"Challah is the bread of choice for this sweet entrée."

1	loaf stale bread (I use challah)
8	whole eggs
2	cups milk
½	cup heavy whipping cream
¾	cup sugar
2	Tbsp vanilla
½	cup all-purpose flour
½	cup firmly packed brown sugar
1	tsp cinnamon
¼	tsp salt
1	stick cold butter, cubed
2	cups raspberries

Grease a 9x13-inch pan. Tear the bread into chunks and place them in the pan.

In a bowl, mix together eggs, milk, cream, sugar, and vanilla. Pour the mixture evenly over the bread. Cover and refrigerate overnight.

In another bowl, mix together the flour, brown sugar, cinnamon, and salt. Add the butter and mix until the batter comes somewhat together, like little pebbles. Store in a plastic bag in the refrigerator.

The next morning: preheat oven to 350 degrees F.

Sprinkle the crumb mixture and raspberries on top of the bread mixture.

If you like soggier French toast, bake for 45 minutes. For a firmer French toast, bake for 1 hour.

Serve warm with maple syrup and butter, if desired.

Baked Cinnamon French Toast

Yield: 8–10 servings

12	slices cinnamon bread, divided
¼	cup butter, melted
8	eggs
2	cups whole milk
2	cups whipping cream
¾	cup sugar
1	Tbsp vanilla

Preheat oven to 375°F. Grease a 9x13-inch baking dish.

Line the bottom of the baking dish with 6 slices of bread. Brush remaining bread with butter and place butter side up over bread in pan. In large mixing bowl, beat eggs. Add milk, cream, sugar, and vanilla; mix well. Pour over bread. Let stand for 15 minutes.

Place dish in a larger pan. Pour boiling water into larger pan to a depth of 1 inch. Bake, uncovered, for 40 minutes or until a knife inserted near the center comes out clean.

Let stand for 10 minutes before serving.

Top with any fruit sauce.

Tips and variations: This may be refrigerated overnight, covered, before baking.

Sweet Mornings

Rose & Lydia's Georgia Peach French Toast

Yield: 6–8 servings

1	stick butter
½	cup brown sugar
1	cup dark Karo® syrup
1	(32-oz.) can peaches, drained, reserving juice, and diced or in chunks
9	eggs
2	cups whole milk
1	Tbsp vanilla extract
10–12	slices white or French bread
	cinnamon, to taste

Grease a 9x13-inch baking pan.

Melt butter, add brown sugar and Karo® syrup; bring to a slow boil, and remove from heat. Stir until mixture appears uniform and smooth. Pour mixture into baking pan and let sit to cool. Distribute peaches evenly over the top of butter/syrup mixture.

In large mixing bowl, blend eggs, milk, and vanilla extract. One at a time, dip bread slices into the milk mixture and soak for a few seconds. Lay pieces of bread side-by-side starting at the end of the baking dish, with each row overlapping the previous one.

Once you have filled the baking dish, pour the remaining mixture evenly over the top. Sprinkle generously with cinnamon. Cover and place in refrigerator to sit overnight. (You may also freeze the dish at this point.)

To bake and serve: Preheat oven to 350°F. Thaw the bread mixture or let sit until it reaches room temperature. Bake for 40 minutes or until top is lightly toasted. Let stand to cool for 5–10 minutes.

Sprinkle with powdered sugar and serve with 50/50 mixture of the drained peach juice and pancake syrup on the side.

Tips and variations: Plan out how to arrange the bread in the pan before you start dipping it.

Sweet Mornings

Apple Cinnamon Baked French Toast

Yield: 6–8 servings

"This is a favorite breakfast treat for guests at our inn and is often requested by returning guests. The dish goes great with smoked sausage, bacon, or your favorite breakfast meat."

1	large loaf French bread
8	extra large eggs
1	cup white sugar, divided
2½	cups half & half or whole milk
1	Tbsp vanilla extract
6–8	medium cooking apples, peeled, cored, and sliced
1	Tbsp cinnamon
1	tsp nutmeg
½	stick butter

Slice bread into 1½-inch slices. Spray 9x13-inch glass pan with cooking oil and put bread slices in dish, fitting tightly.

In a separate bowl, beat together eggs, ½ cup sugar, milk, and vanilla with stick blender or whisk. Pour ½ of egg mixture over bread slices. Place apple slices on top of bread to cover. Pour balance of egg mixture over apples and bread. In a small bowl, mix remaining ½ cup sugar with cinnamon and nutmeg and sprinkle evenly over top of apples. Dot with butter. Cover and refrigerate overnight.

Next morning: preheat oven to 350°F.

Uncover dish and bake in oven for 45 minutes to 1 hour, or until golden brown. It will rise high and brown nicely. Remove from oven and allow to rest for 10 minutes.

Cut into squares and serve with heated maple syrup.

Sweet Mornings

J. Paule's Fenn Inn

Pecan French Toast

Yield: 8–10 servings

"The aroma of this dish along with the fragrance of our own Spicy Sausage patties really gets everyone up in the morning."

¾	cup packed brown sugar
½	cup butter
2	Tbsp light corn syrup
1	tsp cinnamon
½	cup chopped pecans, toasted
5	eggs
1½	cups milk
1	tsp vanilla
1	loaf French or Italian bread (supermarket style), cut in ¾-inch slices

Grease a 9x13-inch baking dish.

In a saucepan over medium heat, mix and melt brown sugar, butter, syrup, cinnamon, and pecans. Pour the syrup mixture into the bottom of the baking dish.

In a mixing bowl, combine the eggs, milk, and vanilla. Arrange the bread slices in the baking dish and pour the egg mixture over top. Cover and refrigerate overnight.

One hour before baking, remove dish from refrigerator. Preheat oven to 350°F.

Bake uncovered 30 minutes.

Serve immediately.

Chateau Chantal Winery and B&B

Cherry Cheese Strata

Yield: 8–10 servings

"This dish by Chef Christine Campbell incorporates the inn's own Chateau Chantal Cherry Merlot Jam."

1	(4-oz.) pkg. cream cheese, softened
16	slices French bread
½	cup Chateau Chantal Cherry Merlot Jam (our favorite cherry jam)
1	cup frozen cherries
4	eggs, slightly beaten
2	cups half & half
⅔	cup sugar
1½	tsp finely shredded orange peel
1	tsp vanilla
¼	cup turbinado sugar
¼	cup almonds, sliced
	vanilla yogurt, for serving

Preheat oven to 350°F. Spray a 2-quart square baking dish with cooking spray.

Spread cream cheese on slices of bread and fit them into the baking dish in a single layer.

Spread Cherry Merlot Jam over top. Scatter frozen cherries on top. Top each bread slice with another bread slice. Tear remaining bread into bite-size pieces and fill in around the slices.

In a medium bowl, combine eggs, half & half, sugar, orange peel, and vanilla. Pour over bread in baking dish. Sprinkle with turbinado sugar and sliced almonds.

Bake uncovered about 45 minutes or until a knife inserted in the center comes out clean. Let stand 15 minutes before serving.

Serve with vanilla yogurt.

Buttermilk Belgian Waffles

Yield: 4–6 waffles

"Another Ginkgo Tree Inn favorite."

1	tsp canola or corn oil, for waffle iron
1	cup all-purpose flour
2	Tbsp sugar
1¼	tsp baking powder
½	tsp baking soda
½	tsp salt (I only use ¼ teaspoon)
1½	cups buttermilk
4	Tbsp unsalted butter, melted
2	large eggs
1	tsp vanilla extract (I like to use a tablespoon)

Preheat a waffle iron for 5 minutes. Brush with oil.

In a large bowl, whisk together the flour, sugar, baking powder, baking soda, and salt.

In another bowl, whisk together the buttermilk, butter, eggs, and vanilla. Add to the flour mixture and whisk just until blended. There will be some small lumps.

Following the manufacturer's directions, ladle enough batter for 1 waffle into the center of the waffle iron (usually about a half-cup) and spread with a spatula to fill the holes. Close the waffle iron and cook until the steam stops escaping from the sides and the top opens easily, or according to the manufacturer's directions, 4–5 minutes. The timing will depend on the specific waffle iron used.

The waffle should be browned and crisp. Transfer each waffle to a warmed platter and repeat with the remaining oil and batter.

Tips and variations: I also sift all the dry ingredients together except the sugar and salt before whisking.

Yin Yang Overnight Waffles, with Zero Baking Powder

Yield: 6 waffles

These great waffles are crispy on the outside while remaining creamy and moist on the inside, thus—Yin-Yang. The recipe uses no (aluminum) baking powder, and uses a touch of yeast for the rising. It also cuts the butter in half if desired. The slow rise through the night makes the flour more digestible and gives it its lightness.

½	tsp yeast
2	cups of a mix of flours, at least 1 cup should be all purpose flour
1	Tbsp sugar or agave nectar
½	tsp salt
2	cups milk
4–8	Tbsp butter, melted (4 is really okay)
½	tsp vanilla or almond extract
2	eggs IN THE MORNING, separated and whites whipped

Combine all the ingredients, except the eggs, in the evening before bed. Cover and let it sit at room temperature until morning. In the morning, separate the eggs. Add the yolks to the mixture, and whip the egg whites to soft peaks. Fold the egg whites into the batter. Bake in oiled waffle iron about 2 minutes per side.

Tips and variations: Sprinkle with powdered sugar to dress them up; have a berry mix ready or maple syrup to enjoy these melt in your mouth waffles.

Fluffy Pumpkin Pancakes

Yield: 6–8 servings

2	cups flour
1	tsp cinnamon
1	tsp pumpkin pie spice (optional)
4	tsp baking powder
1	tsp salt
2	Tbsp sugar
2	cups milk
1	Tbsp butter, melted
1	cup mashed pumpkin
2	eggs, separated

In a large bowl, sift dry ingredients. In a blender or using an immersion blender, mix milk, butter, pumpkin, and egg yolks. Stir into dry ingredients. Beat egg whites until stiff peaks form. Fold in gently.

Depending on the size of the pancake desired, ladle your mix onto a hot, greased skillet. When bubbly around the edges, flip over. Cook until done.

Tips and variations: For children's pancakes you can add mini chocolate chips to make them special.

Claire's Light Multi-grain Pancake Mix

Yield: 6–8 servings

"In keeping with our philosophy of healthy indulgence, I wanted a pancake recipe that both tasted good, was good for you—and a snap to mix up. So often multi-grain pancakes are heavy, dense, and bland—so I played around with several different recipes until I created a blend I like. Our guests tell us these pancakes taste too good to be good for you! I make the mix up ahead of time and always have it ready to go."

2	cups all-purpose flour
2	cups whole-wheat flour
1	cup quick oats
½	cup cornmeal
½	cup brown sugar
2	tsp salt
2	tsp baking soda
1½	cups buttermilk
1	egg, lightly beaten
1	Tbsp oil

Blend the dry ingredients together and store in an airtight container. This is your pancake mix. This makes approximately 6 cups. You will have enough pancake mix left over to make 3 more batches.

When you are ready to cook the pancakes, mix buttermilk, egg, and oil together in a bowl. Put 1½ cups of the pancake mix in a medium bowl and add the wet ingredients. Whisk together just until blended. Allow mixture to sit about 10 minutes for fluffier pancakes.

Pour mix ¼ cup at a time onto hot, greased griddle. When bubbles form and begin to burst, it's time to flip your pancakes. Remove from the griddle when golden brown on both sides. Serve with real Michigan maple syrup.

Tips and variations: May also serve with honey or sautéed apples, peaches, pears or a fresh berry compote. Yogurt can be substituted for part or all of the buttermilk. For vegan pancakes, substitute the egg with mashed banana and use soy or almond milk instead of buttermilk. Chopped, toasted pecans are also nice added to the mix or sprinkled on top of the pancakes.

Sweet Mornings

Puffed Apple Pancakes

Yield: 4–6 servings

"Just add a side of sausage to this dish for a perfect Sunday brunch."

2	Granny Smith or McIntosh apples, peeled and sliced thin
1½	Tbsp lemon juice
4	Tbsp brown sugar
5	Tbsp granulated sugar, divided
1	tsp ground cinnamon
⅛	tsp ground cloves
3	Tbsp salted butter, divided
¾	cup whole milk
3	large eggs
⅔	cup all-purpose flour
¼	tsp salt
1	tsp vanilla

Preheat oven to 425°F.

In a bowl, mix apples with lemon juice, brown sugar, 3 tablespoons granulated sugar, cinnamon, and ground clove.

Heat 1½ tablespoons butter in a 10-inch ovenproof pan over medium heat. Add apples and sauté, stirring occasionally until tender. When cooked, put apples in a large bowl and let cool.

Heat cleaned pan in the oven for 5 minutes.

Combine milk, eggs, flour, remaining granulated sugar, salt, and vanilla in a blender and blend until smooth.

Remove pan from oven and add the remaining butter to the pan. When butter has melted; pour batter into pan. Spoon apple mixture evenly over the top of batter mixture.

Bake pancake until puffed and golden, about 15–20 minutes. Pancake is done when wooden skewer inserted into center comes out clean.

German Apple Pancakes

Yield: 6 servings

3	Tbsp butter
3	Tbsp sugar
1	tsp cinnamon
1/8	tsp nutmeg
3	apples, peeled and sliced
3	eggs
1/2	cup flour
1/2	cup milk
1	tsp baking powder
1/4	tsp salt

Preheat oven to 400°F.

In an ovenproof skillet, melt together butter, sugar, and spices. When well combined, add sliced apples. Sauté over medium heat until apples are just tender. In a bowl, beat eggs, flour, milk, baking powder, and salt together until well blended. Pour batter over apple mixture.

Bake for 15–18 minutes or until puffy and golden on top.

Remove and let stand about 5 minutes before cutting. Serve warm with crème fraîche or sour cream.

Sweet Mornings

Pumpkin Pancakes with Apple Cider Syrup

Yield: 8–12 servings

1½ cups buttermilk
1 cup pumpkin purée
1 egg
2 Tbsp vegetable oil
2 cups all-purpose flour
3 Tbsp brown sugar
2 tsp baking powder
2 tsp baking soda
1 tsp ground allspice
1 tsp cinnamon
½ tsp ground ginger
½ teaspoon salt

Apple cider syrup
½ cup white sugar
1 Tbsp cornstarch
1 tsp ground cinnamon
1 cup apple cider
1 Tbsp lemon juice
2 Tbsp butter

In a large bowl, mix together the buttermilk, pumpkin, egg, and oil.

Combine the flour, brown sugar, baking powder, baking soda, allspice, cinnamon, ginger, and salt in a separate bowl. Stir this into the pumpkin mixture just enough to combine.

Heat a lightly oiled griddle or frying pan over medium-high heat. Pour or scoop the batter onto the griddle using approximately ¼ cup for each pancake. Brown on both sides and serve hot.

To make the syrup, stir together sugar, cornstarch, and cinnamon in a saucepan. Stir in the apple cider and lemon juice. Cook over medium heat until mixture begins to boil. Boil until the syrup thickens. Remove from heat and stir in the butter until melted. Serve warm.

Apple Puff Pancakes

Yield: 6–8 servings

¼ cup sugar
¼ tsp cinnamon
3 large eggs
¼ cup warm milk or light cream
4 Tbsp melted butter plus more
    to drizzle over as topping
½ cup all-purpose flour (may
    substitute rice flour for
    gluten-free)*

½ tsp vanilla extract
3 cups Granny Smith apples,
    peeled (or not), cored,
    sliced
confectioners' sugar or syrup,
    for topping

Preheat oven to 450°F. Butter the bottom and sides of an ovenproof 12-inch skillet, a 9x13-inch pan, or individual ramekins. If using an ovenproof skillet, place the buttered skillet or pan in the oven to preheat for 5 minutes while you prepare the batter.

Mix sugar and cinnamon together in a small bowl; set aside. In a large bowl, whisk together the eggs, milk, and melted butter. Gradually add the flour to create a smooth batter (does not need to be "lump" free). Stir in the vanilla extract; set aside.

Remove the pan from the oven. Layer the apples into it. Pour the batter over the apples and return the pan to the oven immediately. Bake for 25 minutes (18 minutes if using convection). Remove from the oven. Drizzle melted butter over the top. Sprinkle with the cinnamon sugar mixture.

Return to oven for 5 minutes until the pancake is puffy and golden brown with sugar cinnamon melted. Remove from the oven, sprinkle with confectioners' sugar (or drizzle with syrup). Cut in wedges. Serve warm.

If using individual ramekins: Sauté the apples in stick-free skillet with 4 tablespoons butter until lightly browned. Distribute apples among ramekins. Whisk together the eggs, milk, vanilla, and flour. Pour batter over apples. Place in oven for 20 minutes (15 minutes if using convection.) Remove from oven; drizzle each with melted butter. Sprinkle with cinnamon and sugar mixture. Place back in oven for 5 minutes, or until cinnamon sugar is crusted. During this time, prepare plates by placing a dollop of warmed caramel sauce on each plate. Remove ramekins the from oven. Remove "pancakes" from ramekins. Place on caramel sauce on plates and sprinkle with confectioners' sugar.

* If using rice flour, reduce cooking time by 3 minutes.

Sweet Mornings

Hungarian Crêpes Suzette (Palacsinta)

Yield: 4–6 servings

"We always came running when we knew Grandma was making crêpes. They were just perfect and so delicious. We ate them warm and filled with fruit."

5 whole eggs
½ cup sugar
1 tsp vanilla
1 tsp salt
3 cups milk, divided
2 cups flour

In a bowl, beat eggs, sugar, and vanilla until frothy. Add salt and 1½ cups milk. Beat flour in slowly until very smooth. Add remaining milk to make a very thin batter.

Butter a 10-inch nonstick frying pan. Pour about ¼ cup of batter into pan and swish around until the entire bottom of the pan is covered. When lightly browned, using a spatula, flip the crêpe over. Let it warm briefly on this side. Remove and keep warm.

Butter the pan well after each crêpe.

Tips and variations: Crêpes can be served hot or cold. See the cottage cheese and apple fillings Torch Lake B&B uses on the following page. Crêpes can be filled with any fresh fruit, cooked fruits, even pie filling. Crepes are easy to freeze for future use.

Torch Lake B&B

Cottage Cheese Filling for Hungarian Crêpes

Yield: 8–10 crêpe fillings

"This is one of the fillings we often use with the Hungarian Crêpes Suzette recipe that Grandma used to make."

½   cup sugar
2   whole eggs
¼   tsp salt
3   Tbsp sour cream
1   lb. dry or pressed-dry cottage cheese
     prepared Hungarian Crêpes Suzette (See recipe on
        page 215)

Preheat oven to 350°F. Butter a glass baking dish.

In a medium bowl, beat the sugar, eggs, salt, and sour cream together. Mix in the cottage cheese. Fill each crepe; roll up and place in baking dish. Spread top with sour cream and bake for 35 minutes.

Torch Lake B&B

Apple Filling for Hungarian Crêpes Suzette

Yield: 8–10 crêpe fillings

"This recipe came from a book my grandmother gave me called An Outstanding Collection of Treasured Hungarian Recipes and Family Favorites. *This filling is wonderful with our Hungarian Crêpes Suzette."*

¾   stick butter
8   large apples, cored and sliced thin
¾   cup sugar
     prepared Hungarian Crêpes Suzette (See recipe on
        page 215)

Melt butter in a large saucepan. Add sliced apples and top with sugar.

Cover and slowly steam for ½ hour, turning occasionally until apples are soft. Keep warm until ready to use.

Chelsea House Victorian Inn

Crêpes

Yield: 20+ servings

"Our crêpes are a delicious way to include Michigan's French Canadian heritage at our Victorian-era breakfast table. These are a light and refreshing beginning to the day, filled with fresh fruit and healthy non-fat yogurt. Some people make crêpes in the base of a non-stick frying pan using a special crêpe spatula. This can make for thicker crêpes and a longer process of finishing the batter. We have found that upside-down non-stick electric crêpe makers are the easiest and quickest approach, providing a more consistent and thinner, lighter crêpe."

¼ tsp salt

3 eggs (one additional egg yolk is optional)

⅔ cup milk

⅔ cup water

1 cup flour

1 Tbsp sugar (not to be used if crêpes will be used as a savory entrée)

1 Tbsp canola oil

1 tsp vanilla (not to be used if crêpes will be for a savory entrée)

Place salt in the bottom of glass mixing bowl. Add 3 eggs (and one optional egg yolk if you prefer). Using electric beaters, beat eggs with salt only long enough to break up the eggs.

In a small bowl combine milk and water. Set aside.

Sift ⅛–¼ cup of flour into eggs and mix again just until blended. Pour ⅛–¼ cup of milk/water mixture into egg/flour mixture, then blend again. Continue alternately adding flour, mixing, then liquid and mixing until all flour and liquid mixture is gone. Use spatula to scrape the sides as flour can build up on bowl through the mixing process.

Once all flour and liquid are gone, add sugar and blend. Add oil and blend. Add optional vanilla and blend.

Cover and place batter in the refrigerator for at least 5–10 minutes. After the batter has rested in the refrigerator, there will be a foam that has risen to the top. Skim this from the top using your spatula.

If using an upside-down crêpe pan, pour the batter into a dinner plate until it is 2/3 full. Refill plate with remaining batter as your crêpes are made.

Use crêpe pans, turn them upside down and dip them into the batter until the pans are lightly coated. Leave crêpe batter on pans until they appear to separate from the pan—which is an indication they are done cooking, or until they start to slightly brown on the edge. Once a crêpe is cooked it will fall off from the crêpe pan, and cooked crêpes can be stacked onto another dinner plate until the batter is completely utilized.

Tips and variations: If you have a large gravy separator it will be helpful in separating the foam from the batter. Removing the foam from the top just helps to reduce the number of bubbles that will appear in the first couple of crêpes. Your first 1–2 crêpes will have a lot of bubbles in them but this will stop usually by the third crêpe.

You will also want a spatula on hand to scrape the batter out of the mixing bowl to reduce waste. It can also be used to fill some of the holes that will occur from time to time in the crêpes in the cooking process.

Crêpes should be carefully and completely sealed for storage in plastic wrap. Dampen a paper towel and place it between the top crêpe and the plastic wrap to help retain moisture in the crêpes while they are stored.

Crêpes can last up to 3 days sealed and stored in the refrigerator, but they are best within 24–48 hours of preparation.

You can also place wax paper between every 4–6 crêpes for easier separation and with Ziploc freezer bags and a protective plate-sized plastic container, the crêpes are easily stored in the freezer for a longer period of time.

Suggested combinations range from simple to tropical:

- Mandarin orange wedges with vanilla or peach yogurt (Greek yogurt upon request)
- fresh peaches (careful to select ripe ones), dusted with cinnamon and vanilla yogurt
- strawberries, blackberries, and blueberries with vanilla or berry yogurt
- banana and pineapple with key lime yogurt

Crêpes can be used as an appetizer, entrée or dessert:

- As an entrée, savory ingredients like smoked salmon with sautéed onion, chives, and a tablespoon of cream cheese in scrambled eggs are delicious.
- As a dessert, crêpes with chocolate mousse, raspberries or strawberries and shavings of white, milk and/or dark chocolate are awesome with raspberry wine, cappuccino, or a favorite cordial.

John's Famous "Dust Bunnies"

Yield: 8–10 servings

"I'm always looking for new and unique breakfast ideas and our regular guests look forward to each new treat. One afternoon a guest asked my hearing-impaired husband what new treat was in store in the morning. He replied. 'Dust Bunnies.' He had overheard me tell someone I was making Dutch Bunnies, and of course, he misheard. So here is the recipe for John's now-famous 'Dust Bunnies.'"

1	stick butter
3	eggs
¾	cup milk
¾	cup flour
1½	tsp salt
1	tsp vanilla
2	tsp lemon juice

Preheat oven to 425°F. Spray cooking oil in the bottom of a 9x13-inch baking pan or in two large cast-iron skillets. Melt 1 stick of butter in baking pan (or ½ stick in each cast-iron skillet).

In a large bowl, mix all remaining ingredients together. Pour into baking pan or skillets and bake for 20 minutes.

Dust with powdered sugar and serve with maple syrup.

Kathleen's the Morning Dove's Baked Oatmeal

Yield: 6–8 servings

"Kathleen is a Morning Dove who is descended from the mysterious Spirit of the Cloud tribe that inhabits a remote part of the Southwest. There are six daughters who travel the continent and look for signs and marks that they experience that mankind no longer appreciates or has taken for granted. They place omens creating hallowed ground for future generations who will gain insight on what really matters the most— a clean food chain, fresh air to breathe and good water to drink. Kathleen, one of the daughters, stopped by the bed and breakfast on her journey north. Quietly sipping some fresh sassafras tea, she wove tales that have been in her lineage for generations. She shared with us a delicious recipe her mother had created. It's so mysteriously pleasant."

½	cup canola oil
½	cup raw sugar
2	eggs, slightly beaten
3	cups oatmeal
1½	tsp baking powder
1	tsp salt
1	cup milk
1	Tbsp butter
1	banana, medium, sliced
½	cup raisins
1	apple, medium, sliced
1	peach, medium, sliced
	granola or sliced almonds, optional

Preheat oven to 350°F.

In a medium bowl, combine oil, raw sugar, and eggs. In a large bowl, combine oatmeal, baking powder, salt, and milk. Combine wet and dry ingredients. Melt butter in a 9x9-inch or similar pan (to save energy and a pot, melt the butter in the baking pan in the preheated oven.) Add a layer of sliced bananas, raisins, sliced apples, and sliced peaches to the pan. Pour oatmeal mixture over fruit layers.

Optional: sprinkle granola or sliced almonds on top of the oatmeal mixture.

Bake for 35–40 minutes or until lightly brown on edges.

Sweet Mornings

Baked Oatmeal with Fruit and Nuts

Yield: 6–8 servings

"This vegan recipe served at Arcadia House can be substantially prepared the night before, keeping the wet and dry ingredients separate until time to bake."

2	cups organic multi-grain oats
1/3	cup organic natural brown sugar
1/2	cup dried fruit (I use a combo of raisins, cranberries and dates)
	handful of chopped organic walnuts
	few shakes of cinnamon
	shake of nutmeg
1	tsp aluminum-free baking powder
2	tsp ground flaxseed
2	Tbsp warm water
1¾	cup almond milk
1	tsp pure natural vanilla
1/2	cup mashed banana or unsweetened applesauce
	wheat germ

Preheat oven to 375°F. Grease a large casserole-type dish.

In a large bowl, combine oats, brown sugar, fruit, walnuts, spices, and baking powder. In a small bowl, mix together flaxseed and water. Set aside to thicken slightly.

Combine almond milk, vanilla, mashed banana or applesauce and flax-seed mixture in a bowl. Add this mixture to the dry ingredients. Stir until combined. Pour into the dish and sprinkle with wheat germ. Bake for 30 minutes.

This recipe has been adapted from www.vegfamily.com.

Homemade Granola

Yield: 9 cups

*"Guests of our inn love this with yogurt or to put on top of cold cereal.
It is also great with baked oatmeal."*

5	cups old-fashioned rolled oats (not quick oats)
1	cup shredded sweetened coconut
1	cup wheat germ
1	cup chopped raw almonds
½	cup sesame seeds
½	cup raw sunflower seeds
¼	tsp salt
½	cup honey
½	cup corn oil
2	tsp vanilla
1	cup raisins

Preheat oven to 300°F. Grease a 10x15-inch pan.

In a large bowl combine the oats, coconut, wheat germ, almonds, sesame seeds, sunflower seeds, and salt. Set aside.

In small saucepan over medium heat, warm honey with oil and vanilla. Add to dry ingredients and mix thoroughly.

Spread mixture evenly into pan. Bake for 40 minutes, or until cereal is lightly browned.

Add raisins when done cooking.

Sweet Mornings

Candlewyck House B&B

Fruit Smoothie

Yield: 1 smoothie

"Each day we serve a large bowl of fresh fruit with our breakfast. Whenever we have fruit left over, I freeze it in plastic sandwich bags and use it to make smoothies"

- ½   cup orange juice
- ½   cup vanilla yogurt
- 1   Tbsp honey
- 2   sandwich bags fruit (thaw in microwave for a few seconds)

Place all ingredients in a blender. Blend until smooth and serve immediately.

Tips and variations: Banana or strawberries make a nice addition. Do not add ice cubes.

Candlewyck House B&B

Blueberry Syrup

Yield: 8 ounces of syrup

"I developed a recipe for use with my friend Karen Way's baked pancakes. Karen is the innkeeper of our neighboring Pentwater Abbey B&B."

- 1   cup plus ¼ cup orange juice, divided
- 2   cups blueberries (fresh, Michigan-grown preferred)
- 1   cup sugar
- ½   cup light Karo® syrup
      dash cinnamon
- ¼   cup lemon juice
- 2   Tbsp cornstarch

In a saucepan, combine all ingredients except ¼ cup orange juice and the cornstarch. Bring to a boil and simmer 15 minutes. Just before serving, add cornstarch to the ¼ cup orange juice in a small bowl. Mix well. Add to hot syrup mixture. Cook until thickened.

Tips and variations: Of course, this syrup is equally good on everything from pancakes and waffles to ice cream.

Cream Cheese Filling

Yield: 1½ cups

"This is a wonderful cream cheese filling for homemade pastries, or for stuffed French toast. It mixes beautifully with strawberries, blueberries, or any fruit of your choosing for the French toast options."

1	(8-oz.) pkg. cream cheese at room temperature
1/3	cup granulated sugar
½	tsp salt
1	egg
3	Tbsp butter
½	tsp vanilla
1	tsp lemon zest
2	Tbsp flour
¼	cup milk (you may not need all of it)

In a bowl, cream the cheese, sugar, and salt until smooth. Add egg, butter, vanilla, lemon zest and blend well. Add the flour. Mix until just incorporated. Add the milk, a bit at a time while mixing, until mixture is a smooth spreadable consistency.

Tips and variations: You can substitute ¼ teaspoon lemon extract if you do not have fresh lemons.

This recipe has been adapted from Michael Whitman, chef at Grand Rapids Community College.

Frittatas, Omelets, Soufflés & Casseroles

"Savory" is a word from the foodie world often used to categorize dishes that are primarily not sweet and instead are redolent of ingredients like onion or garlic and herbs such as basil, oregano or tarragon. Many Michigan B&B innkeepers are known for the breakfast miracles they create with eggs or potatoes and the addition of a few other ingredients. Here are some dishes to try at home.

Recipes in the Featured Recipes chapter

In this chapter

Savory Breakfasts

Southwestern Breakfast Casserole

Yield: 8–10 servings

"Sue, the Original Siren of Sherwood, created this dish a few years back after we took a trip out to the great southwest and hiked the Grand Canyon."

1	(8.5-oz.) pkg. corn muffin mix
3	cups cubed (1/2-inch) Italian bread
8	oz. Italian sausage
1	cup onion, chopped
2	cups milk
1	tsp ground cumin
1/8	tsp black pepper
1	(10-oz.) can diced tomatoes and green chilies. Do not drain.
4	eggs
2	cups Colby Jack cheese, shredded, divided

Prepare corn muffin mix according to package directions; cool. Crumble muffins into a large bowl and stir in bread. Set aside.

Remove casings from sausage and cook in a large skillet with onion over medium heat until browned, stirring to crumble. Drain.

Combine milk, cumin, pepper, tomatoes, and eggs in a bowl: stir until blended. Add sausage mixture; stir well. Stir into bread mixture. Coat a 9x13-inch baking dish. Spoon half of bread mixture into the baking pan coated with cooking spray. Top with 1 cup cheese. Spoon remaining bread mixture over cheese; top with remaining cheese. Cover and refrigerate 8 hours or overnight.

In the morning: remove baking dish from the refrigerator and preheat oven to 350°F. Bake for 40 minutes or until set. Let stand 10 minutes before serving.

Savory Breakfasts

Dutch Colonial Inn

Southwest Sausage Bake

Yield: 12–15 servings

"A delicious egg dish with a Southwest flair."

6   (10-inch) flour tortillas cut into 1-inch strips
4   (4-oz.) cans chopped green chilies, drained
1   lb. sausage, cooked and drained
2–3 cups Monterey Jack cheese, shredded
10 eggs
½   cup milk
½   tsp of each: salt, ground cumin, garlic salt, pepper, onion salt
    paprika
2   Roma tomatoes, sliced
    sour cream and salsa, for serving

In a greased 9x13-inch baking dish, layer half of the tortilla strips, chilies, sausage, and cheese. Repeat layers. In a bowl, beat eggs, milk, and seasonings. Pour over cheese. Sprinkle with paprika. Cover and refrigerate overnight.

Remove from the refrigerator 30 minutes before baking. Preheat oven to 350°F. Bake uncovered for 50 minutes. Arrange sliced tomatoes over top and bake for an additional 10–15 minutes (until knife comes out clean). Let stand for 10 minutes before cutting. Serve with salsa and sour cream.

Tips and variations: For a nice change, serve with pineapple salsa.

Savory Breakfasts

Garden Fresh Italian Frittata

Yield: 6 servings

"I like to gather vegetables and herbs from my own garden early in the morning for this frittata recipe and use eggs I gathered from the chickens the night before."

2	Tbsp olive oil
3–4	green onions, finely chopped
	handful of green beans, trimmed and cut into 1 inch pieces
1	small zucchini, cut into half or quarter round slices
½	red bell pepper, chopped
	grape or Roma tomatoes, chopped and drained
1	Tbsp minced fresh basil (or 1 tsp dried)
1	Tbsp minced fresh parsley (or 1 tsp dried)
1	tsp minced fresh oregano or a pinch or two dried
	a sprig or two of thyme, leaves stripped from stem
	salt and pepper
6	eggs, beaten well and seasoned with salt and pepper
½	cup Italian-blend shredded cheese

Heat olive oil in an 8 or 10-inch sauté pan over medium heat. Add green onions and sauté 1 or 2 minutes. Add green beans, sauté another minute or two. Add zucchini and red pepper, sauté 2–3 minutes. Add tomatoes and herbs and sauté 1 more minute. Salt and pepper vegetables to taste.

Pour eggs over vegetable mixture in pan and cook over medium heat. Allow eggs to begin to set. With a spatula, pull eggs away from the edge of the pan slightly and tilt pan, allowing uncooked egg to run under set eggs. Continue this process until eggs are mostly cooked. Sprinkle cheese on top of eggs and place pan in the oven under a low broiler for 2–3 minutes, until eggs puff up and cheese melts.

Cut into 6 wedges and serve.

Tips and variations: Potatoes are a nice addition, but should be at least partially cooked before adding to the pan. Ham or sausage also works well with a frittata, but I usually make vegetarian frittatas and serve meat on the side to accommodate meat lovers.

Savory Breakfasts

Tomato-Leek Soufflé Frittata

Yield: 4 servings

"A frittata usually is made by sautéing vegetables, adding egg and cheese to the pan, and finishing in the broiler. We separate the eggs first and whip the whites into a stiff peak. If mixed in just enough but not too vigorously, the foamy egg whites add a light and fluffy dimension to the frittata."

1	Tbsp plus 1 tsp butter, divided
1–2	leeks, white part only, washed and sliced
1/4	cup water
	salt & pepper to taste
1	cup grape tomatoes, halved
4	egg yolks
4	oz. grated Asiago cheese
1	tsp dried Italian herb mix
6	egg whites
	dash of salt for egg whites

Preheat oven to 350°F.

Melt 1 tablespoon butter in a 10-inch ovenproof nonstick skillet. Add leeks and water. Season with salt and pepper. Cook uncovered over medium-low heat until all the water has boiled away. Do not brown.

Remove from heat and add tomatoes, egg yolks, cheese, and herbs. In a separate bowl, whisk egg whites and salt to form stiff peaks. Gently fold into the leek/tomato/cheese mixture in the skillet making sure that all the vegetables are evenly covered. Melt 1 teaspoon butter in an empty skillet and transfer all ingredients to the new skillet. Cook over medium heat for 5–10 minutes until bottom begins to set.

Transfer to the oven and bake 20–30 minutes until center is set and a golden brown crust has developed. Cut into quarters and enjoy.

Tips and variations: Customize this frittata by combining your choice of sautéed ingredients with any type of cheese.

Frittata

Yield: 4 servings

"A Dewey Lake favorite. This recipe is easy and tastes great."

3 large eggs
1 sausage link, browned and cut into small pieces
⅓ cup half & half or milk
4 oz. shredded hash brown potatoes
⅓ cup shredded cheese (your choice)
1 Tbsp onion, finely chopped
1 Tbsp red and/or green pepper, finely chopped
    dash of salt & pepper

Preheat oven to 350°F. Grease an ovenproof skillet.

In a large bowl, whisk eggs and add the rest of the ingredients. Pour into an ovenproof skillet. Bake uncovered for 25–30 minutes

Tips and variations: Add 1 tablespoon of shredded carrots. You can also increase the amount of ingredients for a larger skillet. You may leave out the sausage if you are serving vegetarians.

Savory Breakfasts

Frittata Roll with Pancetta

Yield: 4 servings of 2 slices each

"We almost called this the Cambridge Roll in honor of a guest to whom we served it. He had driven 13-plus hours from Massachusetts just to spend one night at Adventure Inn with his long-time love who runs a family business in Michigan."

5–6 oz. diced pancetta
8 large eggs
½ cup milk
½ cup half & half
⅓ cup all-purpose flour
a couple shakes of Morton Nature's Seasons seasoning blend

½ red pepper, finely diced
4 green onions, finely chopped, including green part
12 basil leaves or more, depending on size, cut into confetti
shredded cheese for topping

Preheat oven to 350°F. Cover a 15x19x1-inch jellyroll pan with parchment paper, allowing it to extend beyond the pan on all sides. Give it shape by making creases in the paper with your finger along the edges. Coat paper with cooking spray.

Sauté pancetta in a skillet until cooked. Remove and drain on paper towels.

In a bowl, whisk together eggs, milk, half & half, flour and seasoning. Flour will retain tiny lumps. Pour egg mixture onto prepared paper in pan. Sprinkle in pancetta, red pepper, onions, and basil to distribute. Bake 14–16 minutes or until edges appear set.

Sprinkle cheese on top. Bake 2 more minutes.

Starting at one of the short ends of the pan, use the combination of a spatula, the paper and a second pair of hands, if available, to roll the frittata. Remove the paper as you go.

Slice and serve hot.

Tips and variations: Other finely diced vegetables can be substituted. Don't pre-cook them, except for mushrooms, which should be drained and pressed after sautéing to remove moisture.

Cornbread makes an excellent accompaniment.

Tortilla & Egg Casserole

Yield: 8–12 servings

1½	cups cooked ham, cubed (OR)
8	fully cooked sausage patties, crumbled (do not use both)
¾	cup onion, chopped
2	cups (8-oz.) cheddar cheese, shredded, divided
12	(7-inch) flour tortillas
2½	cups milk
8	eggs
¼	cup salt
1	Tbsp flour
	dollop of sour cream, to garnish
¼	cup salsa, to garnish

Combine ham or sausage, onions, and 1 cup cheese in a medium bowl. Spoon a scant ¼ cup down the center of each tortilla. Roll up and line up, seam side down (two along the edge) in a greased, 15x9x2-inch glass-baking dish.

In a large bowl, beat milk, eggs, salt, and flour until smooth. Pour over tortillas. Cover with foil and refrigerate for 8 hours, or overnight. Remove from refrigerator 30 minutes before baking.

Preheat oven to 350°F. Bake covered for 30 minutes, uncovered for 10 minutes. Sprinkle with remaining 1 cup cheese and return, uncovered to oven until cheese melts—about 4 minutes.

Let stand 10 minutes before serving.

Garnish with a dollop of sour cream and salsa.

Savory Breakfasts

Egg-Chilada Casserole

Yield: 12 servings

1	lb. ground sausage (pork or turkey)
¾	cup fresh salsa (mild or medium)
1	capful Mrs. Dash Southwest Chipotle
1	cup tomatoes, diced
1	cup sweet onion, diced
1	cup cheese, shredded
12	eggs
1½	cups heavy cream (may substitute half & half or buttermilk)
8	wheat-flour tortillas

Lightly coat 2 (9-inch) pie pans with olive oil.

Brown meat with salsa and spices, drain and set aside to cool. Combine tomatoes, onion, and cheese in a separate bowl. After meat mixture has cooled, combine with vegetable and cheese mixture. Whisk together eggs and cream in another bowl.

Cut tortillas into triangular pieces. Layer about ⅓ of meat mixture into the bottom of the pie pans, cover with a layer of tortilla triangles, add another layer of meat mixture, another layer of wheat flour tortillas, and a light layer of meat mixture on the top.

Pour ½ of the egg mixture over the top of each pie pan with the layered meat mixture and tortillas. Cover with foil and refrigerate overnight.

The next morning, preheat oven to 350°F. Bake for 30 minutes. Uncover, sprinkle with a layer of shredded cheese and continue baking for about 20 more minutes until a knife inserted in the center comes out clean.

Sausage and Cheese Omelet Bake

Yield: 8–10 servings

12 oz. sausage links
12 slices multigrain or wheat bread, crusts removed and
      lightly toasted
 1 (10-oz.) pkg. frozen broccoli, thawed and drained
 ½ cup onion, chopped
 2 cups cheddar cheese, shredded, divided
 6 large eggs
 ¼ tsp salt and pepper
 3 cups milk

Cook sausage links according to package directions and drain on paper towels.

Cut sausage in small pieces.

Place slices of bread in a 9x13-inch baking pan. Top with alternating layers of the broccoli, onion, sausage and 1 cup cheese.

Beat the eggs, salt, and pepper in a bowl with a whisk until blended and then add the milk; combine well. Pour over the ingredients in the baking pan. Cover and refrigerate overnight.

In the morning, preheat the oven to 350°F. Bake uncovered 45 minutes.

Top with remaining 1 cup of shredded cheese and bake additional 15 minutes or until cheese is melted.

Let stand 10 minutes before cutting.

Savory Breakfasts

Frankenmuth B&B

Oven Breakfast Omelet

Yield: 4–6 servings

*"This is the one casserole I have been making for over
30 years and every bit of it gets eaten every time."*

8	eggs
½	cup milk
¼	cup butter, melted
½–¾	cup sharp cheese, shredded
½–¾	cup ham, chopped
1	Tbsp parsley flakes

Preheat oven to 375°F. Grease a 9-inch glass casserole dish.

In a large bowl, mix all ingredients together. Pour into baking dish. Bake uncovered for 30–40 minutes or until mixture is no longer liquid, and the texture is the same all across the top. It is perfect when it is just starting to brown.

Tips and variations: This is a good and quick recipe to double and bake in a 9x13-inch pan for 30–40 minutes.

Innkeeper's Egg and Bacon Casserole

Yield: 6 servings

12 eggs, scrambled
1   lb. bacon, fried, drained
1   (8-oz.) can mushrooms, drained
1   (8-oz.) pkg. cheddar cheese, shredded

Topping
1   can cream of chicken soup
2/3 cup half & half or 1 (5-oz.) can evaporated milk
    salt and pepper to taste

The evening before serving, layer all ingredients in a greased 9x13-inch pan, except for the topping ingredients. Use the order of the ingredients above when layering.

The next morning: preheat oven to 350°F.

In a bowl, mix cream of chicken soup and half & half (or evaporated milk). Pour over layers in the baking dish. Bake for 50 minutes.

Savory Breakfasts

Egg & Fresh Italian Sausage Bake

Yield: 12 servings

"Using fresh Italian sausage from the local farmers adds a lot of flavor. This is a great bake when you have a large number of guests to feed."

12	large eggs
1/3	cup sour cream
1	lb. Italian sausage
1	cup sliced fresh mushrooms
1	onion, chopped
2	tomatoes, chopped
1	(8-oz.) pkg. shredded cheese
	slices of tomato, to garnish
	Italian parsley, to garnish

Preheat oven to 400°F. Grease a 13x9-inch baking dish.

In a large bowl, beat eggs and sour cream until well blended. Pour into baking dish.

Bake for 10 minutes or until egg mixture is softly set. Cook sausage, mushrooms, and onion in a large skillet over medium heat until sausage is done, stirring occasionally. Drain. Reduce oven temperature to 325°F. Spoon tomatoes over egg layer. Cover with sausage mixture and cheese. Bake 30 minutes or until center is set.

Tips and variations: You can also add sautéed spinach on the top of sausage mixture and cover with cheese. I also like to add sliced tomatoes on the top (before baking). Cut the dish into squares—sliced tomatoes will be in the middle of each square for a nice presentation. Garnish with a small stem of Italian parsley. Serve with salad or freshly cut vegetables.

This recipe has been adapted from a local cooking class.

Savory Breakfasts

Herbed Popovers with Buttered Eggs

Yield: 6 servings

"This is always a great 'go to' recipe—different yet easy."

Popovers
¾ cup flour
½ tsp celery salt
2 large eggs
1 cup milk
1 Tbsp butter, melted
2 Tbsp fresh mixed herbs, such as chervil, parsley, chives or tarragon, chopped

Eggs
¼ cup butter
6 large eggs, beaten
2 Tbsp chopped fresh mixed herbs
2 Tbsp half & half

Popovers: Generously grease a 12-cup muffin tin. Sift flour and celery salt into a large bowl. Add eggs, milk, and butter; beat well. Stir in mixed herbs. Pour batter into muffin tins.

Place in cold oven. Set temperature to 425°F. Bake 30 minutes without opening the oven door.

Eggs: Melt butter in a skillet over low heat. Add eggs, stirring constantly until thickened.

Remove from heat. Stir in herbs and half & half.

Serve each person 2 popovers and a mound of eggs.

Tips and variations: I usually use 2 eggs per person and serve with a breakfast meat and a fruit side such as a pineapple soufflé, soufflé lemon custard or a fruit crisp.

Dried herbs can be substituted. Decrease amount by half.

Savory Breakfasts

Miner's Breakfast

Yield: 4–6 servings

"A husky breakfast fit for the hard life of a miner."

4	Tbsp butter
4	large russet potatoes boiled, peeled and cubed
½	bell pepper, chopped
	minced garlic, to taste
	salt and pepper, to taste
8	large eggs, lightly beaten
8–9	strips of bacon, fried crisp and crumbled
1	cup cheddar cheese, shredded

Preheat oven to 350°F.

Melt butter in a large ovenproof skillet. Add cooked potato cubes and bell peppers.

Cook until potatoes are lightly browned. Add garlic and cook for another 30 seconds or so. Salt and pepper to taste. Pour beaten eggs over potatoes and cook until eggs form soft curds, stirring occasionally. Mix in crumbled bacon. Sprinkle cheese over the top. Place skillet in oven or under broiler until cheese is melted.

Serve hot.

Mining in Michigan has been one of the state's most valuable industries for over 150 years. Although mining towns were rather rough in their early days, they soon developed into stable communities. Social life centered around churches, athletic clubs, opera houses, drama and singing groups, and the saloon.

Savory Egg & Hash Brown Bake

Yield: 8 servings

"This dish is unique in the breakfast casserole world because it does not include bread. It's a hearty, country breakfast with a pretty presentation of color."

1   pkg. frozen hash brown patties or 8 square patties.
¼   cup butter, melted
1   lb. ground sausage
2   cups cooked kernel corn
1   red pepper, diced
1   cup cheddar cheese, shredded
8   eggs
1   cup milk
¼   tsp seasoned salt
    Tri-color tortilla chips & salsa

Preheat oven to 425°F.

Place hash browns in 9x13-inch pan. Pour melted butter over hash browns and bake for 20 minutes. Remove and lower oven temperature to 350°F.

Brown and drain sausage. (Can be done the night before to save time.)

Spread meat, corn, and diced red pepper over potatoes and sprinkle cheese on top. In a bowl, beat eggs, milk, salt together; pour over top. Bake for 30–40 minutes until set and golden brown.

When serving, sprinkle with broken tri-colored tortilla chips as a garnish and serve salsa on the side.

Savory Breakfasts

Baked Egg Casserole

Yield: 4–6 servings

"A guest sent me this recipe about 20 years ago. It most likely came from a Kraft cookbook. The old English cheese is so tasty."

4   slices bread, buttered, no crust, cubed
3   eggs
2   cups milk
1   tsp dry mustard
     salt and pepper
1   jar Kraft Old English Cheese, chilled

Prepare bread and place in a buttered casserole dish. In a mixing bowl, combine eggs, milk, dry mustard, salt, and pepper. Pour over the bread. Break cheese up into small pieces. Lightly mix into above mixture. Refrigerate overnight.

Take out of refrigerator 1 hour before baking. Preheat oven to 325°F. Bake covered for 1 hour.

Eggs in a Basket

Yield: 12 baskets, 6–12 servings

"These are a yummy way to serve individual egg casserole portions. They look great on a plate alongside some fresh melon and berries."

12	slices Black Forest ham, very thin but not shaved
8	eggs
1½	cups half & half or light cream
½	tsp lemon pepper
½	tsp onion powder
½	tsp garlic powder
6–8	oz. sharp cheddar cheese, shredded

Preheat oven to 325°F. Spray nonstick muffin pan(s) very lightly with vegetable oil spray.

Place ham slice in muffin cup, carefully arranging each slice to form a "basket."

Beat eggs, cream and seasonings in a bowl with a stick blender. Pour egg mixture into a large measuring cup with spout. Fill ham baskets about ¾ full with egg mixture.

Sprinkle a heaping tablespoon of shredded cheese on top of each basket.

Bake 30 minutes or until toothpick comes out clean.

Tips and variations: Chopped chives or scallions are also great added to the egg mixture.

These can be served with a side of salsa.

Savory Breakfasts

Sausage & Cream Cheese Bake

Yield: 8–12 servings

"Easy to assemble. Great taste."

12	eggs
½	cup milk
1	lb. breakfast sausage
8	oz. cream cheese
2	(8-oz.) cans crescent rolls
2	cups cheddar cheese, shredded

Preheat oven to 375°F.

In a bowl, beat eggs and add milk. Cook in a skillet until eggs are scrambled; set aside. In a large skillet, brown sausage. When cooked, add cream cheese; stir to combine. Add scrambled eggs and combine.

In an ungreased 9x13-inch baking dish, unroll 1 can of crescent rolls. Press down. Spread sausage mixture on top. Top with shredded cheese. Then top with the remaining can of crescent rolls. Bake 25 minutes.

Herbed Brie Scrambled Eggs

Yield: 6-10 servings

"A quick and easy way to put a little something special into your breakfast. I like to serve this with buttermilk biscuits."

18	eggs
½	cup milk
1	bunch of green onions, finely diced
¼	tsp salt
½	tsp pepper
1	Tbsp butter
6	oz. Aloutte Crème de Brie spreadable herbed cheese

In a mixing bowl whip together eggs, milk, onions, salt, and pepper until well blended.

Melt butter in a large skillet. Add egg mixture and scramble by gently folding eggs over and drawing to the side of the pan until firm.

Remove from heat and fold in cheese until melted.

Serve immediately.

Savory Breakfasts

Amish Breakfast Casserole

Yield: 6–8 servings

"An all-in-one hearty breakfast. Guys especially love it."

1	lb. bacon
1	sweet medium onion
6	eggs
4	cups frozen shredded hash browns, thawed
1½	cups cottage cheese
2	cups cheddar cheese, divided
1½	cups shredded Swiss cheese, divided

Preheat oven to 350°F.

Cook bacon and onions until crispy.

In a large bowl, mix eggs and hash browns. Add cottage cheese, half of the cheddar cheese and half of the Swiss cheese. Mix together well. Add crispy bacon bits and onions. Place mixture in a 9x13-inch baking dish. Sprinkle remaining cheeses on the top. Bake 35–40 minutes.

Remove from oven and let stand for 10 minutes. Cut and serve.

Tips and variations: I sometimes add additional meat, fried sausage, or ham cubes.

Savory Breakfasts

Individual Strata

Yield: 1 serving

"This is a very versatile dish in which you may use any meat or vegetables you wish. This works well for 1-3 or more people who may be eating at different times. This often happens with our corporate guests."

¼	cup any meat, cooked, (bacon, ham or sausage) optional
¼	cup vegetables and mushrooms (optional)
1	slice bread, crust removed or 1/2 English muffin
1	egg
⅓	cup milk
	dash each salt, pepper, ground mustard, onion powder
	Tabasco sauce, to taste
2	Tbsp sharp cheddar cheese, shredded

Preheat oven to 350°F. Grease an 8-ounce custard dish.

In a small skillet, sauté any meat, vegetables, or mushrooms you may be using. Cube bread, place in the custard dish and add meat and/or vegetables.

In a small bowl, mix egg, milk, and seasonings together. Pour mixture over the top of the bread and other ingredients. Sprinkle with cheese. Bake uncovered for 25–30 minutes.

Tips and variations: This dish may be prepared the night before and placed in the refrigerator until the following morning.

Savory Breakfasts

Zesty Sausage & Egg Casserole

Yield: 8 servings

"I found this basic casserole recipe and have been making changes to it over time. It can easily be cut in half for 4 people and using a 9x9 or 8x8 pan. Our return guests often request this zesty version as well as our milder Italian sausage version. It is also a good choice for low carbohydrate eaters as it does not include the bread base that many casseroles or stratas call for."

1½–2	lbs. hot sausage in a roll
2	cups cheddar, Colby, or Colby Jack mix
6–7	eggs
2	cups half & half

Grease a 9x13-inch baking dish with cooking spray.

Brown sausage in nonstick skillet until fully cooked with no pink showing.

Drain excess fat and spread sausage in the baking dish. Sprinkle cheese over the sausage.

In a mixing bowl, lightly beat eggs until well blended; add the half & half; mix well.

Pour egg mixture over casserole. Cover and store in the refrigerator over-night.

The next morning preheat the oven to 350°F. Bake for 45–55 minutes until bubbly and golden. Allow to cool a few minutes. Cut into desired squares and serve.

Tips and variations: Use different flavored sausages, cheeses and spices.

Cheesy Scrambled Eggs

Yield: 5 servings

*"These scrambled eggs go especially well with our
Blueberry German Pancakes." (see page 147)*

10	eggs
2	tsp milk
½	cup peppers (orange, yellow, or red), diced
½	cup sweet onions, diced
1	cup shredded cheese, Mexican flavor

Spray an 11-inch skillet with vegetable oil and set aside. Whisk eggs
and milk together; set aside. Sauté peppers and onion in skillet. Add
egg/milk mixture to skillet. Cook until set. Add shredded cheese and
cook until melted. Serve hot.

Tips and Variations: Fresh fruit is a perfect compliment to this dish.

Savory Breakfasts

Bruschetta Eggs Benedict

Yield: 2 servings

"Who doesn't like eggs Benedict and bruschetta? We have combined these two culinary favorites into one delightful breakfast. Using both fresh tomatoes and basil in this recipe will transcend it to sublime."

2   tomatoes, seeded & diced (approximate amount)
    balsamic vinegar & olive oil (You may substitute a
      Greek dressing.)
    fresh or dried basil, for marinade
4   slices Italian or French bread (2 slices per serving)
    olive oil, to garnish bread
    garlic salt, to garnish bread

Béarnaise Sauce (you may substitute hollandaise sauce)
2   egg yolks
1   Tbsp water
1   Tbsp rice vinegar
2   Tbsp whipping cream
1   Tbsp half & half
½   tsp salt
    dash of hot pepper sauce
4   Tbsp butter
4   poached eggs (2 per serving)

For Bruschetta: Combine tomatoes, dressing and basil to marinate overnight in the refrigerator.

When you are ready to prepare, sprinkle bread lightly with olive oil and garlic salt. Toast until golden brown.

For Béarnaise Sauce: Mix egg yolks, water, vinegar, cream, half & half, salt, and hot pepper sauce in a bowl. Place in a double boiler pan over low heat. Stir with a whisk until mixture begins to thicken. Add butter, bit by bit. This makes about ¾ cup of sauce.

To serve: Place a spoonful of tomato mixture over toasted bread. Add poached eggs and béarnaise sauce to serve.

Crazy Benedicts with Cheese Sauce

Yield: 6–8 servings

"The innkeepers and new owners (as of late 2012) of Wind in the Pines can't wait to serve this recipe bequeathed to them by former innkeepers Cindee and Chuck McLaughlin."

Cheese Sauce
1 Tbsp butter
1 Tbsp flour
½ tsp salt
½ tsp Penzey's Mural of Flavor blend
½ cup milk, 2% low fat
½ cup white wine
⅓ cup cheese

Spinach sauce
3 Tbsp olive oil
½ cup sweet onion, diced
4 tsp garlic, minced
6 cups spinach leaves
½ cup tomato, diced and seeded
2 cups Swiss cheese, shredded, plus more for serving

Egg Mixture
2 Tbsp butter
12 whole eggs
2 Tbsp sour cream
2 tsp prepared mustard

6 whole English muffins

Cheese Sauce: melt butter in a saucepan and whisk in flour, salt, and Penzey's seasoning until smooth. Gradually stir in milk and wine, cooking over direct heat and stirring constantly until sauce boils. Add cheese and continue stirring until cheese melts and sauce becomes smooth and thick. Simmer for an additional 10 minutes over very low heat, stirring occasionally. Set aside but keep warm.

Savory Breakfasts

Spinach Sauce: In a sauté pan over medium-low heat, sweat onion and garlic in oil until softened, about 5 minutes. Add spinach and cook until just starting to wilt. Stir in tomato and cheese. Remove from heat. Season to taste.

Preheat oven to 350°F.

Egg Mixture: Melt butter in a frying pan over medium heat. Whisk together eggs, sour cream and mustard. Add to pan and scramble eggs until fluffy. Eggs should be slightly wet when done so they don't overcook when placed in the oven.

For muffins: Cover a cookie sheet with aluminum foil. Toast muffin halves and lay out on the cookie sheet.

To serve: Place about ¼ cup of the egg mixture on each muffin half.

Place about ¼ cup of the spinach mixture over the eggs. Top with a little shredded Swiss cheese.

Put in the oven and warm through for about 10 minutes.

Remove from oven, put two muffin halves on each plate and cover with cheese sauce.

Italian Breakfast Casserole

Yield: 8–12 servings

1 lb. bulk Italian sweet sausage
½ cup shallots, chopped
2 garlic cloves, minced
½ cup oil-packed, sun dried tomatoes, drained, chopped
4 Tbsp fresh parsley, chopped, divided
5 large eggs
3 large egg yolks
1 cup half & half
1 cup whipping cream
2 cups mozzarella cheese, shredded, divided
½ tsp salt

Preheat oven to 375°F. Butter a 13x9x2-inch glass baking dish.

Sauté sausage in a nonstick skillet over medium heat until brown and cooked through, about 10 minutes. Break sausage into small pieces with the back of a fork. Add shallots and garlic; sauté 3 minutes. Add sun dried tomatoes and 2 tablespoons of parsley; stir 1 minute.

Spread sausage mixture in the prepared baking dish. (Can be made a day ahead to this point. Cover and refrigerate.)

Whisk eggs, egg yolks, half & half, whipping cream, 1½ cups cheese, and salt in large bowl, blending well.

Pour egg mixture over sausage mixture in dish. Sprinkle remaining ½ cup cheese and 2 tablespoons parsley over the top. Bake until the top of the casserole is golden brown and knife inserted into the center comes out clean, about 30 minutes. Let stand 5 minutes before serving.

Savory Breakfasts

J. Paule's Fenn Inn

Layered Breakfast Casserole

Yield: 1 serving

"All ingredient amounts are for 1 individual casserole. Increase incrementally for the number of people you are serving."

⅓ cup Southwest-style frozen hash browns, thawed
¼ cup Jimmy Dean Original Sausage Crumbles (fully cooked)
⅓ cup shredded cheese of your choice
½ Tbsp onions, finely chopped and sautéed briefly in a little vegetable oil
1 Tbsp green or other sweet pepper, finely chopped
2 eggs
⅓ cup milk
   dash of salt and pepper (optional)

Spray individual casserole dishes with cooking oil.

Layer hash browns, sausage, cheese, onions, and peppers in the prepared casserole dish. Mix eggs and milk in a bowl. Pour egg mixture over the top of the mixture in the casserole dish. Gently combine with a fork. (May be refrigerated overnight.)

To cook, preheat oven to 350°F. Bake uncovered. Check in 35 minutes to see if the eggs are set by inserting a knife in the center. When it comes out clean, it is done.

Tips and variations: Broccoli or spinach may be used. Use any sausage you prefer, or ham or bacon.

Savory Breakfasts

Herbed Baked Eggs

Yield: 4 servings

"We inherited this recipe from the former innkeeper, Chuck McLaughlin. Thanks, Chuck!"

- 4 eggs
- 1 tsp Dijon mustard
- ⅓ cup sour cream
- 1 tsp dried chives, chopped
- 1 tsp dried parsley, chopped
- 1 Tbsp onion, finely chopped
- ¾ cup cheddar cheese, shredded

Preheat oven to 350°F. Spray 4 ramekins with cooking oil.

In a medium bowl, beat eggs, mustard, and sour cream. Add herbs and onions.

Beat well and pour mixture into prepared ramekins. Add 3 tablespoons of shredded cheese to each ramekin and gently mix in.

Place filled ramekins in a pan filled with about ½-inch water.

Bake for 45 minutes or until firm and golden. Turn out onto serving plates.

Tips and variations: A tomato salad goes well with this.

Savory Breakfasts

Hash Brown Bacon & Egg Cups

Yield: 3 servings (2 cups per guest)

"This is a gluten-free dish. If you like your bacon crispy, pre-cook bacon until half done."

6–8	Tbsp hash brown potatoes, shredded (enough to line 6 muffin cups)
4	Tbsp butter, melted
6	slices bacon
6	eggs
	salt and pepper, to taste
6	tsp grated cheese (your choice) (approximately 1 tsp per muffin cup)

Preheat oven to 350°F.

Using a muffin tin, cupcake tin, or ramekin, line bottom and up sides with potatoes. Drizzle with butter. Place in oven until potatoes are lightly browned, 20 minutes (15 minutes in convection).

Line each cup with a slice of bacon, pressing the bacon around the sides—not on the bottom. Crack one egg into the center of the cup or ramekin.

Sprinkle with salt, pepper, and cheese if desired.

Bake for 20 minutes (15 in convection oven) or until the egg is done to the consistency you like.

These bacon and egg cups should pop right out of the pan.

Tips and variations: Serve with sweet bread, or toasted and buttered sourdough English muffins.

Arcadia House

Eggs Carbonara

Yield: 6–8 servings

"Bacon lovers—take note. Our guests like this tasty gluten-free dish. The recipe comes from an inn in California by way of epicurious.com."

- 6 bacon slices
- 12 large eggs
- 1 oz. (½ cup) Parmesan cheese, finely grated
- ¼ cup heavy cream
- 1 Tbsp fresh basil, chopped, plus extra for garnish
- ½ tsp salt
- ½ tsp black pepper
- 2 tsp garlic, minced
- 1 Tbsp fresh flat-leaf parsley, chopped
- 2 Tbsp scallions, chopped, plus extra for garnish

Cook bacon in a 12-inch nonstick skillet over moderate heat, turning over occasionally, until crisp, then transfer with tongs to paper towels to drain. When cool, finely crumble bacon.

Reserve 2 tablespoons bacon fat in a small bowl and discard remainder. Wipe skillet clean with paper towels. Pour reserved fat back into the skillet and set aside.

Vigorously whisk together eggs, Parmesan, cream, basil, salt, and pepper in a bowl until foamy.

Over moderate heat, cook garlic and parsley in the skillet with the reserved bacon fat for 1 minute (do not brown garlic). Add scallions and cook, stirring occasionally, until softened, about 3 minutes. Add egg mixture and cook, stirring occasionally to scramble eggs and form large curds, lifting up cooked egg around edge with a heatproof rubber spatula to let raw egg flow underneath, until eggs are just set. Stir in crumbled bacon, top with chopped scallions and basil, and serve immediately.

Brunch Eggs

Yield: 6–10 servings

2   cups sharp cheddar cheese, grated
¼   cup (½ stick) butter
1   cup half & half
½   tsp salt
2   tsp dry mustard
¼   tsp pepper
14   eggs, slightly beaten
     paprika, to garnish
     parsley sprig, to garnish

Preheat oven to 325°F.

Sprinkle the cheese in the bottom of a 9x13-inch baking dish.
Dot with butter.

In a bowl, combine the half & half, salt, dry mustard, and pepper. Pour
half over the cheese. Pour the slightly beaten eggs over the cheese.
Pour the remaining cream over the eggs. Bake for 45 minutes.

Sprinkle with paprika and top with a sprig of parsley.

This recipe has been adapted from *The American Country Inn
and Bed & Breakfast Cookbook: Volume Two.*

Lunch & Dinner & All the Extras

Some Michigan bed and breakfasts serve lunch or dinner regularly, others on special occasions. Some inns offer a late afternoon social hour at which appetizers are served. At other B&Bs, you'll find canapés or another homemade snack in your room at check-in time. Several of our B&Bs offer cooking classes where you'll learn to make soups, fresh bread or more—even beer. In this section, Michigan innkeepers share some of their favorite recipes for main entrées, hors d'oeuvres, soup, salad, veggies and other side dishes.

Recipes in the Featured Recipes chapter

In this chapter

Lunch & Dinner

Greek Quiche

Yield: 6 servings

"Great brunch dish."

3	large eggs
1½	cups half & half
½	tsp oregano
½	tsp salt
⅛	tsp pepper, fresh ground or seasoned
6	oz. fresh spinach, cooked, chopped, and squeezed dry
1	cup mozzarella cheese, shredded
¼	cup sun-dried tomatoes, chopped, soaked in boiling water for 5 minutes, drained
¼	cup green onions, sliced
¼	cup kalamata olives, sliced
1	(9-inch) refrigerated pie crust, unbaked
½	cup feta cheese, crumbled

Preheat oven to 350°F.

In a medium bowl, whisk together eggs, half & half, oregano, salt, and pepper.

Stir in spinach, mozzarella, sun-dried tomatoes, green onions, and olives: mix well.

Pour into pie shell. Sprinkle with crumbled feta cheese. Bake 40–45 minutes or until a knife inserted in the center comes out clean and the top is golden brown.

Let stand for 10 minutes. Cut into wedges and serve warm.

Lunch & Dinner

Crustless Spinach & Feta Quiche

Yield: 6 servings

"This lovely quiche is one of the recipes most-often requested at our inn. We make it in individual boat-shaped ramekins, but it can easily be done in any pie plate that you might have. Besides being delicious, this quiche is gluten-free, lactose-free, and meat-free, so it's enjoyed by many guests on special diets."

1	Tbsp vegetable oil
1	large onion, chopped
1	(10-oz.) pkg. frozen spinach, thawed and squeezed dry
5	large eggs
10	oz. feta cheese, crumbled
	fresh ground pepper

Preheat oven to 350°F. Grease a 9-inch pie plate.

Heat oil in skillet. Add onion and sauté until soft. Add spinach. Cook until excess moisture is evaporated. Let cool. Beat eggs in a bowl; add cheese. Stir eggs and cheese into cooled spinach mixture. Season with pepper. Pour into pie plate and spread evenly.

Bake 40–45 minutes until top is nicely browned and tester comes out clean.

Tips and variations: Variations to this recipe are endless, so let your imagination run free. As a matter of fact, this recipe was given to us by a friend when we bought our B&B, and her version used ¾ lb. grated Muenster cheese—which is also delicious! We've also done it with about ¾ lb. Havarti dill and added extra dill—fantastic! You could also add other vegetables.

Tomato and Onion Quiche

Yield: 8 servings

"A delicious vegetarian quiche—use as your main entrée and serve a meat on the side."

1	9-inch pie crust
1	cup cheese, your choice, shredded
½	cup onions, chopped
1	Tbsp butter
2	oz. tomatoes, sliced ¼-inch thick, and quartered. Lay to dry on paper towel.
3	eggs
3	Tbsp flour
½	cup cream
¼	cup milk
1	Tbsp fresh basil
1	tsp dry basil
½	tsp salt
1/8	tsp black pepper
¼	tsp mustard
	paprika, to garnish
	shredded cheese, to garnish
	fresh parsley, to garnish

Preheat oven to 350°F. Bake pie crust until light brown, 7–10 minutes. Cool.

Sprinkle cheese on crust. In a small pan, sauté onions and butter until soft and translucent. Spoon onions on cheese. Arrange a layer of tomatoes on onions.

In a mixing bowl, combine eggs, flour, cream, milk, and remaining herbs and seasonings. Pour egg mixture on top of tomatoes. Sprinkle with paprika. Cover and refrigerate overnight.

The next morning: remove casserole from the refrigerate and preheat oven to 350°F. Bake uncovered 40–60 minutes. Just before it's done, sprinkle with cheese and parsley. Cover and bake 5 more minutes. Let stand 10 minutes before serving.

Tips and variations: You could add cooked sausage if desired.

Lunch & Dinner

Zucchini Quiche

Yield: 6 servings

*"My British mother served this dish to us for our afternoon teas.
I fondly make this dish for my guests with all the good memories that
come with it."*

4	eggs, lightly beaten
1	cup baking mix (such as Bisquick® or "Jiffy")
½	cup Parmesan cheese, grated
1	cup Swiss cheese, shredded
¼	cup vegetable oil
5	green onions, sliced
2	Tbsp snipped fresh dill or 1½ Tbsp dried dill
3	cups zucchini (about 2 medium or 1 large), shredded

Preheat oven to 350°F. Spray a 9-inch quiche dish with cooking oil.

Combine all ingredients in a large bowl, making sure you add the zucchini last.

Pour batter into quiche dish. Bake uncovered for 40–45 minutes.

This recipe has been adapted from Jean Turczyn.

Lunch & Dinner

Hankerd Inn

Zucchini Onion Pie

Yield: 6 servings

*"Here is a way to use up your zucchini! It is a great side dish
with chicken."*

3	eggs
½	cup Parmesan cheese, grated
½	cup canola oil
½	cup sharp American cheese, grated
1	garlic clove, minced
¼	tsp salt
½	garlic pepper
3	cups zucchini, sliced
1	cup biscuit baking mix
1	large onion, chopped

Preheat oven to 350°F. Grease a 9-inch deep-dish pie plate.

In a large bowl, whisk the first seven ingredients. Stir in the zucchini, biscuit mix, and onion. Pour into the prepared pie plate and bake 25–35 minutes or until lightly browned.

Zucchini are usually picked when under 8 inches in length, when the seeds are still soft and immature. Mature zucchini can be as large as three feet in length. The larger ones are often fibrous. A zucchini with the flowers attached is a sign of a truly fresh and immature fruit, and are especially sought after by many people for its sweeter flavor.

Lunch & Dinner

Meat & Potato Quiche

Yield: 4 servings

"A guest gave me one of their family cookbooks over 20 years ago, and I am still using this recipe which came from it."

3	Tbsp vegetable oil
3	cups shredded raw potatoes (I buy frozen and thaw.)
1	cup cheddar cheese
¾	cup meat (I use ham and fried bacon.)
¼	cup chopped onion
	parsley flakes
¾	can evaporated milk
2	eggs

Preheat oven to 425°F.

In a 9-inch pie pan, stir together oil and potatoes. Press evenly to make a crust.

Bake for 15 minutes. Remove from the oven and layer with cheese, meat, onion, and parsley. In a separate bowl, mix together the milk and eggs. Pour over the dish. Return to the oven and bake for 30 minutes. Allow to cool 5 minutes before cutting.

Tips and variations: To serve more guests, double the recipe and bake in a 9x13-inch pan. I like it the best with a lot of bacon.

Lunch & Dinner

Brian's Tomato Pesto Quiche

Yield: 6–8 servings

"We often serve this with brown sugar bacon, fresh fruit, and muffins."

Pesto

1   cup sun-dried tomatoes
1   clove garlic
     fresh basil
½   cup olive oil
     dash of lemon juice
     pine nuts (optional)

Quiche

4   eggs
1   cup half & half
1   cup feta cheese
1   (9-inch) homemade or purchased pie crust, unbaked

Preheat oven to 350°F.

Place pesto ingredients in food processor and pulse. Combine all other quiche ingredients and add to pie pan.

Bake 45 minutes or until golden brown.

Lunch & Dinner

Crustless Quiche

Yield: 6–8 servings

"After preparing quiche many different ways and usually in a crust that guests didn't eat, I started preparing it with no crust. It always gets compliments. It can be adapted easily, leaving out meat, changing the vegetable or the cheese. It doesn't take long to prepare and always looks nice on leafy lettuce with a grape tomato garnish. Leftovers reheat well. It can be baked, cooled, and frozen for future use."

½ cup French fried onion rings, divided
½ lb. bacon, cooked, drained and crumbled
1 cup cooked broccoli or asparagus, chopped (optional)
6 eggs
1½ cups milk or half & half, or a combination
½ cups small curd cottage cheese (low-fat)
1 tsp dill
1 tsp parsley
1 tsp pepper
1½ cups Swiss cheese, shredded

Preheat oven to 375°F. Grease a deep-dish pie plate, flan, or quiche pan with cooking spray.

Sprinkle ¼ cup crumbled French fried onions on bottom of baking pan. Top with the meat and vegetable(s). In a bowl, mix together eggs, milk, cottage cheese, and spices. Stir in the shredded cheese. Pour liquid ingredients over items in the pie plate. Sprinkle the remaining crumbled French fried onions.

Bake immediately for 45–60 minutes.

Tips and variations: There is a lot of leeway in this recipe to make it your own with your selection of breakfast meats, vegetables, herbs, and toppings.

Potato Rosemary Garlic Fontina Cheese Strata

Yield: 12 servings

"This recipe is a wonderful amalgamation of local potatoes, fresh rosemary, garlic, and fontina cheese—great for serving larger groups of guests and friends. We continue the Italian theme by serving a first course of grapes marinated in grappa or local wine served in a grape juice-thinned mascarpone cheese sauce."

1	loaf Italian bread, sliced (You will need approximately 8 slices to cover a 2-qt. casserole dish.)
4–5	medium red potatoes
1	stick softened butter, divided
1	medium shallot, finely chopped
1	large or 2 small cloves garlic, minced
1	Tbsp fresh rosemary, chopped
16	oz. fontina cheese
12	jumbo or large eggs
1	Tbsp parsley (fresh or dried), chopped
3½	cups half & half
	rosemary or thyme sprig, to garnish

Preheat oven to 200°F.

Place bread slices on baking sheet in the oven for 20 minutes, then turn over and put back in oven for 20 more minutes. Meanwhile boil 2–3 quarts of water in a saucepan and put in diced (about 3/8 inch size) potatoes with skins on for approximately 7 minutes until just tender, but still firm. Drain. Melt 4 tablespoons of butter in a frying pan on medium heat and fry the potatoes until they begin to brown.

Add shallot pieces to potatoes and continue to sauté until shallots begin to soften or turn translucent (about 3 minutes). Push potato/onion mixture to one side of pan and put a small sliver of butter into other side. Press garlic into this butter and cook briefly to separate then toss with potato mixture. Turn heat off and add rosemary, toss. Cool slightly while bread continues to dry in the oven. Grate fontina cheese (can use a special blade on food processor for this if you like, or with handheld grater). Remove bread from oven and cool.

Lunch & Dinner

(Continued from previous page)

Liberally butter a casserole dish, and lightly butter one side of now dried and cooled bread slices. Place a layer of bread slices, buttered side up, in casserole dish, trimming as necessary to fit bottom of dish. Sprinkle ½ potato mixture on top of bread, then ½ of cheese. Place a second layer of bread slices on top of cheese, then remaining potato mixture followed by cheese.

Whisk eggs and parsley in a large bowl until well beaten; whisk in cream. Pour mixture evenly over surface of layer casserole. Place plastic wrap over dish and push down slightly. Put casserole in refrigerator overnight (or at least 4 hours), applying enough weight on top of casserole to assure bread is completely covered by egg mixture but doesn't overflow.

When ready to cook, allow strata to sit at room temperature for 20 minutes before putting into the oven preheated to 325°F. Cook for 1 hour and 10 minutes or up to 1½ hours (depending on oven temperature variance). When done, the crust should be lightly browned and puffed (although this will deflate). Let strata rest for at least 10 minutes at room temperature, and up to 20 minutes is fine, to solidify the layers. Serve warm, garnished with either a fresh rosemary or thyme sprig.

This recipe has been adapted from *Cook's Illustrated*.

Sausage & Wild Rice Brunch Casserole

Yield: 6 servings

"This recipe can be a lunch, brunch, or breakfast dish."

¾ cup wild rice	**White sauce**
2 quarts water	2 Tbsp butter
¾ cup long grain brown rice	2 Tbsp flour
1 lb. bulk sausage, regular or hot	1 cup milk
2 Tbsp butter or margarine, divided, for casserole dish and skillet	¼ cup mushroom liquid
½ cup onion, chopped	½ tsp chicken base or salt
1 cup celery, chopped	½ cup sour cream
1 sweet red pepper, chopped	
1 (8-oz.) jar mushroom stems and pieces, drained (Reserve liquid for sauce)	

Rinse wild rice under running water for 2 minutes; drain thoroughly. Simmer in the water for 15 minutes. Add the brown rice; continue gently simmering for 35 minutes. Drain any remaining water.

Preheat oven to 350°F. Butter a 2½ quart casserole dish.

Brown sausage in a skillet until crumbly. Pour off fat. Set aside. Melt butter in a skillet. Add onion, celery, and pepper. Sauté until tender; set aside.

Prepare white sauce by melting butter in skillet. Blend in flour. Cook 1 minute, then whisk in milk, mushroom liquid, and chicken base. Cook until thickened and smooth. Remove from heat and add sour cream. Combine rice, sausage, vegetables, mushrooms, and white sauce. Pour into casserole dish. Cover with lid or aluminum foil. Bake for 60 minutes. (If you wish to prepare the day ahead, cool casserole uncovered, then cover and refrigerate overnight.)

Tips and variations: This recipe also makes great stuffing for portobello mushrooms.

Time-pressed cooks may choose to substitute 1 can condensed soup (chicken or mushroom) and ½ soup-can of milk for the white stock. The resulting casserole will be higher in sodium content.

Lunch & Dinner

Crêpes du Nord

Yield: 12 crêpes (2 per person)

*"The recipe is an original recipe but styled a bit
after a wild rice scrambled egg dish from Minnesota."*

Crêpe
1¼ cups all-purpose flour, sifted
½ tsp salt
4 eggs
1 cup milk
3 Tbsp unsalted butter, melted
1¼ cups cold water

Cream sauce
1½ Tbsp butter
1½ Tbsp flour
1¼ cups half & half plus additional to achieve desired
     consistency
½ tsp herbs de Provence

Filling (enough for 12 crêpes)
6 dried morel mushrooms, medium size (about 2-inch
   length, 1-inch girth)
3 green onions, medium size, white part plus 2 inches of
   green
12 button mushrooms, medium size (or substitute 2 large
    mini portabellas or 3   small for the above amounts)
¾–1 cup cooked 7-grain wild rice mix from Oryana's
6 eggs, extra large or jumbo
   orange slice twist, to garnish

Crêpes: In a blender or food processor blend all ingredients at high
speed for 30 seconds, scrape down sides and blend 30 more seconds.
Pour batter into a mixing bowl, cover, and refrigerate for 1 hour. To
make 6-inch crêpes pour a scant ⅓ cup of batter (or heavy ¼ cup) into
a hot, buttered crêpe pan. Cook over medium-high heat until surface
is bubbly, loosen edge with spatula and flip crêpe from one to the
other pan, cooking until golden brown, about 30 seconds. Do not
wash crêpe pans, just wipe out and re-season with butter as you make

crêpes. Stack 4 crêpes each on two plates to cool while you continue cooking the remainder of batter. If you are freezing for future use: wrap each set of 4 gently in cling wrap, close wrap over 4, then stack next 4 so you end up with packets of 4. Take whole stack and put into Ziploc bag, and onto a plate to keep flat, then freeze.

Cream Sauce: Melt butter in a saucepan then add flour, whisk together, then cook over low heat until bubbly and the mixture begins to brown just slightly (this removes flour taste). Continue to whisk while gradually adding half & half. Add herbs de Provence seasoning. Heat over low until sauce thickens and reduces slightly. Add small amounts of additional cream as you continue to cook for 10 minutes to retain desired sauce consistency, then turn heat to simmer and cover until ready to use (can be held up to 30 minutes). Re-whisk prior to pouring over crêpes and add cream as necessary. Reduce proportionately for smaller numbers of guests.

Filling: Reconstitute dried morels in simmering water for 15 minutes. Slice green onions and button mushrooms into ¼-inch wide pieces. Dice morels into smaller ⅛–¼-inch pieces. Sauté onions and mushrooms over medium heat until just turning slightly brown, about 7 minutes. Filling can hold at this point while you make the sauce. When ready to continue, add cooked rice, then eggs. Cook all over low-medium heat until eggs are cooked but still slightly runny.

To assemble, place 1 crêpe on each plate and fill with enough filling to provide a 1-inch tube of egg mixture across the middle of each crêpe from left to right. Then fold the crêpe edge nearest you over the filling and gently turn the crêpe away from you, thus rolling the filling into the crêpe. This procedure helps to avoid too much handling of the delicate crêpes.

Garnish plate with 3 cooked asparagus spears if large size or 5 if small and thin (or about ½ cup of roasted roots in winter), and 2–3 slices Canadian bacon depending on thickness of cut and size of meat round (you cut in half across mid-section to form half slices). Then reheat entire plate for 45 seconds on microwave high to heat crêpes thoroughly. Pour ¼ cup of cream sauce over length of crêpes, garnish with edible flower (violets or nasturtium), thyme sprig from garden, or two chive sprigs; and in all cases an orange slice twist and serve.

Olive Oil Shiitake Mushroom Bread Pudding

Yield: 4 servings

"Shiitakes, native to East Asia, are the second most commonly cultivated edible mushroom. This savory side dish could be served with any meal of the day. Kingsley House uses olive oil from the innkeeper's Olive Cart—an oil and balsamic vinegar store."

1²/₃	cups whole milk
2	eggs, lightly beaten
1	baguette, preferably stale, cut into cubes
3	Tbsp Olive Cart Organic Extra Virgin Olive Oil, plus more for greasing pan(s)
1	onion, diced
8	shiitake mushrooms, chopped roughly
1	sprig fresh rosemary, roughly chop leaves
¼	cup Parmesan cheese, plus more for sprinkling salt and pepper, to taste

Preheat oven to 375°F. Lightly grease an 8-inch pie pan or four 4-inch ramekins. Set aside.

Combine milk and eggs in a mixing bowl and whisk lightly to combine. Add bread cubes and stir to ensure all are thoroughly soaked. Set aside.

Heat the olive oil in a frying pan over low heat. Add onion and cook slowly for 8–10 minutes. Increase to medium and add the mushrooms. Cook for another 2–3 minutes until mushrooms begin to shrink. Remove from heat.

Stir the onion-mushroom mixture into the soaking bread. Gently fold in the rosemary and Parmesan. Season with salt and pepper to taste.

Spoon the bread mixture into the prepared pan or ramekins. Sprinkle with a pinch of Parmesan and bake for 25–30 minutes, or until pudding sets and the tops are golden-brown and crisp. Allow to cool 5 minutes before serving.

Chili Cheese Puff

Yield: 8 servings

"This has a touch of southwestern flavor, is easy to prepare and great with salsa on the side."

½   cup flour
1   tsp baking powder
10   eggs
2   cups cottage cheese
4   cups Monterey Jack cheese, shredded
½   cup butter, melted
1   can green chilies, chopped

Preheat oven to 350°F. Grease a 9x13-inch glass baking dish with cooking spray.

Mix flour and baking powder in a small bowl.

In a separate bowl, beat 10 eggs and add the flour mixture. Add remaining ingredients and blend. Pour into prepared baking dish. Bake 45 minutes. Cut into squares.

Tips and variations: For flavoring, use cumin, garlic, and pepper. Serve with salsa.

Lunch & Dinner

Italian Pasta Frittata

Yield: 12 servings

"Knock them out with this one."

2 Tbsp olive oil, divided for coating ramekins and
sautéing
6 oz. dried spaghetti
4–5 cloves garlic, minced
2 Tbsp fresh or dried basil
1–2 medium zucchini, sliced
1 cup medium red pepper, diced
1 cup sweet onion, diced
1½ cups mushrooms, diced
10 eggs
1 cup buttermilk or heavy cream
1 tsp dry mustard
1 (8-oz.) pkg. cream cheese, cubed and softened
1 cup Parmesan cheese
24 grape tomatoes

Preheat oven to 350°F. Place 12 individual ramekins on a large, rimmed baking tray and lightly coat each one with olive oil.

Cook spaghetti according to directions. Drain and divide equally into bottom of each ramekin. In a sauté pan, heat olive oil and sauté garlic, basil, zucchini, red pepper, onion, and mushrooms just until tender. Layer the vegetables over the pasta in each ramekin.

In a bowl, mix eggs, buttermilk/heavy cream, dry mustard, cream cheese and Parmesan cheese until slightly lumpy. I use a stand-mixer for this step. Ladle the mixture over pasta and vegetables, top with 4 sliced grape tomatoes. Bake uncovered for 1 hour, turning at 30 minutes. Serve with garlic toast points.

Tips and variations: Most any vegetable combination works in this dish. Just remember to change your spices to complement your vegetable blend. For example, with rice noodles use carrots, red onion, crimini mushrooms, snow peas, and water chestnuts with coriander or five-spice to create an Asian-inspired feast. This dish can be refrigerated overnight.

Lunch & Dinner

Voyager's inn

Asparagus Frittata

Yield: 4 servings

- 1 tsp butter
- ½ lb. asparagus spears, fresh
- 1 cup mushrooms, sliced
- 6 eggs
- ¾ cup cottage cheese
- 2 tsp yellow mustard
- ⅛ tsp salt
  dash of pepper
- 1 medium tomato, chopped

Preheat oven to 400°F.

Melt butter into a 10-inch ovenproof skillet. Cut asparagus spears into ½-inch pieces.

Sautée 2–3 minutes. Add mushrooms. Sauté 2–3 additional minutes.

In a bowl, whisk eggs until foamy. Mix in cottage cheese, mustard, salt and pepper.

Pour over asparagus/mushrooms. Cook over low heat until mixture bubbles and begins to set around edges. Bake uncovered for about 10 minutes or until set.

Garnish with chopped tomato.

Spinach Strudel

Yield: 10 slices

"This savory strudel is perfect when you are in the mood for something fast, fresh, and flavorful."

10 oz. frozen spinach, thawed, squeezed dry, and chopped coarse	2 Tbsp pine nuts, toasted
	2 Tbsp lemon juice
¾ cup whole-milk ricotta cheese	2 garlic cloves, minced
¾ cup feta cheese, crumbled	½ tsp ground nutmeg
6 scallions, sliced thin and sautéed	salt and pepper
	10 (14x9-inch) phyllo sheets, thawed
½ cup golden raisins	olive oil spray or melted butter

Preheat oven to 400°F. Line baking sheet with parchment paper.

Mix all ingredients together in bowl, except phyllo sheets and olive oil.

On a cooking sheet or cutting board, layer phyllo sheets on top of one another, coating each sheet with oil spray or melted butter. Mound spinach mixture into a narrow log shape along bottom edge of the stack of sheets, leaving about a 2-inch border at bottom and a ½-inch border on sides. Fold bottom edge of dough over filling, then continue to roll dough around filling into a tight log. (Roll 14-inch edge of the phyllo to form the log.) Fold in the sides or leave them open.

Transfer filled log, seam side down, to lined baking sheet. Lightly spray dough with cooking oil, or brush with melted butter. Bake for about 20 minutes until golden, rotating sheet halfway through baking. Let cool on the sheet for 5 minutes, then slice and serve.

Tips and variations: Keep the phyllo covered with damp towels while working. Do not use fewer than 10 layers of phyllo or roll will have a weak structure.

Substitute ½ cup chopped pitted kalamata olives for raisins and 3 ounces crumbled goat cheese for feta. Sautéed mushrooms are an excellent addition.

This recipe has been adapted from *Cook's Illustrated*.

Asparagus & Red Pepper Tart

Yield: 2–3 servings

"This fresh asparagus entrée features a no-fuss crust and fresh ingredients, perfect for a quick assembly. The end result is an impressive treat for all your senses. Add a fresh salad and you have the makings for a delicious light summer dinner."

1	Tbsp olive oil
½	lb. asparagus, trimmed and cut in 1-inch pieces
½	cup red pepper, chopped
¼	cup onion, diced
1	tsp dried basil, additional for garnishing
	salt and pepper, to taste
½	(15-oz.) pkg. refrigerated pie crust, room temperature, unbaked
2	oz. mozzarella cheese, shredded
2	oz. feta cheese, crumbled
2	Tbsp Parmesan cheese, grated

Preheat oven to 400°F.

In a large skillet, lightly sauté asparagus, red pepper, and onion in olive oil. Season with basil, salt, and pepper. Unroll pie crust and place on ungreased baking sheet.

Sprinkle mozzarella cheese on pie crust within an inch of the edge. Spread sautéed vegetable mix evenly over mozzarella. Top with feta cheese. Fold edge of the pie crust over vegetable/cheese mix. The crust should not cover the vegetables completely.

Bake for 20–25 minutes or until dough is lightly browned. Remove from oven, sprinkle Parmesan cheese and additional basil evenly over the crust and exposed vegetables. Bake 5 more minutes. Cool on wire rack for 5 minutes before serving.

Lunch & Dinner

Asparagus Wraps

Yield: 12–16 wraps

"This recipe has been a favorite of our guests for some time and living near the 'Asparagus Capital' makes it representative of Hart. We received this from a friend living in Hart."

12–16	stalks asparagus, ring-finger size or smaller
1	(8-oz.) carton Philadelphia Cream Cheese, not whipped
12–16	salami slices, sliced thinner than normal, (ask your butcher for help)

Line up the tips of the asparagus and trim off the bottom part of the stem (as much as 2 inches) so they are all the same length. Place in boiling water and boil for about 2 minutes depending on the diameter (only one minute for thinner asparagus). Plunge immediately into ice water, and let sit for about 15 minutes. Drain on a paper towel.

Line up salami on a straight edge (i.e., counter, cutting board, cooking sheet) and with an angled butter knife spread a thin layer of cream cheese on each salami slice.

Place the asparagus on the salami and roll up and store in the refrigerator.

Tips and variations: These can be made two days in advance.

Spoon Cornbread Casserole

Yield: 10 servings

"Cornbread with additional ingredients makes a perfect side dish for a Southwest breakfast menu or egg dishes."

- ½   cup margarine or butter, melted
- 1   (8-oz.) can whole kernel corn, drained
- 1   (8-oz.) can cream style corn
- 1   cup sour cream
- 2   eggs
- 1   (8.5-oz.) pkg. "Jiffy" Corn Muffin Mix
  Optional ingredients: chopped pecans or chopped jalapeño peppers or sun-dried tomatoes

Preheat oven to 375°F. Grease or spray a 1½-quart casserole dish with cooking oil.

Combine butter and corn in prepared casserole dish. Blend in sour cream. Beat eggs and stir into casserole along with corn muffin mix. Blend thoroughly. Bake 35–40 minutes or until center is firm. Serve in hot casserole dish with butter or honey on the side.

Tips and variations: Add optional ingredients for variations in flavor. Double ingredients for a 13x9-inch baking dish.

This recipe has been adapted from *"Jiffy" Mix Recipe Cookbook*, Chelsea, Michigan.

Lunch & Dinner

Crisp Roasted Fingerling Potatoes

Yield: 4 servings

"Crispy and creamy potatoes? The secret is baking soda. Baking soda breaks down pectin and draws the starch to the surface. Surface starch encourages browning. This side dish combines the delicate flavor of fingerlings with the satisfying crispiness of traditional roasted potatoes."

2	lbs. fingerling potatoes, unpeeled, halved lengthwise
½	cup salt
½	tsp baking soda
2	Tbsp olive oil, divided
¼	tsp pepper

Adjust oven rack to lowest position, place rimmed baking sheet on rack, and preheat oven to 500°F.

Bring 8 cups water to boil in a large saucepan. Add potatoes, salt, and baking soda. Bring to a simmer. Potatoes are done when they are tender but the centers offer slight resistance when pierced with the tip of a knife, about 7–10 minutes.

Drain potatoes in colander and shake vigorously to roughen edges. Transfer potatoes to a large platter lined with a dish towel and arrange cut side up. Let sit until no longer steaming and surface is tacky, about 5 minutes.

Transfer potatoes to large bowl and toss with 1 tablespoon oil and pepper. Working quickly, carefully remove baking sheet from oven and drizzle remaining 1 tablespoon oil over surface. Arrange potatoes on baking sheet, cut side down, in an even layer. Bake until cut sides are crisp and skins are spotty brown, about 20–25 minutes, rotating sheet halfway through roasting.

Remove from oven and flip potatoes cut side up. Let cool on sheet for 5 minutes and serve.

Tips and variations: Don't skip the step of letting potatoes cool before roasting, otherwise they will become soggy.

This recipe has been adapted from *Cook's Country*.

Lunch & Dinner

Hash Browns Mit Onions

Yield: 6–8 servings

"For vegetarian and vegan guests of our inn, this is one of our often made dishes, but really everybody likes these flavorful hash browns. This dish uses our very own Grandpa's Seasoning, an old family blend of eight kinds of flour, powdered garlic, powdered onion, and seasoned salt. We tell guests how to make it for themselves."

2	medium red potatoes, scrubbed, with eyes removed, and shredded
½	large onion, diced
1	tsp extra virgin olive oil
	sea salt
	ground black pepper
	Grandpa's Seasoning or your favorite all-purpose seasoning

Add oil to a large skillet over low heat. Spread one-half of the shredded potatoes evenly in the skillet. Distribute diced onion over the potatoes. Add seasonings, using your judgment as to amount. Add the remaining potatoes.

Use a flat-end wooden spoon to unify the circular shape by pushing the outside edges in, toward the center. When the underneath side of the mixture begins to brown, after about 15 minutes, flip it (if you are brave and able), or lay a flat skillet on top and flip it over.

Reshape with the flat end of wooden spoon. When the second side begins to brown, after about 10 minutes, slide the hash brown onto an oval serving dish and present to guests. Serve warm.

Tips and variations: We usually cut these hash browns into wedges and serve like pizza slices with a triangular pie server. For a romantic touch, we've been known to make these into a heart shape instead of a circle.

Lunch & Dinner

East Meets West in a Pita

Yield: 6–8 servings

"This cool summer sandwich combines grilled pork tenderloin teriyaki—that's east—with ranch dressing—Hidden Valley has got to be west, right?—and vegetables in a pita pocket."

2 pork tenderloins with silver tissue removed

Marinade
- 4 Tbsp soy sauce
- 2–3 cloves garlic, minced, crushed or sliced
- 2 tsp brown sugar
- 1 tsp ground ginger
- ½ tsp freshly ground black pepper

Dressing
- 1 (6-oz.) container of sour cream
- 1 packet of Hidden Valley Ranch Seasoning and Salad Dressing Mix

Vegetables
- any combination of red onion and bell peppers, chopped
- tomatoes, chopped and drained
- English cucumbers, sliced

- pita pocket bread

Place the meat in a Ziploc bag. Blend marinade ingredients and add to bag. Close tightly. Let stand three to four hours at room temperature or in the refrigerator for up to 12 hours.

When ready to cook, grill over medium-high heat 12–15 minutes, turning once. Baste frequently with reserved marinade. Don't overcook pork tenderloin. Take it off the grill when the inside is still just a little pink. When ready to serve, at room temperature or cold, slice thinly.

Place vegetables and ranch dressing in individual bowls. Serve everything buffet-style, allowing diners to assemble their own sandwiches.

This recipe has been adapted from a Teriyaki Pork Tenderloin recipe from *Detroit Free Press Cookbook*, 1984.

Lunch & Dinner

Mexican Grille

Yield: 2 loaves, 10 sandwiches

*"A spicy/sweet grilled sandwich good for breakfast, lunch, or dinner.
Change the cheese or use another salsa to give it your own style."*

Mexican Bread
½ cup warm water
2 pkgs. dry yeast
¾ cup cornmeal
1 tsp salt
1 Tbsp sugar
½ tsp baking soda
2 eggs
1 cup buttermilk or sour milk
½ cup oil
1 cup cream style corn
5 cups flour, divided
1½ cups sharp cheddar, grated
1 (4-oz.) can green chilies, chopped

Pineapple Salsa
1 ripe pineapple, diced small
1 red pepper, diced small
1 green pepper, diced small
1 small red onion, diced small
½ hot chili pepper, seeded and minced (optional)
½ cup fresh cilantro or mint, chopped
4 Tbsp lime juice
1 Tbsp olive oil
1 Tbsp brown sugar
dash of ground ginger or more to taste

sliced cheese, your choice, for the sandwich

Bread: In a large bowl, dissolve yeast in warm water, let stand 5 minutes.
Add cornmeal, salt, sugar, and baking soda. Beat until well-mixed. Add
eggs, buttermilk, oil, corn, and 2 cups flour. Beat vigorously until well-
blended. Add cheese, chilies, and the remaining flour. (Use just enough
flour to make dough manageable.) Knead until cheese and chilis are well

distributed. Let rest 10 minutes. Resume kneading until smooth and elastic. Place in greased bowl. Cover and let rise until double. Punch down and knead to remove large pockets of air. Shape into 2 loaves. Place seam side down in bread pan. Cover and let rise to top of pan.

Preheat oven to 350°F. Bake for 50-60 minutes. The loaf should sound hollow when rapped on the bottom with your knuckle. Cool on wire rack.

Pineapple Salsa: In a large bowl, mix all ingredients together in a bowl. Chill 1 hour.

To assemble: Make a cheese sandwich with the Mexican bread (your choice of cheese) and grill until cheese is melted. Cut in half and serve with salsa.

Tips and variations: The bread slices easier on the second day. Slice and freeze 1 week. Salsa can be diced the night before and mixed in the morning.

Sarah's Oriental Salad

Yield: 4–6 servings

"Sarah, our English Siren friend extraordinaire, from the far southern side of Saugatuck, said (in a language all her own) when she tried this salad, 'Topper!'—which we trust was a compliment since she ate all that was on her plate and asked for seconds."

- ⅓ cup rice or cider vinegar
- ¼ cup sugar
- 3 Tbsp vegetable oil
- 2 Tbsp honey
- 2 Tbsp low-sodium soy sauce
- 1 Tbsp butter
- ⅓ cup slivered almonds
- ¼ cup sunflower seed kernels
- 2 (5-oz.) pkgs. Japanese curly noodles (soba), crumbled
- 8 cups Napa (Chinese) cabbage, shredded
- 2 cups carrots, shredded
- 5 green onions, thinly sliced

Combine first 5 ingredients in a small saucepan and bring to a boil. Cook for 1 minute, stirring constantly. Spoon into a bowl, cover and chill. Set aside.

Melt butter in large nonstick skillet and add almonds, sunflower kernels, and noodles. Cook 3 minutes or until lightly toasted, tossing occasionally. Spoon mixture into a large bowl, cover and chill. Add vinegar mixture to noodle mix; let stand 15 minutes. Add cabbage, carrots, and onions, tossing to coat.

Lunch & Dinner

Q's Soon-to-be-Famous Tuna Salad

Yield: 3–4 servings

"Q (we won't reveal her real name) is our secret agent baker, a legend in her own time. She enters the bed and breakfast utilizing her secret agent baker disguise, works her magic, and right before our very own eyes a new dish has appeared."

½	cup plain yogurt
1	Tbsp mayonnaise
1	Tbsp Dijon mustard
	ground black pepper, to taste
½	cup radishes, chopped
½	cup celery, chopped
2	(6-oz.) cans tuna, drained

In a bowl, combine first 4 ingredients. Place radishes, celery, and tuna in a bowl, then add yogurt mixture. Combine well. Refrigerate at least 1 hour before serving.

Canned tuna was first produced in 1903, and quickly became popular. Tuna is canned in edible oils, in brine, in water, and in various sauces. In the United States, 52% of canned tuna is used for sandwiches; 22% for salads; and 15% for casseroles. In the United States, only Albacore can legally be sold in canned form as "white meat tuna." —Wikipedia

Lunch & Dinner

Crunchy Napa Cabbage Salad

Yield: 6–8 servings

"My college roommate, Patty, married a minister and entered a world of weekly potluck dinners. She assures me that this dish has everything you want for a buffet table: easy to make, tasty, somewhat healthy, and it stays crisp at room temperature."

Dressing
¾ cup canola oil
2 Tbsp soy sauce
½ cup sugar
½ cup red wine vinegar

2 pkgs. ramen noodles, any flavor, unopened
½ cup butter
½ cup almonds, sliced
⅓ cup sesame seeds
1 large head Napa cabbage
6 scallions, chopped, including green part

Whisk all dressing ingredients together in a bowl. Chill.

Pound noodle packages lightly with a mallet to break up noodles. Open packages and either discard flavor packets or reserve for another use. Melt butter in a skillet over medium heat. Add noodles. Stir to coat. When noodles turn golden, add almonds. Stir frequently. Add sesame seeds about a minute before removing skillet from heat. Drain noodle mixture on paper towels. Let cool to room temperature.

To assemble, lay cabbage on its side on a cutting board as if it were a loaf of bread and cut thin slices with a long, sharp knife. Break up curls of cabbage as you transfer to bowl. Add scallions. Pour dressing over cabbage and toss. Top with crunchy noodle mixture and serve.

Lunch & Dinner

Bavarian Cabbage Chowder

Yield: 4 servings

"I have always loved to cook and it's a pleasure to fill our B&B with the wonderful smell of this creamy soup. It has lots of flavor and it's simple to make all in one pot. We love to slice and dip a buttered baguette into it. It's so good I always make a double batch because it's even better the second day!"

1   lb. fully cooked smoked kielbasa, cut into bite-size pieces
2   cups carrots, diagonally sliced
¼   tsp caraway seeds
2   Tbsp butter
2   cans cream of celery soup
1   soup can milk
1   soup can water
3   cups cabbage, cut into long thin shreds or a bag of pre-sliced cabbage slaw

In a large heavy pan, brown kielbasa, add carrots with caraway seeds and butter. Brown until carrots are tender. Stir in remaining ingredients. Bring to a boil, reduce heat and simmer till cabbage is done; stirring occasionally.

Tips and variations: You can add diced fresh potatoes.

Big Bay Point Lighthouse B&B

Tomato Basil Soup

Yield: 4 servings

"This is a favorite at a local Marquette eatery and now one of my favorites when the 'girls' come for lunch."

2	Tbsp butter
1	medium onion, finely chopped
1	clove garlic, minced
1	(14.5-oz.) can diced tomatoes, drained
2½	cups tomato juice
1	bay leaf
⅛	tsp ground pepper
4	oz. softened cream cheese, cut in small chunks
¼	cup snipped fresh basil (you can use dried but fresh gives a better taste)

Melt butter in large saucepan. Sauté onion and garlic until onion is tender but not brown.

Add tomatoes, tomato juice, bay leaf, and pepper. Bring to boil and reduce heat. Simmer uncovered 20 minutes, stirring occasionally. Remove from heat. Discard bay leaf.

In a food processor or blender, place half of the tomato mixture and the cream cheese. Cover and process until smooth. Add basil to the remaining half of the tomato mixture and gently mix together. Combine the blended tomato mixture and the non-blended mixture together. This gives the soup more texture and chunks.

Tips and variations: If you don't want chunks of tomatoes in the soup, you can blend all of it and the taste is just as good.

Lunch & Dinner

Harvest Soup

Yield: 4 servings

"November is Murder Mystery Month at the Munro House. The soup course during the dinner party usually includes this seasonal favorite."

2   Tbsp butter
8   oz. fresh mushrooms, sliced
½   cup onion, chopped
2   Tbsp flour
1   tsp curry powder
3   cups vegetable broth
1   (15-oz.) can solid packed pumpkin
1   (12 oz.) can evaporated milk
1   Tbsp honey
½   tsp salt
¼   tsp pepper
¼   tsp ground nutmeg
     chives (optional)

In a large saucepan, sauté the mushrooms and onion in butter until tender. Stir in the flour and curry powder until blended. Gradually add the broth. Bring to a boil; cook and stir for 2 minutes or until thickened. Add the pumpkin, milk, honey, salt, pepper, and nutmeg.

Heat through. Garnish with chives.

Lunch & Dinner

Sue's Springtime Cream of Spinach Soup

Yield: 6 servings

"This is a nice light soup for the springtime."

1	large onion, chopped
2	medium potatoes, peeled and chopped
3	cups water
2	tsp salt
14	oz. fresh spinach, cleaned and stemmed
4	medium cloves garlic, peeled only
2	Tbsp butter
3	Tbsp flour
1½	cups hot milk
	white pepper to taste
	nutmeg, for garnish

Boil onion, potatoes, water, and salt in a large saucepan. Cover and simmer until potatoes are tender. Remove from heat. Add spinach and garlic; set aside.

Melt butter over low heat in small saucepan and whisk in flour. Keep whisking over low heat 5 minutes then drizzle in the milk and continue to whisk until smooth (5-8 minutes).

In a food processor, purée vegetables in their cooking water and return to saucepan. Stir in the white sauce and add white pepper to taste. Serve hot, topped with a sprinkle of nutmeg.

Lunch & Dinner

Black & White Chicken Chili

Yield: 4-6 servings

"Everyone has a favorite version of chili with different options of beans, meat or no meat. Here's a delicious chili variation. Enjoy the flavors!"

1	tsp olive oil
1	small onion, chopped
2	cloves garlic, chopped
1	6-8 oz. boneless chicken breast, cooked and chopped
1	(14.5 oz.) can chicken broth
1	(15.5 oz.) can black beans, rinsed and drained
1	(15.5 oz.) can white beans, rinsed and drained
1	(10.5 oz.) can cream of celery soup
8	oz. corn, frozen or canned
1	rib celery, chopped
¼	large red pepper, seeded and chopped
¼	cup cornmeal
1	tsp cumin
1	tsp oregano
1	tsp chili powder
1	tsp parsley
	dash of red pepper flakes
	dash of cinnamon

In a Dutch oven or soup kettle, heat oil and sauté onion until translucent. Add garlic, sauté one minute more. Add all remaining ingredients and simmer for minimum of 45 minutes.

Tips and variations: Equally delicious simmered in a crockpot for 6 hours on low.

Fajita Beef Stew

Yield: 8 servings

*"We serve this hearty soup filled with steak and vegetables
for dinner with its yummy fajita beef broth!"*

- 12 oz. raw lean beef filet, thinly sliced into bite-sized strips
- 2 Tbsp (about half of a 1-oz. packet) dry fajita seasoning, divided
- 1 (14.5-oz.) can diced tomatoes with chilies, undrained
- 1 large russet potato, peeled and cubed
- 1 large onion, thinly sliced into bite-sized strips
- 2 bell peppers, seeded, thinly sliced into bite-sized strips
- 2 portabella mushrooms, sliced into bite-sized strips
- 4 cups (32 oz.) reduced-sodium fat-free beef broth
- 1 tsp chopped garlic
- 2 Tbsp cornstarch
- 2 Tbsp cold water
  sour cream for garnish
  fresh cilantro, chopped, for garnish

Season beef with ½ tablespoon fajita seasoning; set aside. Put remaining fajita seasoning and all other ingredients except beef, cornstarch, water, and garnishes into a crockpot and gently stir to combine. Add beef and stir again.

Cover and cook on high for 3–4 hours or on low for 7–8 hours, until beef is cooked through and vegetables are soft. In a small dish, combine cornstarch and cold water; stir to dissolve. Turn off the crockpot. Add cornstarch mixture and stir well. Allow to thicken, uncovered, about 5 minutes.

Tips and variations: You can add a can of black beans and a can of corn. I like to top each serving with a spoonful of sour cream and a little freshly chopped cilantro.

Lunch & Dinner

Crimson Cottage Inn the Woods

Easy Shepherd's Pie

Yield: 6–8 servings

"I finally came up with this version of Shepherd's Pie after repeatedly ordering it at a favorite English Pub-type restaurant. I knew there was a distinct spice flavoring so I asked what the spices were. The answer was pickling spice. Given that pickling spices would have to be ground for this dish, I made my own spice mixture based on the contents of the jarred version."

2	lbs. ground beef
1½	(12-oz.) jars of beef gravy (I have used fat-free which lowers the calories and still tastes great.)
1	Tbsp pickling spice*
1	(15-oz.) can corn (drained)
1	(15-oz.) can peas and carrots (drained)
	mashed potatoes
	grated cheese of your choice (I use Colby, Colby Jack mix, or cheddar.)

Preheat oven to 350°F.

Brown the ground beef in a large skillet and drain fat. Add gravy and spices; mix well.

Add vegetables. Pour mixture into a 9x13-inch casserole dish. (I have also used individual casserole dishes.)

Top with mashed potatoes, enough to cover entire mixture. (I have used flavored boxed mashed potatoes in a pinch but you can make fresh or use leftovers. I use both packages and it is just enough) Top with cheese.

Bake for 25–40 minutes or until bubbly. Remove from oven and allow to stand a few minutes before serving.

*For the pickling spice: add 2–3 shakes each of turmeric, cinnamon, ground ginger, ground cloves, coriander, cumin, allspice, salt, and pepper. The spices can be adjusted according to your taste. Though they may sound strange, I believe they "make" the difference! I often make a large mix of these spices (equal parts of each) and keep in an air-tight container. Then I use a tablespoon or more in this recipe.

This dish can be made ahead and refrigerated.

Lunch & Dinner

Scottish Jeans Savory Pot Roast

Yield: 6 servings

"From the County of Cromarty came this Scottish lass, who delighted us with her Savory Pot Roast. She appeared on our doorstep claiming we had met in a previous life sometime in the 1700s—that we used to have a small dinner group that met once a week and shared meals with the clan. She requisitioned our kitchen with the understanding that it was her turn, while she asserted that we left for the new world without a forwarding address and it took her a couple of centuries to find us. Well, I for one sure am glad she tracked us down. This pot roast is delicious! "

1	(3 lb.) blade pot roast
	oil for frying
	sea salt
¼	cup wine vinegar
¼	cup oil
¼	cup catsup
2	Tbsp soy sauce
2	Tbsp Worcestershire sauce
1	tsp dried crushed rosemary
½	tsp garlic powder (use the real thing and more of it)
½	tsp dry mustard

In a skillet (Dutch oven) brown meat in a small amount of oil. Sprinkle meat with a little salt. In a large bowl, combine remaining ingredients; pour over meat. Cover tightly. Simmer 2 hours or until tender. Remove meat to heated platter. Skim excess fat from sauce. Spoon sauce over meat.

Lunch & Dinner

Cranberry Chicken

Yield: 4–6 servings

"This is my daughter-in-law's recipe. The grandchildren love it."

1 can whole cranberry sauce
1 (8-oz.) bottle French dressing
1 pkg. dry onion soup mix
1 whole chicken, cut up

Preheat oven to 350°F.

Combine cranberry sauce, French dressing, and dry soup in a bowl. Place chicken in flat baking dish and cover with the cranberry mixture.

Bake for 2 hours. Cover with aluminum foil for the last ½ hour.

Tips and variations: Instead of a whole chicken, you may use two packages of chicken parts or boneless chicken breasts. If using boneless breasts, reduce baking time to1 hour.

Mustard Rosemary Chicken

Yield: 2–4 servings

2 Tbsp butter
2 Tbsp olive oil
2 whole chicken breasts, boned, skinned, and cut in
    1-inch cubes
3 Tbsp Dijon mustard, divided
1 Tbsp onion, minced fine
1 tsp rosemary, crushed
¼ tsp ground pepper
¼ tsp garlic powder
½ cup dry white wine
2 cups chicken bouillon
½ cup sour cream
2 Tbsp parsley

Melt butter with olive oil in large skillet. Add chicken, 2 tablespoons mustard, onion, and all dry spices. Mix well and sauté over medium-high heat until golden brown. Deglaze the pan with white wine and boil until reduced by one-third. Add bouillon and remaining tablespoon of mustard. Mix well and simmer uncovered until slightly thickened, about 20 minutes. Remove from heat; add sour cream. Mix well and return to medium-low heat.

Heat until nearly boiling. Stir in parsley. Reduce heat to low and cook 5 minutes more.

Lunch & Dinner

Braised Chicken with Cherry Sauce

Yield: 4 servings

"Michigan cherries with chicken? Try it!"

Sauce

- 1 lb. (2½ cups) sweet cherries, pitted, divided
- ½ cup orange juice
- ¼ cup honey
- 4 Tbsp brown sugar
- 2 tsp fresh ginger, grated
- 1 small clove garlic, minced
- ½ cup soy sauce
- 2 Tbsp lemon juice

Chicken

- 1 3 lb. chicken, cleaned, cut in pieces
- 2 tsp butter (you can use vegetable or olive oil instead of butter)

Reserve ¾ cup of pitted cherries. Put rest of cherries with orange juice in blender and blend until smooth. Combine this with remaining ingredients for sauce. Set aside.

Preheat oven to 350°F.

Melt butter in a large skillet and sauté chicken pieces until lightly browned.

Arrange pieces in a 9x13-inch baking dish, skin side down. Pour cherry sauce over chicken. Bake for 20 minutes.

Remove pan from oven, turn chicken pieces; sprinkle with the reserved ¾ cup whole cherries. Return to oven and bake 30 minutes more or until chicken is tender.

Lunch & Dinner

Poppy Seed Chicken

Yield: 8 servings

"This is a recipe I use when we host special event dinners. You can make it ahead of time and hold in the refrigerator overnight. It works well when using chafing dishes. We like to serve it with home-style buttered noodles and fresh steamed broccoli. There's only one problem—it's so good you won't have any leftovers!"

2½	lbs. chicken tender strips
1	cup chicken broth
1	cup sour cream
1	can cream of chicken soup w/herbs
1	onion, diced
1	red or green pepper, diced
1	cup fresh mushrooms, diced
1	bag of wide egg noodles (or you can use rice)

Topping

1	sleeve Ritz crackers
1	Tbsp poppy seed
1	stick butter, melted

Preheat oven to 350°F.

Boil chicken for 10 minutes, drain, cut into chunks. Mix chicken broth, sour cream, and soup in the bottom of a glass 9x13-inch casserole pan. Sauté onion, peppers, and mushrooms (if you like them); add to the pan. Add chicken and blend well. Bake covered for 30 minutes.

For the topping:

Crush Ritz crackers in a Ziploc bag. In a bowl, mix poppy seeds, crackers, and melted butter. Spread on top of casserole and bake 20 minutes uncovered. Serve over a bed of boiled wide egg noodles or rice.

Tips and variations: I love veggies so I often add any fresh or leftover vegetables that I have in the refrigerator.

Lunch & Dinner

State Street Inn B&B

Curried Ham Steak

Yield: 4–6 servings

"This dish fits in well with any meal. For breakfast, I would make scrambled eggs with onions or chives and either scones or biscuits. For lunch or dinner, you can serve it with rice, quinoa, or couscous and a green vegetable."

- ¼ cup butter
- ¼ cup brown sugar
- 1 Tbsp curry powder
- 2 ham steaks, ½-inch thick
- ¼ cup raisins
- 1 (16-oz.) can pineapple slices, drained
- 1 (16-oz.) can apricot halves, drained
- 1 (16-oz.) can pear halves drained

Preheat oven to 350°F.

In a saucepan, melt together butter and brown sugar. Stir in curry powder. Place ham steaks in a large shallow baking dish. Top with fruit. Pour brown sugar sauce over all and bake 30–45 minutes until it bubbles and sizzles.

Lunch & Dinner

Mary Jane's Raisin Sauce

Yield: 2–3 cups of sauce

"Serve this hot over ham. The recipe comes from my mother Mary Jane, a marvelous cook who passed in April 2012, three weeks shy of her 91st birthday."

⅓	cup brown sugar
1	Tbsp flour
½	Tbsp dry mustard
	dash salt
	dash pepper
1¾	cup water
¼	cup apple cider vinegar
¾	cup seedless raisins
1	Tbsp butter

In a saucepan mix together the sugar, flour, mustard, salt, and pepper. Stir in water and vinegar, mixing well. Bring to boil, stirring constantly.

Add raisins and butter and simmer for 10 minutes, giving the sauce an occasional stir.

Shrimp Dip

Yield: 1 large bowl of dip

"This is one of our favorite holiday dips. It's great served with club crackers. My husband, Paul, says it's the sole reason he puts on 10 pounds between Thanksgiving and Christmas. He just can't leave it alone!"

- 2 cans tomato soup, condensed (Do not dilute with water.)
- 2 (8-oz.) pkgs. cream cheese
- 1 (16-oz.) jar mayonnaise
- 1 large sweet onion, finely chopped
- 1 small can chopped black olives, drained
- 1 (2-lb.) bag frozen cooked shrimp/thawed, remove tails and put through food processor or mince with a knife.
- 1 box of Club or Ritz crackers, for dipping

In a saucepan, cook tomato soup and cream cheese on very low heat to melt, whisking together. Cool for ½ hour.

Add mayonnaise, onion, black olives, and shrimp. Blend well; cover and let set for 1 day in the refrigerator for flavors to mingle. Serve with crackers. This will hold for a week in the refrigerator, or you can freeze into smaller quantities.

Tips and variations: Perfect just the way it is.

Sicilian Nachos

Yield: 8–12 servings

"This is a very tasty appetizer for which most of the ingredients can be prepared a couple of days in advance."

1	lb. ground beef
1	small red onion, finely chopped
1	medium carrot, finely chopped
4	cloves of garlic, minced
1	tsp crushed red pepper flakes
½	cup dry red wine or beef broth
1	(15-oz.) can crushed tomatoes, undrained
1	(8-oz.) can of tomato sauce
2	bay leaves
¼	tsp salt
¼	tsp pepper
2	tsp dried basil (or 2 Tbsp fresh minced basil)
50	slices French baguette bread, 1/4-inch thick
⅔	cup olive oil
4	cloves garlic, crushed, added to olive oil
1	cup Parmesan cheese, shaved
1	cup mozzarella cheese, shredded

In a large skillet cook the first 5 ingredients until the beef is no longer pink and then add red wine. Stir in the crushed tomatoes and tomato sauce. Rinse the sauce can with a little water and add. Add bay leaves, salt, and pepper.

Bring to a boil, lower to simmer, leave uncovered for 30–40 minutes until thickened. Remove bay leaves, and add basil.

Preheat oven to 400°F. Place baguette slices tightly on a cookie sheet. Brush tops with the olive oil and garlic mixture. Bake for 3–5 minutes or until very lightly browned. Remove from oven and place a large teaspoon of the beef mixture on top of each slice. Sprinkle Parmesan cheese on top, and then mozzarella. Return to the oven for 10–15 minutes

Remove to a large platter and you are ready to serve.

This recipe has been adapted from *Taste of Home Appetizer Book*.

Lunch & Dinner

Homemade Salsa

Yield: 6 pint jars

"We are located in the heart of the thumb of Michigan, where fresh produce is always available in the summer. This recipe has been a family tradition for the last 17 years. I was given this recipe by a lady I met in the canning section of our local grocery store. I never saw her again, but I think of her every year when I make this salsa."

6	tomatoes (skins off), chopped
2	cups sweet peppers, about six peppers (green, red, yellow, orange or any combination depending on the flavor or color you want), chopped
1	cup onion, chopped
4	jalapeño peppers, diced. Leave the seeds in one to all, depending on the amount of heat you like.
3½	tsp kosher salt
1	cup cider vinegar
¼	cup sugar

Mix all ingredients together. Bring the salsa to a boil.

Fill 6 hot pint jars using a slotted spoon to drain excess liquid, and a jar funnel.

Place sterilized lids on the jars and put them in a water bath canner for 30 minutes.

Remove and allow jars to sit overnight without disturbing.

Tips and variations: The great thing about this recipe is that you can leave in more jalapeño seeds or add different peppers to make it hotter. You can leave out all seeds to make it milder, or use fewer jalapeño peppers and more sweet peppers.

Gorgonzola Cheese Spread

Yield: 2 cups

"I first tasted this spread at a downstate wine event and fell in love with its unusual combination of flavors. I traveled to Fenton's French Laundry Deli, the store that had provided the dish for the event. As the recipe for specific ingredients was not offered, I purchased 2 quarts of the spread and then set about trying to duplicate it at home. One weekend I made 3 versions of the spread and asked my guests which one most closely resembled the original. This is my closest approximation."

1	(8-oz.) pkg. cream cheese at room temperature
1	(4-oz.) pkg. blue cheese at room temperature
2	slices cooked bacon, crumbled
1–2	green onions, chopped
2	Tbsp apricot jam
1/8	tsp cayenne pepper, or to taste for hotness

Mix cream cheese and blue cheese together in a bowl; blend well. Add bacon bits, green onion, apricot jam, and pepper; blend well. Serve with water crackers.

Lunch & Dinner

Party Pretzels

Yield: 1 pound

"Guests of Sand Castle Inn love these pretzels so much,
we bag them up and hand them out along with the recipe."

1   (1-lb.) bag small pretzel twists
1   Tbsp dry ranch dressing mix
1   Tbsp lemon pepper seasoning
1   Tbsp dried dill
1   cup oil

Preheat oven to 300°F.

Put everything in a one-gallon Ziploc bag and mix, turning the bag to evenly coat the pretzels. Lay out on a baking sheet. Bake for 8 minutes. Stir the contents well. Bake for another 8 minutes.

Tips and variations: If a holiday is near, I add candies or M&Ms after baking and the pretzels are cooled.

Lunch & Dinner

Sweet Endings

Cakes, Cookies, Pies & Fruit Specialties

From your favorite Michigan B&B stay, do you have the memory of a fabulous cookie awaiting you when you returned from dinner? Or maybe some homemade chocolates left on your nightstand? Bed and breakfast innkeepers all have different practices when it comes to offering these tempting extras. In this section, Michigan innkeepers share some of their favorite yummy dessert recipes and other sweet treats.

Recipes in the Featured Recipes chapter

In this chapter

Sweet Endings

German Apple Cake

Yield: 10–12 servings

"My sister who lives in Montana had a German neighbor who gave her this recipe. Here in Oceana County we grow a lot of apples. I commonly use Jonagolds to make this. On a cool fall day this adds a heavenly aroma in the house."

5	apples, sliced thin
5	Tbsp sugar
2	tsp cinnamon
⅓	cup orange juice
3	cups flour
2⅓	cups sugar
2	tsp vanilla
½	tsp salt
4	eggs
1	cup cooking oil
1½	tsp baking soda
½	tsp baking powder

Preheat oven to 350°F. Grease a tube pan.

Toss apples with sugar and cinnamon; set aside. In a mixing bowl, blend on low speed for one minute the orange juice, flour, sugar, vanilla, salt, eggs, and cooking oil. Then mix 3 minutes on high speed. Add baking soda and baking powder. Mix 1 minute.

Fill pan, alternating 3 layers of batter and 2 layers of apples. Bake for 1½ hours.

Take out of the oven and let cool for 10 minutes. Loosen around the edges and invert onto a cake plate.

Tips and variations: You could use any baking apple to make this.

Orange Crunch Cake

Yield: 8–12 servings

"This cake is so easy and delicious, light and sweet—a house favorite."

- 1 pkg. yellow cake mix
- 1 (11-oz.) can mandarin oranges with juice
- 1 small box vanilla instant pudding
- 4 eggs
- 1 cup oil
- ½ cup chopped pecans

Sauce
- 1 cup sugar
- 1 stick butter
- ¼ cup orange juice

Preheat oven to 350°F. Grease a standard Bundt pan or 13x9-inch pan.

In a large bowl combine cake mix, oranges, pudding mix, eggs, oil, and pecans with a hand mixture. Pour into prepared pan.

Bake for 45 minutes or until done.

For sauce, place all ingredients in a small saucepan over low heat and simmer until sugar is melted; stirring frequently.

Pour sauce over warm cake in Bundt pan, wait a few minutes then flip Bundt pan onto serving platter. It will soak into the cake. If using a 13x9 pan leave in the pan and cut pieces.

Dove Nest B&B St. Joseph

Clementine Cake

Yield: 8–10 slices

"This excellent gluten-free cake is enjoyed by all the guests of Dove Nest B&B in St. Joseph, not just guests who have a gluten allergy."

4–5	clementines (slightly less than 1 lb.)
6	eggs
1	cup, plus 2 Tbsp sugar
2⅓	cups ground almonds
1	heaping teaspoon baking powder
	confectioners' sugar

Preheat oven to 375°F. Grease and line an 8-inch springform pan with parchment paper.

Put clementines in a pot of cold water and cover; bring to a boil. Cook for 2 hours. Drain and let cool. Cut clementines in half and remove seeds. Finely chop the skins, pith, and fruit by hand or use a food processor.

In a bowl, whisk eggs. Add sugar, almonds, and baking powder. Mix well. Add the chopped clementines.

Pour the cake mixture into prepared pan and bake for 30–50 minutes. Remove from the oven and let cool in the pan on a rack. When the cake is cold, you can take it out of the pan and dust it with confectioners' sugar.

This recipe has been adapted from Martin's Grocery Store Cooking School.

The Painted Turtle Inn

No Name Cake

Yield: 8–12 servings

I'm not quite sure how this cake got its name—or lack thereof—but we have always called it No Name Cake as long as I can remember. Perhaps it's too good to be restricted to a name! This cake is wonderfully moist and great for breakfast as a coffee cake or as dessert. The layering of the batter and filling creates a swirl in the cake that looks beautiful and tastes even better!

Cake

1 box yellow cake mix
1 (3¾ oz.) pkg. instant
  vanilla pudding
¾ cup vegetable oil
¾ cup water
1 tsp vanilla
4 eggs

Filling

½ cup fine ground pecans
⅓ cup sugar
2 tsp cinnamon

Glaze

1 cup powdered sugar
2–3 Tbsp milk
1 tsp butter, melted

1 tsp butter, softened

Preheat oven to 350°F. Blend cake mix, pudding, oil, water, and vanilla in the bowl of an electric mixer. Add eggs 1 at a time, mixing until incorporated. Beat 8 minutes on medium speed.

Mix the filling ingredients together in a small bowl.

Mix the glaze ingredients together in a separate bowl. Glaze should be fairly thick so it doesn't all run off the warm cake.

Grease Bundt pan with butter. Sprinkle some filling into pan and shake all over bottom and sides. Pour extra back into bowl. Pour some of the batter into the pan (to just cover the bottom of the pan), then some of the filling, then batter again and filling, ending with batter. (I also put a little filling on the top of the batter at the end.) Bake for 1 hour.

Turn cake out of pan and prick holes into it with toothpick while still warm, then pour the glaze over and let it run down the sides of the cake. Freezes well, also.

Orange Olive Oil Pumpkin Cake

Yield: 12–16 servings

"Ever since Dave Drees, innkeeper at Kingsley House B&B, opened a store selling olive oil and balsamic vinegar, he finds lots of ways to work these tasty and healthy ingredients into recipes."

2	cups all-purpose flour
2	tsp baking powder
1	tsp salt
1	tsp cinnamon
½	tsp baking soda
½	tsp ground ginger
¼	tsp nutmeg
¼	tsp cloves
4	eggs
1½	cups sugar
1	(15-oz.) can pumpkin purée
1	cup Olive Cart Blood Orange Olive Oil
1	cup chopped toasted pecans, optional

Preheat oven to 350°F. Lightly oil two 9-inch round cake pans; line each with wax paper and oil the paper. Set aside.

In a large bowl, sift together flour, baking powder, salt, cinnamon, baking soda, ginger, nutmeg, and cloves.

In a separate large bowl, beat together eggs, sugar, pumpkin, and oil. Add dry ingredients. Mix until just combined. Gently fold in pecans, if using.

Transfer batter into prepared pans, spreading evenly. Bake until a toothpick inserted in the center of each cake comes out clean, 30–35 minutes.

Cool cakes in pans for 10 minutes; invert onto wire racks and cool completely.

Tips and variations: You can order blood orange olive oil from the Olive Cart in South Haven, or find something similar at a local specialty store.

Sweet Endings

Select Harvest Gewürztraminer Cake

Yield: 16 servings

½ cup pecans, chopped
1 (18 oz.) yellow cake mix
1 small package vanilla instant pudding
½ cup water
1 cup Chateau Chantal Select Harvest Gewürztraminer, divided
½ cup vegetable oil
4 eggs

Icing
¼ lb. butter
1 cup sugar
¼ cup water

Preheat oven to 325°F. Line bottom of greased 10-inch tube pan with chopped pecans. Blend boxed cake mix, pudding, water, ½ cup Select Harvest Gewürztraminer, vegetable oil, and 4 eggs with mixer and pour into pecan-lined tube pan. Bake for 50–60 minutes.

In a small saucepan, mix and boil the butter, sugar, and water for 3 minutes. Remove from heat and then add remaining ½ cup Select Harvest Gewürztraminer. Pour this mixture over hot cake and leave in pan until completely cool before turning out.

Caramel Banana Cake with Walnuts

Yield: 8-12 servings

"What a combination of flavors—exciting and different."

- 1 pkg. white cake mix, pudding included (18½ oz.)
- 4 eggs
- ¾ cup water
- ⅓ cup cooking oil
- 1 cup bananas, mashed
- ¾ cup chopped walnuts
- 1 pkg. Instant butterscotch pudding (3¾ oz.)
  confectioners' sugar, to garnish

Preheat oven to 350°F. Grease and flour a 12-cup Bundt pan.

In a large bowl, combine cake mix, eggs, water, cooking oil and bananas. Blend just to moisten; beat 2 minutes at medium speed. Stir in walnuts.

Set aside 1½ cups batter. Stir pudding into remaining batter until blended. Pour batter into Bundt pan. Top with reserved batter.

Bake about 50 minutes or until cake tests done with a tooth pick. Cool in pan 10–15 minutes, turn out on wire rack or serving plate to compete cooling. Sprinkle with confectioners' sugar.

Tips and variations: Substitute instant banana pudding mix in place of butterscotch, and decrease the amount of bananas to ½ cup.

Sweet Endings

Hankerd Inn

Pumpkin Dessert

Yield: 8–12 servings

"Enjoy this sweet treat as you enjoy the colors of fall."

- 1 (29-oz.) can pumpkin
- 1½ tsp cinnamon
- 1 cup Carnation milk
- ¼ tsp nutmeg
- 1 cup white sugar
- 1 cup brown sugar
- 4 eggs
- 1 box yellow cake mix
- 1 cup nuts
- 1 cup butter, melted

Preheat oven to 325°F. Grease a 9x13-inch pan.

Mix the first seven ingredients together. Pour into prepared baking pan. Sprinkle dry cake mix over the pumpkin mixture. Press cake mix slightly. Sprinkle nuts over cake mix and pour melted butter over all.

Bake for one hour.

Tips and variations: This is good topped with whipped cream when serving.

Susan's Brownie Pie

Yield: 6–8 servings

"I have my mom to thank for this recipe. This easy pie is the only birthday cake my sister Susan ever requests. To share the recipe and yet hold back vital information, my mother neglects to mention that the cookies required are almost always found in a grocery's baking aisle, not with the other cookies."

4	egg whites, use large eggs
¾	cup sugar
16	Nabisco Famous Chocolate Wafers, finely crushed
½	cup chopped walnuts
½	tsp vanilla
	dash salt
8	oz. whipping cream
3	Tbsp confectioners' sugar, to taste
⅓	cup Hershey's Semi-Sweet Mini Morsels

Preheat oven to 325°F. Grease a 9-inch pie plate.

Whip egg whites in a bowl with electric mixer until stiff peaks form. Add sugar slowly while continuing to whip. Stir in by hand the wafers, walnuts, vanilla and salt.

Pour into prepared pie plate.

Bake 35 minutes or until tester inserted in center comes out clean. Let pie cool.

Whip cream with electric mixer until soft peaks form. Add confectioners' sugar slowly while continuing to whip. Spread whipped cream over cooled pie with a knife or metal spatula. Garnish with chocolate mini morsels.

Tips and variations: Curled shavings of semi-sweet chocolate look more impressive than mini morsels. Don't cop out and use Cool Whip. Susan wouldn't approve.

Sweet Endings

Sugar Cream Pie

Yield: 8–12 servings

"In summer we serve this with fresh-from-the-garden raspberries. In winter I make frozen raspberries into a velvety sauce … yummy. The original recipe came from a fabulous recipe book, Hollyhocks & Radishes *by Bonnie Stewart Mickelson, which is jam-packed with recipes and stories of the beautiful Upper Peninsula."*

1	cup sugar
½	cup minus 1 tablespoon flour
2	cups heavy cream
½	tsp vanilla
1	9-inch pie shell, unbaked
1	Tbsp butter

Preheat oven to 425°F.

Combine sugar with flour in a mixing bowl. Add cream and mix well. Add the vanilla. Pour into pie shell and dot with butter slices.

Bake 15 minutes.

Reduce heat to 350° and bake 45 minutes more, or until the center is bubbly and thickened. If the edges of the crust begin to overly brown, cover it with strips of foil.

Tips and variations: Best served with raspberries, but fresh sliced peaches are good, too.

Sweet Endings

Key Lime Cheesecake

Yield: 8–12 servings

"Using the same basic recipe, I've flavored this light cheesecake in many different ways. It's been a turtle cheesecake, a strawberry cheesecake and a Chambord cheesecake, but key lime is my favorite."

Crust
- 2 cups honey graham cracker crumbs
- ½ cup walnuts, finely chopped
- 1 tsp cinnamon
- ⅓ cup butter, softened
- ¼ cup sugar

Filling
- 3½ (8-oz.) pkgs. cream cheese, room temperature
- 1 cup sugar, or less
- 5 eggs, separated
- 1 Tbsp vanilla
- ¼ cup juice of key limes

Topping
- 1⅔ cups sour cream
- 1 Tbsp sugar or more to taste
- 1 tsp vanilla

Preheat oven to 350°F. In food processor, pulse crust ingredients until combined and crushed. A pinch of the crust ingredients should hold its shape. Add more butter if necessary. Press firmly into the bottom and part way up the sides of a 10-inch springform pan. Bake 10–15 minutes. Remove from the oven and let cool.

Blend cream cheese, sugar, 5 egg yolks, and vanilla until smooth in a clean food processor bowl, stopping to scrape the sides a couple times. Add lime juice slowly through the feeding tube and stop to taste periodically until you achieve the balance of sweet and tart. If filling seems runnier than a cake batter, add a bit more cream cheese.

In large bowl, beat egg whites until stiff. Fold in the cream cheese mixture. Pour onto cooled, baked crust. Bake until a toothpick removes cleanly from center, 45–60 minutes. Increase heat to 400°F. Blend ingredients for the topping and spread on top of the cheesecake. Bake 10 minutes. Cool for several hours before serving.

Tips and variations: If cracks develop in the top of the cheesecake, skip the sour cream topping and, just before serving, slather on 8 ounces of heavy cream that you've whipped and sweetened with confectioners' sugar. Nobody ever objects to that.

Sweet Endings

Chocolate Chip & Cranberry Brownies

Yield: 48 pieces

"Greet guests and family with the delicious scent of chocolate when they arrive at your door. Our guests love these moist, flavorful brownies."

1⅓	cups all-purpose flour
⅔	cup granulated sugar
⅔	cup brown sugar, packed
½	cup cocoa
½	tsp baking powder
½	tsp salt
½	cup chocolate chips
½	cup dried cranberries
½	cup butter
3	eggs
1	tsp vanilla

Preheat oven to 350°F. Grease a 9x13-inch baking pan.

In a large mixing bowl, combine flour, sugars, cocoa, baking powder, and salt. Stir in chocolate chips and dried cranberries.

Melt butter. Add eggs and vanilla to dry ingredients; stir in melted butter. Batter will be very thick.

Spread evenly in baking pan. Bake for 25–30 minutes. Do not over bake. Cool in pan on wire rack. When cool, cut into desired pieces and enjoy.

Tips and variations: Make up several batches of the dry mix, label and store in large Ziploc bags. When you need a quick dessert, just melt butter, stir in eggs and vanilla and pop into the oven.

Chocolate Decadence

Yield: 12–16 servings

"This is our "REAL" Signature recipe. The name Chocolate Decadence reflects the intense chocolate flavor, not the level of expertise required to succeed at this recipe. The five ingredients required are more than likely in your pantry. The simplicity of this dessert belies its sumptuousness.

For chocoholics, this is to die for. Served with whipped cream, stout beer, or mixed berries, this is the kind of dessert for which your friends will remember you best. It is better than any we have sampled in any restaurants across North America—and we have 'researched' many. It is best served cold (and a day or more old) as the texture and taste get better and better. Enjoy!"

Cake

16 oz. semisweet or bittersweet chocolate, cut into pieces, or chocolate chips
5 oz. unsalted butter
5 large eggs, separated (room temperature)
1 Tbsp flour
¼ tsp cream of tartar
3 Tbsp granulated sugar

Whipped cream topping

4 cups heavy cream
3 Tbsp sugar

Preheat oven to 425°F. Butter an 8x2-inch round cake pan and line bottom with a round of parchment or wax paper.

Melt chocolate and butter in a small bowl set over a saucepan of simmering water or a double boiler over low heat. Stir until smooth. Whisk in egg yolks and flour until well mixed. Set aside.

Beat egg whites and cream of tartar in a cold, clean dry mixing bowl at medium speed until soft peaks form. Gradually sprinkle in granulated sugar, beating at high speed until stiff but not dry. Mix about ¼ of the egg white mixture into chocolate mixture to lighten it; mix well. Quickly but gently, fold in remaining egg white mixture.

Sweet Endings

(Continued from previous page)

Pour batter into prepared cake pan. Bake for exactly 15 minutes (top will be set, but a tester will not come out clean). Remove from oven and cool in pan. Cake will rise somewhat, especially around the edges. It will appear undercooked, but this is OK! It will shrink and sink in the center as it cools, do not worry! This is perfectly normal. Let cool completely in the pan on the rack. Run a thin knife around the edge of cake. Cover and chill completely in the refrigerator.

Run a thin knife around the edge to release it from the pan. Warm the bottom of the pan on a stove burner on low heat for just a few seconds, moving the pan around on the burner; invert onto a plate to unmold. Peel the parchment liner from the bottom of the cake and invert on serving plate. At this point, the cake will be higher around the edges than in the center. The cake can be made up to 4 days in advance. Wrap well and refrigerate until needed or freeze up to 3 months.

For sweetened whipped cream, whip together the heavy cream with sugar until soft peaks form.

To serve: Remove from refrigerator 1 hour before serving. Cut in wedges and serve with sweetened whipped cream and fresh fruit. Our favorite is raspberries or strawberries!

To serve more formally: Serve with fruit coulis: Purée 1 cup fresh raspberries with ½ cup sugar in a food processor or blender, then force through a fine sieve into a bowl. Chill until ready to serve.

Or, frost with a whipped chocolate ganache: In a food processor chop 12 ounces of good quality chocolate into small pieces. Heat 10 ounces heavy whipping cream in a small saucepan just until bubbles form on the edges. With the motor running pour hot cream into chocolate and process until smooth. Transfer to bowl and cool until frosting consistency.

This recipe has been adapted from *Cocolat*, by Alice Medrich.

Banana Cupcakes with Peanut Butter Frosting

Yield: 12 cupcakes

Cupcakes
1¼ cups all-purpose flour
1½ tsp baking powder
½ tsp baking soda
¼ tsp salt
2 very ripe large bananas, peeled
½ cup sour cream
1½ tsp vanilla extract
¾ cup sugar
½ cup (1 stick) unsalted butter, room temperature
1 large egg
1 large egg yolk

Frosting
1½ cups powdered sugar
1 (8-oz.) pkg. cream cheese, room temperature
½ cup (1 stick) unsalted butter, room temperature
½ cup smooth peanut butter (do not use old-fashioned or freshly ground)
lightly salted roasted peanuts, chopped (optional)

For cupcakes: Position rack in center of oven and preheat to 350°F. Line standard (⅓ cup) muffin cups with paper liners.

Whisk flour, baking powder, baking soda, and salt in a medium bowl to blend. Mash bananas with a fork in another medium bowl until smooth. Mix sour cream and vanilla into bananas. Using electric mixer, beat sugar and butter in large bowl until light and fluffy, about 3 minutes. Add egg and egg yolk and beat until well blended.

Add flour mixture in three additions alternately with banana-sour cream mixture in two additions, beginning and ending with flour mixture and beating just until blended after each addition.

Divide batter among prepared muffin cups (generous 1/4 cup for each). Bake cupcakes until tester inserted into center of each comes out clean, about 20 minutes. Transfer cupcakes to rack and let cool completely.

For frosting: Sift powdered sugar into large bowl. Add cream cheese, butter, and peanut butter. Using electric mixer, beat mixture until smooth. Spread frosting over top of cupcakes, dividing equally. Sprinkle lightly with chopped peanuts, if desired.

Tips and variations: Can be made one day ahead. Store air-tight at room temperature.

Blueberry Buckles

Yield: 8 servings

Topping

1	cup sugar
1	cup all-purpose flour
1	tsp cinnamon
½	cup cold butter

Batter

½	tsp salt
¾	tsp baking powder
¾	cup plus 2 Tbsp all-purpose flour
1½	tsp grated lemon zest
1	tsp vanilla
½	cup milk
6	Tbsp whipping cream
1	egg
¼	cup soft butter
¼	cup sugar
1¾	cups fresh or frozen blueberries

Preheat oven to 425°F. Generously grease eight ½-cup porcelain ramekins.

For topping, using your fingers, blend first four ingredients, cutting in the butter until mixture resembles a coarse meal. Chill while making batter.

In a medium bowl, sift together salt, baking powder, and flour. Stir in lemon zest with a fork. In a small bowl, combine vanilla, milk, and whipping cream. In another small bowl, beat egg well. Cream soft butter and sugar together in a large bowl. Mix in half of the beaten egg. Mix in dry ingredients and milk/whipping cream mixture. Then add the other half of the beaten egg.

Into each prepared ramekin, layer in order: 2 tablespoons topping, ½ cup berries, 2 tablespoons batter, more berries, 2 tablespoons topping.

Bake in center of oven for 15 minutes or less, until golden. Serve warm.

Rhubarb Crisp

Yield: 4–6 servings

*"We put something sweet on the breakfast table every morning.
Of course, this could be a dessert, too."*

- 3 cups rhubarb, chopped
- 2 eggs
- ½ cup sugar
- ⅓ cup buttermilk
- 3 Tbsp flour
- ½ tsp nutmeg

Topping
- ½ stick butter, softened
- ½ cup brown sugar
- ½ cup white sugar
- ½ cup flour
- 1 Tbsp cinnamon
- ½ cup chopped nuts

Preheat oven to 350°F.

Combine rhubarb, eggs, sugar, buttermilk, flour, and nutmeg in a 9x9-inch square baking dish until well blended. For the topping, blend the butter, sugars, flour, and cinnamon in a small bowl until crumbly. Stir in nuts. Sprinkle over rhubarb mixture. Bake 25 minutes. Top with whipped cream.

Rhubarb "Good-Anytime-of-the-Day" Crisp

Yield: 8–9 servings

"This is good any time of day. For breakfast, you can top with a little Greek yogurt or sweet cream. For lunch or dinner, French vanilla ice cream is just the ticket. It seems everyone in our area has rhubarb growing in the garden."

5	cups rhubarb, finely chopped
1⅓	cups sugar
⅔	cup flour
½	tsp salt
1	Tbsp cinnamon
½	tsp nutmeg
3	Tbsp water, divided

Topping

¾	cup brown sugar
¾	cup flour
1	cup quick oats
½	cup butter, softened
½	tsp salt
½	cup walnuts or pecans, chopped

Preheat oven to 350°F.

In a bowl, mix rhubarb, sugar, flour, salt, cinnamon, and nutmeg. Divide mix among 8 or 9 eight-ounce ramekins.

Sprinkle water over rhubarb mixture, dividing among the ramekins.

Combine brown sugar, flour, oats, butter, salt, and nuts into a crumbly mixture for topping. Sprinkle over each ramekin of rhubarb.

Bake for 30 minutes.

Tips and variations: This recipe is good with apples or peaches if you do not care for rhubarb.

Sweet Endings

Rhubarb & Strawberry Crisp

Yield: 6 servings

*"At Dewey Lake Manor we love to bake with freshly picked fruit
from our garden. This recipe came from a friend of mine
who is a great gardener and a very good cook."*

Fruit Mixture

1½	cups strawberries, diced
2	cups rhubarb, diced
1	cup sugar
1	egg, beaten
2	Tbsp self-rising flour
2	Tbsp lemon juice
½	tsp cinnamon

Topping

1	cup self-rising flour
⅓	cup butter, softened
½	cup sugar

Preheat oven to 350°F.

For fruit mixture, mix all ingredients together in a large bowl. Pour into a 9x9-inch pan.

For topping, mix ingredients together in a small bowl. Place on top of fruit mixture.

Bake 45–50 minutes.

Sweet Endings

Mango Pear Crisp

Yield: 8–10 servings

6 medium pears (about 2 lbs.) firm but ripe, peeled, cored
3 mangoes, firm and slightly ripe, peeled, cut into 1/2-inch slices
¾ cup all-purpose flour
½ cup sugar
½ tsp salt
8 Tbsp (1 stick) cold butter, cut into small pieces

Position a rack in the lower third of the oven. Preheat the oven to 375°F.

Slice the pears in half and then each half into 4 wedges. Place in an unbuttered 2-quart baking dish that is 2-inches deep. Add the mangoes and toss to combine with the pears.

In a bowl, stir together the flour, sugar, salt. Add the butter.

Using a pastry blender or 2 knives, cut the butter into the dry ingredients until the mixture resembles coarse crumbs. This can be done with a mixer or a food processor, taking care not to blend the butter too thoroughly. Scatter the topping evenly over the fruit. Tap the dish on the counter once or twice to settle in the crumbs. Bake until the topping is golden brown, the juices are bubbling, and the fruit is tender when pierced with a skewer, about 50–60 minutes. Serve warm.

Flourless Oatmeal Peanut Butter Cookies

Yield: 2 dozen cookies

"These cookies get raves from our guests and lots of requests for the recipe. They are great for the health-conscious people wishing to avoid white flour. Trying to keep them in the cookie jar and away from my husband is the challenge."

1¾	cups peanut butter
½	cup butter, softened
1	cup sugar
1	cup packed brown sugar
3	eggs
1	tsp vanilla extract
4½	cups old-fashioned oats
2	tsp baking soda
1	cup semi-sweet chocolate chips
1	cup dried cherries or cranberries
1	cup chopped walnuts

Preheat oven to 350°F.

In a large mixing bowl, cream peanut butter, butter, and sugars. Add eggs one at a time, beating well after each addition. Beat in vanilla.

In a medium bowl, combine oats and baking soda. Gradually add oats and baking soda to the creamed mixture. Stir in chips, cherries or cranberries, and walnuts.

Drop by heaping tablespoon 2 inches apart onto ungreased baking sheets. Bake for 12–14 minutes. Adjust baking time for crispy or moist cookie. Remove to wire racks or brown paper bag sheets to cool.

Sweet Endings

Peanut Butter Cookies

Yield: 36 cookies

"I found this recipe years ago in a magazine. It is considered a healthy recipe. This is a diabetic-friendly recipe. Many of our guests at A Dove Nest B&B in Kingston comment on the great peanut butter taste of these cookies. And the best thing about these cookies—they only have three ingredients."

1   cup sugar
1   cup peanut butter
1   egg

Preheat oven to 375°F. Grease cookie sheets.

In a small bowl, combine sugar, peanut butter, and egg. Roll mixture into 36 one-inch balls. Place balls 2 inches apart on cookie sheets.

Flatten each ball with a glass that has been slightly greased and dipped in sugar.

Bake for 9 minutes, until edges are set and the bottoms are light brown.

Peanut Butter Oatmeal Chocolate Chip Cookies

Yield: 24 cookies

"A huge favorite with our guests—these cookies are moist, chewy, and easy to make—a perfect treat for cold winter nights. They are guaranteed to satisfy anyone's inner chocoholic cravings."

½	cup butter
½	cup sugar
⅓	cup firmly packed brown sugar
½	cup peanut butter
1	large egg
1	tsp vanilla (or more)
1	cup unbleached all-purpose flour
½	cup oatmeal
1	tsp baking soda
¼	tsp salt
1	(12-oz.) bag semi-sweet chocolate chips*

Preheat oven to 350°F.

Cream butter and sugars together in a bowl. Add peanut butter, egg, and vanilla. Mix well.

In another bowl, mix dry ingredients together and add to butter mixture. Add chips and mix well. Either drop onto pan or roll into small balls. Bake for 10–12 minutes.

Cool for 5 minutes on sheet.

*Milk, dark or white chocolate chips are okay, too.

This recipe has been adapted from Food.com (http://www.food.com/recipe/peanut-butter-oatmeal-chocolate-chip-cookies-145478).

Sweet Endings

Red Velvet Cookies

Yield: 6 dozen cookies

*"Yummy cookie for any time of the year.
They look especially inviting on a holiday cookie tray."*

1 cup shortening	**Frosting**
1 cup sugar	1½ cups butter, softened
¾ cup packed brown sugar	3¾ cups confectioners' sugar
3 eggs, separated	⅛ tsp salt
2 tsp red food coloring	3–4 Tbsp milk
4 cups all-purpose flour	Red sugar sprinkles
3 Tbsp baking cocoa	(optional)
3 tsp baking powder	
1 tsp salt	
1 cup buttermilk	
2 cups chocolate chips	

Preheat oven to 350°F. Grease baking sheets.

In a large bowl, cream the shortening and sugars until light and fluffy. Beat in egg yolks and food coloring. In a separate bowl, combine the flour, cocoa, baking powder, and salt. Add to the creamed mixture alternately with buttermilk, beating well after each addition.

In another bowl with clean beaters, beat egg whites until stiff peaks form; fold into batter. Fold in chocolate chips.

Drop by tablespoonfuls 2 inches apart onto baking sheets. Bake 12–14 minutes or until set. Remove to wire rack to cool completely.

For frosting, in a large bowl, beat the butter, confectioners' sugar, and salt until blended. Add enough milk to achieve desired consistency. Frost cookies. Sprinkle with red sugar sprinkles.

Store in an air-tight container or freeze for up to one month.

This recipe has been adapted from the *Taste of Home Cookbook* (2010).

Sweet Endings

Super-Soft Snickerdoodle Cookies

Yield: 24 cookies

"A favorite at our inn."

1	cup (2 sticks) unsalted butter
½	cup dark brown sugar
1	cup white sugar
3	cups flour
¼	tsp cinnamon
¼	tsp nutmeg
1	tsp baking soda
½	tsp salt
3	eggs
1	tsp vanilla extract

For the cinnamon sugar

¼	cup white sugar
1	Tbsp cinnamon
¼	tsp nutmeg

Preheat oven to 425°F.

Gently melt the butter in a saucepan or in the microwave and let it cool while you mix the dry ingredients. In a bowl, stir together the sugars, flour, spices, baking soda, and salt. Whisk the eggs into the cooled butter and add the vanilla.

Stir the wet ingredients into the dry ingredients, stirring just until it comes together.

In a soup plate or shallow bowl, mix together the white sugar, cinnamon, and nutmeg.

Form small 1½-inch balls of dough and roll them in the cinnamon sugar. Place them on an unlined, ungreased baking sheet and flatten slightly.

Bake for 7 minutes, then remove and let cool on the baking sheet for 5 minutes. Remove to a wire rack.

Tips and variations: The dough can be refrigerated for up to 5 days, well wrapped. It can also be frozen in logs.

Sweet Endings

Chocolate Chocolate-Chip Meringue Cookies

Yield: 48 cookies

"Larry's Chocolate Meringue Cookies are so light and airy, sweet and crispy, that they just melt in your mouth. The outside is nice and crisp, yet the inside remains wonderfully soft and puffy. They are delightful eaten just as they are or they make a very nice accompaniment to a plated dessert, ice cream or port wine. Enjoy!"

3	large egg whites
¼	tsp cream of tartar
¼	tsp salt
1	cup sugar
3	Tbsp unsweetened cocoa
3	Tbsp semisweet chocolate mini-chips

Preheat oven to 300°F. Cover a baking sheet with parchment paper; secure to baking sheet with masking tape.

Beat egg whites, cream of tartar, and salt at high speed with a mixer until soft peaks form. Add sugar, 1 tablespoon at a time, beating until stiff peaks form. Sift cocoa over egg white mixture; fold in. Fold in mini-chips.

Drop batter by level tablespoonfuls onto prepared baking sheet. Bake for 40 minutes or until crisp. Cool on pan on a wire rack. Repeat procedure with remaining batter, reusing parchment paper. Store in an airtight container.

Tips and variations: Add finely chopped walnuts or pecans for a nutty twist!

This recipe has been adapted from *Cooking Light Magazine*.

Sweet Endings

Pumpkin Chocolate Chip Cookies

Yield: 60 cookies

"When pumpkins begin to frost outdoors, it's time to warm up your taste buds indoors with these delicious pumpkin cookies. They are chewy, packed with flavor, and super easy to make."

1	cup (2 sticks) unsalted butter, softened
1	cup white sugar
1	cup light brown sugar
2	large eggs
1	tsp vanilla extract
1	cup canned pumpkin purée
3	cups all-purpose flour
2	tsp baking soda
½	tsp salt
1	tsp ground cinnamon
½	tsp ground ginger
¼	tsp ground nutmeg
¼	tsp ground cloves
2	cups (12-oz. bag) milk chocolate chips, not semisweet

Preheat oven to 350°F. Spray cookie sheets with nonstick spray or line them with parchment paper.

In a large bowl, beat the butter until smooth with a mixer. Beat in the white and brown sugars, a little at a time, until the mixture is light and fluffy. Beat in the eggs 1 at a time, then mix in the vanilla and pumpkin purée. In a large bowl, whisk together the flour, baking soda, salt, cinnamon, ginger, nutmeg, and cloves. Slowly beat the flour mixture into the batter in thirds. Stir in the chips.

Scoop the cookie dough by heaping tablespoons onto the prepared cookie sheets and bake for 15–20 minutes, or until the cookies are browned around the edges. Remove the cookie sheets from the oven and let them rest for 2 minutes. Remove the cookies with a spatula and cool them on wire racks.

Sweet Endings

Grammy's Spice Cookies

Yield: 48 cookies

"A natural for fall and holiday baking. These mouthwatering frosted treats are irresistible. Our guests can't stop eating them!"

2 sticks (1 cup) unsalted butter, softened, divided
1 cup sugar
¼ cup molasses
1 large egg
2 cups all-purpose flour
2 tsp baking soda
¾ tsp ground ginger
¾ tsp ground cloves
½ tsp fine sea salt

Icing
3¾ cups confectioners' sugar
1 tsp vanilla extract
3 Tbsp heavy cream or milk, more as needed
1–2 Tbsp Irish whiskey, optional

Preheat oven to 375°F. Line several baking sheets with parchment paper or nonstick liners.

Using an electric mixer, beat 12 Tbsp butter with the sugar, molasses, and egg until fluffy, about 2 minutes. Slowly beat in flour, baking soda, spices, and salt.

Shape dough into walnut-sized balls and place 2 inches apart on baking sheets.

Bake until firm, about 10–12 minutes. Remove with spatula and let cool on wire racks.

In a separate bowl, beat remaining butter with confectioners' sugar until smooth to make the icing. Go slowly so you don't create a sugar storm. Beat in vanilla and enough cream or milk, and whiskey if using, to make a spreadable frosting. Spread on fully cooled cookies.

Tips and variations: Double the amount of spices (cinnamon, ginger, and cloves) for a more pronounced flavor.

Chocolate Truffles

Yield: 16–20 truffles

"Almost anyone who loves chocolate will also love these truffles. They are easy to make, although a bit time consuming. They are worth the time and trouble. You can make truffles in so many different flavors, but some of my favorites are hazelnut, peppermint and raspberry."

- 1 cup heavy cream
- 16 oz. semi-sweet or bittersweet chocolate (I prefer semi-sweet. Pick only the highest quality.)
- 1 tsp vanilla or other flavorings such as Amaretto (2 Tbsp), Almond extract (1 tsp), hazelnut liquor (2 Tbsp), peppermint extract (1 tsp, or to taste)

Truffle coatings
Dutch cocoa powder
finely chopped walnuts, pecans or almonds
coconut, toasted or not

In a small, heavy saucepan, bring the heavy cream to a simmer (this may take a while). Be sure to stir and scrape down the sides with a rubber spatula every few minutes.

Place chocolate in a separate bowl. Pour the hot cream over the chocolate. Add your chosen flavoring and allow to stand for a few minutes; then stir until smooth. This chocolate base is called ganache.

Allow to cool, then place in the refrigerator for 3–4 hours.

Line a baking sheet with parchment paper. Remove the ganache from the refrigerator and with a melon baller, scoop up balls approximately 1 inch in diameter. Roll quickly in your hands. If you do not work quickly, the chocolate will begin to melt from the warmth of your skin. Place on the baking sheet. When you have finished rolling the truffles, you may roll them in one of the coatings: cocoa, nuts or coconut.

Tip: I put each truffle in a little candy paper cup. We package them in cellophane bags of 5 or 6 truffles each. Best stored in a covered container in the refrigerator.

Sweet Endings

Cherry Brandy Truffles

Yield: 20–25 truffles

1 lb. Callebaut milk chocolate
4 Tbsp unsalted butter
1 cup whipping cream
½ cup Chateau Chantal Cerise (cherry port)
  nuts, finely chopped (optional)
½ lb. Callebaut bittersweet chocolate for dipping

Break chocolate up in small pieces. Melt in double boiler over simmering water. Add butter and whipping cream. Stir in the Cerise. Finely chopped nuts may be added. Chill until firm enough to roll into 1-inch balls. Freeze.

Dip into melted bittersweet chocolate. Can be drizzled with white chocolate or decorated with nuts.

Fudge Caramel Delight

Yield: approximately 100–1-inch bars

"These have gotten rave reviews from all who have tried them!"

1	cup (6 oz.) milk chocolate chips
¼	cup butterscotch chips
¼	cup creamy peanut butter
¼	cup butter
1	cup sugar
¼	cup evaporated milk
1½	cups marshmallow crème (one 7 oz. jar)
¼	cup creamy peanut butter
1	tsp vanilla
1½	cups lightly chopped salted peanuts
1	pkg. (14 oz.) caramels
¼	cup heavy or whipping cream
1	cup (6 oz.) milk chocolate chips
¼	cup butterscotch chips
¼	cup creamy peanut butter

Combine the first three ingredients in a 2–cup container and microwave until melted (about 1½ minutes). Stir until smooth. Spread onto the bottom of a lightly greased 9x13-inch pan. Refrigerate until set.

For the filling: melt butter in a heavy saucepan over medium-high heat. Add sugar and milk. Bring to a boil; boil and stir for 5 minutes. Remove from heat; stir in the marshmallow crème, peanut butter, and vanilla. Add peanuts. Spread over the first layer. Refrigerate until set.

Combine the caramels and cream in a 2-quart glass measuring container; microwave 1½ minutes or so until completely melted and smooth. It may need another 30 seconds. Spread over the layer of filling. Refrigerate until set.

For the icing: repeat the instructions for the first three ingredients. Spread over the top of the caramel layer. Refrigerate for at least 1 hour. Cut into 1 inch squares. Store in the refrigerator.

Sweet Endings

Olive Oil Biscotti Dipped in Chocolate

Yield: 16–18 biscotti

*"Australia produces outstanding extra virgin olive oils. For this dish,
Dave the innkeeper uses one that comes from a region north of Melbourne.
It's a nutty, fruit-intense oil with spicy overtones and a peppery finish.
It's available from the Olive Cart in South Haven."*

½	cup sugar
2	eggs
3	Tbsp Olive Cart Australian Olive Oil
2	Tbsp maple syrup
1	tsp vanilla
1¼	cup all-purpose flour
1½	tsp baking powder
1	tsp cinnamon
¼	tsp salt
½	cup chopped dried cranberries
½	cup chopped pistachios
½	cup semisweet chocolate chips

Preheat oven to 350°F. Lightly oil a baking sheet.

In a large bowl, beat together sugar, eggs, oil, maple syrup, and vanilla until smooth.

In a separate large bowl, sift together flour, baking powder, cinnamon, and salt.

Add to egg mixture; beat until just mixed. Stir in cranberries and pistachios.

Turn dough out onto a lightly floured surface; knead 10 times until dough holds. Divide dough in half; form two flat logs, each about 9 inches long and 3 inches wide.

Bake 25 minutes, until lightly browned. Cool 10 minutes on baking sheet; reduce oven temperature to 325°F. Cut logs on the diagonal into ½-inch thick slices. Return to baking sheet; bake an additional 10 minutes, turning once. Cool on a wire rack.

Meanwhile, place chocolate chips in a microwave and cook until melted, about 1 minute; stirring every 30 seconds. When melted, whisk until smooth, dip biscotti tips into chocolate and place on wax paper to fully dry.

Sweet Endings

Cranberry Chocolate Chip Biscotti

Yield: 2 1/2 dozen

"Biscotti are basically a twice-baked, biscuit-like cookie intended for dunking. Our guests love to enjoy this biscotti dipped into coffee or our homemade hot cocoa. I grew up in an Italian area of New Jersey, so for me this is a little bit of home. These are fun to make and eat."

2¾ cups all-purpose flour	1/8 tsp salt
1 cup sugar	1 Tbsp vegetable oil
½ cup dried cranberries	1 tsp almond extract
1/3 cup semi-sweet chocolate chips	1 tsp vanilla extract
2 tsp baking powder	3 large eggs

Preheat oven to 350°F. Coat a baking sheet with cooking spray.

Lightly spoon flour into dry measuring cups, leveling with a knife. Combine the flour and the next 5 ingredients in a large bowl. In a separate bowl, combine oil, extracts and eggs. Whisk together. Add to flour mixture, stirring until well-blended. (Dough will be dry and crumbly).

Turn the dough out onto a lightly floured surface. Knead lightly 7–8 times. Divide the dough in half. Shape each portion into an 8-inch long roll. Place rolls 6 inches apart on the baking sheet. Flatten each roll to 1-inch thickness.

Bake for 35 minutes. Remove rolls from baking sheet. Cool 10 minutes on a wire rack. Cut each roll diagonally into 15 (½-inch) slices. Place the slices, cut sides down, on baking sheet. Reduce oven temperature to 325°F. and bake for 10 minutes.

Turn cookies over; bake an additional 10 minutes (cookies will be slightly soft in the center but will harden as they cool). Remove from baking sheet, cool completely on wire rack.

Tips and variations: I like to add pistachios. They taste great and give a wonderful color to the biscotti.

Drizzle with a combination of white and dark chocolate (melted in the microwave) or use either to frost with a layer on the bottom, once the biscotti has cooled.

Sweet Endings

Lemon Zucchini Drops

Yield: 24 cookies

½	cup butter or margarine, softened
1	cup sugar
1	egg
1	cup finely shredded zucchini
1	tsp grated lemon peel
2	cups all-purpose flour
1	tsp baking soda
1	tsp baking powder
1	tsp cinnamon
½	tsp salt
½	cup raisins
½	cup walnuts, chopped

Lemon Glaze

2	cups confectioners' sugar
2–3	Tbsp lemon juice

Preheat oven to 375 degrees F. Lightly grease a cookie sheet.

In a mixing bowl, cream the butter and sugar together. Beat in the egg, zucchini, and lemon peel.

In a large bowl, combine the flour, baking soda, baking powder, cinnamon, and salt. Gradually add the creamed mixture. Stir in raisins and walnuts.

Drop by tablespoonfuls 3 inches apart on cookie sheet. Bake for 8–10 minutes or until lightly brown. Remove to wire racks to cool.

For glaze, combine the sugar and enough lemon juice to get a thin spreading consistency.

Spread or just drizzle over the cooled cookies. Enjoy!

Souffléd Lemon Custard

Yield: 10-12 servings

"I found this recipe in 1990 and kept it for years before serving it to a gathering of innkeepers. Many copies of the recipe went home with innkeepers that night."

½	cup unsalted butter, softened
1½	cups sugar
6	large eggs, separated
⅔	cup fresh lemon juice
⅔	cup flour
	grated zest of 3 lemons
2	cups milk
1	cup heavy whipping cream
½	tsp salt

Preheat oven to 350°F. Lightly grease a 9-inch round pan or 10-12 individual ramekins.

Cream butter and sugar together in a large bowl until light and fluffy. Beat in yolks one at a time, beating well after each addition. Beat in juice, flour, and zest. Stir in milk and cream until well combined. Whip egg whites with salt until soft peaks form. Stir ¼ of whites into lemon mixture. Fold in remaining whites gently but thoroughly.

Pour into cake pan. Set into a larger pan and add enough hot water to reach halfway up the side of the cake pan. Place in the middle of the oven. Bake for 50–60 minutes or until just set and top is golden. Cool slightly, serve warm.

Tips and variations: I find this makes more than a cake pan can hold. Ramekins are a good substitute. Decrease baking time to about 35 minutes. Delicious served chilled.

This recipe has been adapted from Hamersly Bistro in Boston.

Sweet Endings

Fruit Pizza

Yield: 12 servings

"Who wouldn't love this decadent fruit course? Just imagine a sugar cookie crust and a sweet cream cheese frosting topped with yummy fresh fruit. One recent guest remarked 'Dessert first is always a good idea!' and then she polished it off. We've also use this dish when we have a High Tea."

1½ cups sugar, plus 2–3 Tbsp for coating crust	**Frosting**
	12 oz cream cheese, softened
14 Tbsp (1¾ sticks) unsalted butter, softened	7½ Tbsp unsalted butter, softened
2 tsp vanilla extract	1 tsp vanilla extract
2 large eggs, room temperature	1¾ cups powdered sugar
2½ cups all-purpose flour	
½ tsp baking powder	fresh fruit, assorted, sliced
½ tsp salt	

Beat the sugar and butter together in a large bowl until fluffy, 3–5 minutes.

Add vanilla and eggs, and mix until combined. In another bowl, mix together flour, baking powder and salt. Add dry ingredients to wet, and mix just until combined, about 30 seconds. Wrap dough in plastic wrap and refrigerate.

When you're ready to bake the crust, preheat oven to 350°F.

Roll chilled dough into one big cookie and place on round baking stone, sprinkle with 2–3 Tbsp of sugar. Bake 17–20 minutes until slightly under baked. Let cool; chill in the refrigerator.

For the frosting: Beat cream cheese, butter, vanilla and powdered sugar in a bowl until well mixed.

Spread on chilled cookie. Chill again to set and thicken the frosting.

Top with colorful fresh fruit in a pleasing pattern. Cut into slices and serve.

Tips and variations: Feel free to make this as one very large "pizza" or in smaller versions. Do under-bake the cookie a bit so that it's a bit soft and easy to slice rather than crunchy.

This recipe has been adapted from pinchofyum.com via America's Test Kitchen.

Sweet Endings

Christmas in July Fruit Cup

Yield: 4–6 servings

"We discovered this recipe from a local grocery store tasting sample."

- 1 pkg. French vanilla instant pudding
- 2 Tbsp cool whip
- 1 banana, sliced
- 2 kiwi, sliced
- 8 strawberries, quartered

Make pudding by box directions. Mix in 2 tablespoons of cool whip. Add cut up banana. Add cut up kiwi. Add cut up strawberries.

Tips and variations: Try raspberry instead of strawberry for variation.

Frozen Fruit 'N Cream

Yield: 14 servings

- 8 oz. cream cheese
- ½ cup sifted confectioners' sugar
- 2 cups frozen whipped dairy topping (do not thaw)
- 1 cup walnuts, chopped, plus 14 walnut halves for garnish
- 14 (9-oz.) plastic cups
- 2 (1-lb.) cans cranberry sauce
- 2 (1-lb.) cans crushed pineapple

In a medium bowl, beat cream cheese, confectioners' sugar, and whipped topping together. Stir in chopped nuts. Neatly spoon a scant 1/4 cup into the bottoms of 14 plastic cups. In a large bowl, mix cranberry sauce and crushed pineapple together well. Spoon ½ cup of mixture into each plastic cup.

Place on a cookie sheet, cover with plastic wrap and freeze. To remove from cup, dip bottom and sides quickly in warm water; store in freezer bags.

To serve: remove desired quantity from freezer and place in small decorative dishes one hour before serving. Press a walnut half in the cream top.

Sweet Endings

Very Berry Yogurt Cream Parfaits

Yield: 1 serving

"These parfaits are a favorite with guests and there are endless possibilities as multiple combinations of fruit make them both beautiful and tasty. Strawberry/blueberry is a patriotic combination, peach/berry with blueberries, raspberries or strawberries is delicious, black and blue parfaits (blackberries and blueberries) are fun, kiwi/grape look great for St. Patrick's Day and Cherry/Berry is very Valentiney."

1	cup heavy whipping cream
1	tsp vanilla
2–4	Tbsp powdered sugar, to taste
1	cup plain (or vanilla) Greek yogurt
1½	cups each of two kinds of fruit, fresh or frozen
	sugar to taste for fruit

Beat cold whipping cream until almost stiff peaks form, adding vanilla and powdered sugar to taste, gradually as you beat. Slowly add in Greek yogurt until just combined.

Leave smaller berries whole. Cut strawberries, peaches, or larger fruits into small pieces. Add sugar to taste.

Spoon fruit and yogurt cream into parfait glasses in layers, ¼ cup at a time. Using a pastry bag to squeeze yogurt cream into parfait glasses keeps things neater.

Garnish with a slice of fruit on the edge of the glass.

Tips and variations: Add sugar to fruit depending on taste. More powdered sugar may be needed for plain yogurt than for vanilla, and less vanilla if using vanilla yogurt.

Sweet Endings

Pineapple with Warm Caramel Sauce

Yield: 6 servings

*"It's the spring of 2012, and Marian Stollenwerk, new innkeeper at Wind in the Pines, is doing what anyone might do who just bought a bed and breakfast—she's building a file of wonderful recipes. Here is one
she found that could either be dessert or a decadent delight at breakfast."*

12	pineapple slices, ½-inch thick
½	cup maple syrup
½	cup heavy cream
	fresh strawberries and mint for garnish
½	cup finely chopped walnuts or pecans

Arrange 2 slices of pineapple overlapping on each plate. Cover and refrigerate until serving time. When almost ready to serve, bring maple syrup to a boil in saucepan, boil for 2 minutes. Immediately stir in the cream, return to boiling and boil for 15 seconds.

Divide the hot sauce evenly over the individual plates. Garnish with a strawberry and mint.

Sprinkle with the nuts and serve immediately.

This recipe has been adapted from *Recipes to Remember*, Reynolds House Bed and Breakfast.

Sweet Endings

Butter Cream Frosting

Yield: 12 ounces of frosting

"This recipe came from a 1959 book, The Best of Cooking in Our Lady of the Lakes Church of Waterford, MI. It was submitted by a Mrs. A.J. Law. This is where I went to church and school. I have been making the frosting since my dad bought the book for my mother when it was first published and sold at church. It is still to this day the best butter cream frosting I have had (and many people agree)."

½	cup butter
½	cup shortening
1	cup granulated sugar
1	tsp vanilla
⅔	cup warm milk

Cream together the butter, shortening, sugar, and vanilla.

Add the warm milk slowly and beat at high speed until ready to spread. This will be just like cream.

Sandtown Farmhouse B&B

Hot Spiced Cider

Yield: 8–12 servings

"Just after Labor Day we begin pressing cider from our farm orchard. Our guests—young and old—eagerly help pick pails of apples, wash, cut, and turn the crank on our press, squeezing out the golden cider."

2   quarts apple cider
½   cup brown sugar
3   whole cloves
1   stick cinnamon
1   cardamom seed pod

Combine all ingredients in a large saucepan. Heat well, but do not boil.

Prairieside Suites Luxury B&B

Hot Chocolate

Yield: approximately 40 servings

"Our guests all enjoy our homemade hot cocoa. I have been tweaking this recipe for years and it is my most asked-for recipe. My favorite way to serve it is with coffee poured over the dry cocoa mix, instead of hot water."

8   cups dried milk
2   cups Chocolate Nestlé's Quik
2   cups powdered sugar or 2 cups Splenda
1⅓ cups non-dairy creamer
⅓   cup instant coffee, decaf or regular
    whipped cream, to garnish
    chocolate shavings, to garnish

Mix all ingredients in a large bowl and stir. Fill a cup ⅓ full of cocoa mix. Add hot water, maybe a little whipped cream, chocolate shavings, or for the holidays stir with a peppermint stick. I put all ingredients into a large Tupperware cereal container and shake. This way you can mix and store … all in one. Nothing could be easier. Then use the pour spout to fill your cup or pour into jars to give as a gift.

Alphabetical Index of Inns
(and pages they appear on)

U.S. Measurement Equivalents

pinch/dash	1/16 teaspoon
½ teaspoon	30 drops
1 teaspoon	1/3 tablespoon
3 teaspoons	1 tablespoon
½ tablespoon	1½ teaspoons
1 tablespoon	3 teaspoons; ½ fluid ounce
2 tablespoons	1/8 cup; 1 fluid ounce
3 tablespoons	1½ fluid ounces; 1 jigger
jigger	1½ fluid ounces; 3 tablespoons
4 tablespoons	¼ cup; 2 fluid ounces
5⅓ tablespoons	1/3 cup; 5 tablespoons + 1 teaspoon
8 tablespoons	½ cup; 4 fluid ounces
10⅔ tablespoons	⅔ cup; 10 tablespoons + 2 teaspoons
12 tablespoons	¾ cup; 6 fluid ounces
16 tablespoons	1 cup; 8 fluid ounces; ½ pint
1/8 cup	2 tablespoons; 1 fluid ounce
¼ cup	4 tablespoons; 2 fluid ounces
1/3 cup	5 tablespoons + 1 teaspoon
3/8 cup	¼ cup + 2 tablespoons
½ cup	8 tablespoons; 4 fluid ounces
⅔ cup	10 tablespoons + 2 teaspoons
5/8 cup	½ cup + 2 tablespoons
¾ cup	12 tablespoons; 6 fluid ounces
7/8 cup	¾ cup + 2 tablespoons
1 cup	16 tablespoons; ½ pint; 8 fluid ounces
2 cups	1 pint; 16 fluid ounces
3 cups	1½ pints; 24 fluid ounces
4 cups	1 quart; 32 fluid ounces
8 cups	2 quarts; 64 fluid ounces
1 pint	2 cups; 16 fluid ounces
2 pints	1 quart; 32 fluid ounces
1 quart	2 pints; 4 cups; 32 fluid ounces
4 quarts	1 gallon; 8 pints
1 gallon	4 quarts; 8 pints; 16 cups; 128 fluid ounces
8 quarts	1 peck
4 pecks	1 bushel

– Index –